THE CAPITOL RIOTS

The Capitol Riots maps out the events of the January 6, 2021 insurrectionary riots at the United States Capitol building, providing context for understanding the contributing factors and ongoing implications of the uprising.

This definitive text explores the rise of populism, disinformation, conspiracy theories, the alt-right, and white supremacy during the lead-up to and planning of the Stop the Steal campaign, as well as the complex interplay during the riots of political performances, costumes, objectives, communications, digital media, datafication, race, gender, and—ultimately—power. Assembling raw data from social media, selfie photos and videos, and mainstream journalism, the authors develop a timeline and data visualizations representing the events. They delve into the complex, openly shared narratives, motivations, and actions of people on the ground that day who violated the symbolic center of U.S. democracy. An analysis of visual data reveals an affective outpouring of mutually amplifying expressions of frustration, fear, hate, anger, and anomie that correspond to similar logics and counter-logics in the polarized and chaotic contemporary media environment that have only been intensified by COVID-19 lockdowns, conspiracy theories, and a call to action at the Capitol from the outgoing POTUS and his inner circle.

The book will appeal to both a general audience of those curious about how and why the Capitol riots unfolded and to students and scholars of communications, political science, media studies, sociology, education, surveillance studies, digital humanities, gender studies, critical whiteness studies, and datafication studies. It will also find an audience within computer science and technology studies through its approach to big data, data visualization, AI, algorithms, data tracking, and other data sciences.

Sandra Jeppesen is Professor in Media, Film, and Communications at Lakehead University Orillia, Canada; activist-researcher; and co-founder of the Media Action Research Group. She is the author of *Transformative Media: Intersectional Technopolitics from Indymedia to #BlackLivesMatter* (UBC Press 2021).

Michael Hoechsmann is Associate Professor in the Faculty of Education at Lakehead University Orillia, Canada. His research focuses on digital and media literacies and cultural studies.

iowyth hezel ulthiin is a PhD Student in Communications and Culture at X University, Canada. Their research centers around embodiment, affect, outsider communities, and hopeful imaginaries engaged through praxis.

David VanDyke is a Data Scientist and Graduate Student in the Faculty of Education at Lakehead University Orillia, Canada. He is interested in data visualization and the use of large datasets to improve education and digital media literacy.

Miranda McKee is a Visual Arts Educator and Curator and a Graduate Student in the Faculty of Education at Lakehead University Orillia, Canada. Her exhibitions and public programs examine the role of photography within the context of contemporary visual culture.

POLITICS, MEDIA AND POLITICAL COMMUNICATION

Titles in this series include:

Communication in Global Jihad
Jonathan Matusitz

Democracy and Fake News
Information Manipulation and Post-Truth Politics
Edited by Serena Giusti and Elisa Piras

Political Communication and COVID-19
Governance and Rhetoric in Times of Crisis
Edited by Darren Lilleker, Ioana A. Coman, Miloš Gregor and Edoardo Novelli

The Capitol Riots
Digital Media, Disinformation, and Democracy Under Attack
Sandra Jeppesen, Michael Hoechsmann, iowyth hezel ulthiin, David VanDyke and Miranda McKee
with chapters by Henry Giroux and Chenjerai Kumanyika

For more information about this series, please visit: https://www.routledge.com/ Politics-Media-and-Political-Communication/book-series/POLMED.

THE CAPITOL RIOTS

Digital Media, Disinformation, and Democracy Under Attack

Sandra Jeppesen, Michael Hoechsmann, iowyth hezel ulthiin, David VanDyke and Miranda McKee

with chapters by Henry Giroux and Chenjerai Kumanyika

Routledge
Taylor & Francis Group

LONDON AND NEW YORK

Cover image: Copyright iowyth hezel ulthiin, ulthiin's impression of photograph by Win McNamee

First published 2022
by Routledge
4 Park Square, Milton Park, Abingdon, Oxon OX14 4RN

and by Routledge
605 Third Avenue, New York, NY 10158

Routledge is an imprint of the Taylor & Francis Group, an informa business

British Library Cataloguing in Publication Data
A catalogue record for this book is available from the British Library

Library of Congress Cataloging-in-Publication Data
A catalog record has been requested for this book

ISBN: 978-1-032-16042-9 (hbk)
ISBN: 978-1-032-16040-5 (pbk)
ISBN: 978-1-003-24686-2 (ebk)

DOI: 10.4324/9781003246862

Typeset in Bembo
by Taylor & Francis Books

This book is dedicated to all those in pursuit of social justice who seek the truth in an era of disinformation, misrepresentation, and injustice.

CONTENTS

FIGURES

TABLES

ACKNOWLEDGEMENTS

Every project has an origin and this one began with a virtual panel discussion at a research showcase hosted by Lakehead University early in 2021. The co-authors assembled here had formed a panel called 'Unmasking the Infodemic: Research in/on Social Media and Algorithms' at Lakehead University's Research and Innovation Week on March 2, 2021. The discussions after the panel turned to the events of January 6 at the U.S. Capitol and a decision was made to collaborate on some writing which ended up becoming this book.

This book is enriched by the contributions of Henry A. Giroux, McMaster University, and Chenjerai Kumanyika, Rutgers University. We are grateful for the participation of these extraordinary activist scholars.

We also want to thank colleagues, mentors and students at Lakehead University and elsewhere who have influenced our thought and approaches to social, cultural and political theory and analysis.

This research was in part supported by the Social Sciences and Humanities Research Council of Canada (SSHRC) Grant #435-2017-0745 and ongoing collaborations with the UNESCO Chair in Democracy, Global Citizenship and Transformative Education (DCMÉT).

We have been grateful for the excellent advice offered by the peer reviewers of our initial proposal and the editorial support of Meghan Murray, a Lakehead University student in Media, Film, and Communications. We also wish to acknowledge Routledge editors Hannah Rich and Emily Ross who have been enthusiastic and thorough sources of advice and instruction along the way.

And finally, we profoundly thank our partners, families, and friends who have tolerated absences, late nights and unending conversations about conspiracies, riots, and contemporary political dystopias.

CONTRIBUTORS

Henry Giroux holds the McMaster University Chair for Scholarship in the Public Interest in the Department of English and Cultural Studies and is the Paulo Freire Distinguished Scholar in Critical Pedagogy at McMaster University, Canada. His website is henryagiroux.com.

Michael Hoechsmann is Associate Professor in the Faculty of Education at Lakehead University Orillia, Canada. His research focuses on digital and media literacies and cultural studies.

Sandra Jeppesen is Professor in Media, Film, and Communications at Lakehead University Orillia, Canada; activist-researcher; and co-founder of the Media Action Research Group. She is the author of *Transformative Media: Intersectional Technopolitics from Indymedia to #BlackLivesMatter* (UBC Press 2021).

Chenjerai Kumanyika is Assistant Professor in the Department of Journalism and Media at Rutgers University, USA. His research and teaching focus on power, race, and promotional culture in the creative industries. He is a podcaster and organizer and serves on the boards of Street Poets and The Moth.

Miranda McKee is a visual arts educator and curator and a graduate student in the Faculty of Education at Lakehead University Orillia, Canada. Her exhibitions and public programs examine the role of photography within the context of contemporary visual culture.

iowyth hezel ulthiin is a PhD student in Communications and Culture at X University, Canada. Their research centers around embodiment, affect, outsider communities, and hopeful imaginaries engaged through praxis.

David VanDyke is a data scientist and graduate student in the Faculty of Education at Lakehead University Orillia, Canada. He is interested in data visualization and the use of large datasets to improve education and digital media literacy.

PART 1

Social, Political, Economic, and Epistemic Contexts of the Capitol Riots

1

INTRODUCTION

The Cascading Crises Propelling the Capitol Riots

*Sandra Jeppesen, Michael Hoechsmann and
iowyth hezel ulthiin*

Making sense of history as it unfolds can be a fraught exercise, an attempt to find order in events taking place across space and time, when it can be difficult to find critical distance. However, occasionally a flashpoint occurs with such intensity that it seems briefly to arrest time. The sense of suspended time lasts long enough to allow for a synchronic snapshot to emerge, peeling back the layers of social and psychological immersion that make up the familiar to lay bare the complex forces of an epoch. The Capitol riots in Washington, DC, on January 6th, 2021, are just such a flashpoint. In years to come, we may see this as a day to be remembered, yet it may also be too easily forgotten, discarded on the junk heap of history like so many social media memes.

At that flashpoint moment, the social, political and economic crises accumulating over decades of American and global history exploded in the chaotic occupation of the US Capitol building by populist groups, organized militias, white supremacist groups, conspiracy theorists, historical re-enactors, and so-called 'inspired believers' (Program on Extremism, 2021). They were in Washington to express fealty to Donald Trump, the outgoing 45th President of the United States (POTUS), a man who ran America like a business, purportedly rejecting the entrenched political elite (while inhabiting this very position) and their social-political norms, to give power back to the ordinary citizen. Leading up to the riots, Trump tweeted incessantly, making use of well-worn rhetorical strategies used by far-right elites in mobilizing the disenfranchised to support white supremacy (Mondon and Winter, 2020). Unsurprisingly, the rioters depicted in the media that day were predominantly white, staking claims for the continued domination of whiteness in America.

The US Political, Economic, and Social Context

The Capitol riots can be understood as the culmination of a fevered period in the US, built up through the Trump presidency and accelerating dramatically through

DOI: 10.4324/9781003246862-2

a series of four ongoing events in 2020. First, the COVID-19 pandemic broke out, with ramifications in terms of state (mis)management that included downplaying the seriousness of the pandemic, in parallel with citizen mobilizations providing mutual aid and 'care-mongering' tempered by reactionary threads against masking, lockdowns, and vaccinations. Second, these reactionary threads were driven by the denial of health science and a concomitant escalation of disinformation, fake news, and conspiracy theories. Third, the reactionary context includes an escalation of white supremacy, racism, populism, and the alt-right (opaquely supported by Trump), not just in the US but also globally, with a simultaneous rise in anti-racist movements exemplified by Black Lives Matter. And, finally, the defeat of Donald Trump by Joe Biden in the Presidential election of November 2020 and the subsequent disinformation campaign falsely claiming Biden had stolen the election, organized under the hashtag #StopTheSteal, can be seen as the inciting incident in the ensuing actions.

In the context of these four trends, discussed below, the 'March to Save America,' also called #MarchForTrump, was organized by a group called Women for America First (Schwartz, 2021) to take place in Washington on January 6, 2021. And take place it did. But how did we get here?

The COVID Conjuncture

The year 2020 opened with the arrival of a COVID-19 epidemic, eventually labeled a pandemic by the WHO on March 11th. In the United States, this health crisis was politicized by a president who engaged in casual COVID denialism, refused to follow public health guidelines such as wearing a mask or social distancing, and rolled out a fragmented, incoherent, and self-absorbed pandemic strategy, including a withdrawal of the US from the WHO, and hijacking high-level COVID strategy meetings to discuss his personal online image. His primary crisis communication strategy centered on the use of Twitter as a digital pulpit for the dissemination of spontaneous exhortations, often very personal, occurring late at night, and unbecoming of the position of POTUS. This lack of science-based leadership created an information gap followed closely on its heels by an *infodemic* (Cinelli et al., 2020), a dangerous viral misinformation epidemic run rampant on social media. The infodemic included not just misinformation but also the outgrowth of conspiracy theories around COVID and beyond, as people attempted to come to terms with emerging health, economic, social, and political realities within an atmosphere of unknowns mixed with outright fabrications or disinformation. Alt-right politics defending anti-masking, anti-vaxxing, and anti-lockdowns further confused the issue, as highly divisive political agendas emerged, taking advantage of the heightened state of confusion and anxiety to mobilize support for Republicans and the alt-right. Moreover, the politicization of public health care through the dismantling of Obamacare and the capitalist-friendly political denial of climate science have both directly promoted distrust of scientists, medical professionals, and public health officials now tasked with managing COVID-19.

This context, which Toby Miller and Pal Ahluwalia (2020) call 'The Covid conjuncture' brought with it not just grievances against governmental overreach—contesting the legislation of mandatory masking, lockdowns, border closures, and business shutdowns—but also fears of mandated vaccinations, quarantine jails, internment camps, and microchipped vaccines, and the limits to freedom and autonomy these seem to imply. The US public has a healthy distrust of state officials at the best of times and is well aware of what happens to society's rebels and out-casts. However far-fetched some of these fears may seem, there is a history of gov-ernment persecution, where outspoken radicals may be silenced, criminalized, jailed, subjected to state violence, or even killed. Moreover, there is a history of unethical psycho-medical experiments in Canada and the US that have received media play in recent years, including the MK Ultra experiments with LSD on unknowing subjects (Bhambra, 2019); the Milgram experiments on the (ir)respon-sibilization of violence (Blass, 2009); the Tuskegee Study in which Black men with syphilis were given placebos such as aspirin and denied antibiotics, without consent, to better understand serious complications of the disease (Jones, 2008); and the historical and on-going non-consensual sterilization of racialized and Indigenous women (Black, Rich, and Felske-Durksen, 2021)—all with long-term negative consequences for participants, up to and including death. In this context, distrust of medical officials and the medical establishment might be understandable, and the fragmented, misinformed, anti-science, and often contradictory crisis communication strategies of the Trump Administration only served to exacerbate this unease.

While populist groups were contesting public health guidelines aimed to keep people safe from COVID, as fragmented as these guidelines were in the US, the facts started to emerge that COVID had served to make visible and amplify vast inequalities across race and gender. Racialized groups in the US, Canada, and other countries have counted disproportionate numbers of cases and deaths (Millet et al., 2020; Lewis et al., 2020). Women, and in particular women of color, are doing the heavy lifting in terms of over-representation as front-line workers such as nurses, grocery store and retail clerks, teachers, daycare staff, long-term-care workers, cleaners, and more—positions that have higher exposure and therefore higher rates of infection and death. In addition, under lockdowns, stark increases for women in job losses, childcare responsibilities, homeschooling supervision, and gender-based domestic violence have led the pandemic to be called 'a disaster for feminism' (Lewis, 2020, n.p.). These unequal impacts have led some to call COVID-19 a *syndemic*, in which social, environmental, and economic conditions have synergistically combined with the pandemic to exacerbate negative health impacts on particular groups and communities (Miller, 2021).

The Crossroads of the Information and Health Crises

The rise of fake news and disinformation during the tenure of President Trump is also of note, as is his dismissal of mainstream news itself as 'fake news,' leading to a confusing meta-mediascape of truths, half-truths, and lies. Trump was found, by a team of fact-checkers at the *Washington Post*, to have lied or made misleading claims a total of 30,573 times during his four-year tenure as President—a rate of 20.9 lies per day (Kessler et al., 2021). A mixed bag of conspiracy theories arose in this wake, with claims as wide-ranging and imaginative as the following: the horrific wildfires in California were started by Antifa or Jewish Space Lasers (Chait, 2021); Hollywood and political elites are harvesting the blood of children through a Satanist pedophile ring, a theory promoted by QAnon (Friedberg, 2020); and 'The Great Replacement,' a populist fear held by white people of being demographically 'replaced' by racialized groups, propagated by such right-wing media pundits as Fox News' Tucker Carlson (Giroux, 2021). These and other conspiracy theories have grown legs in a context where journalists, educators, and other cultural and knowledge producers, in particular those articulating ideas related to social justice, critical race theory, feminism, Marxism, and so on, are increasingly demonized (see Chapter 2). Viral disinformation tidbits—as fascinating as they are false—serve as surplus narratives, underlining the fragility of collective truth, and with it, propelling the growing incoherence of the American consciousness forward (see Chapter 3). These conspiracies and incoherencies both motivate and are reflected in the riotous discourses and material actions of January 6th.

While Trump positions himself as a lone hero, standing up to the very political and economic forces from which he has so richly benefited throughout his lifetime, he continues to blame liberal elites for the pain faced by America's dispossessed, serving to erase the fact that he is part of this same oppressive and extremely wealthy elite class. Thus, despite being deeply embedded in the conduits of power, he is seen by populist publics as an ordinary working man, having pulled himself up by the bootstraps. This claim is patently false. Donald Trump inherited over 413 million dollars from his father's real estate empire (Barstow, Craig, and Buettner, 2018). This (mis)alignment of Trump with the economic concerns of his base is just one more piece in the disinformation puzzle. Disinformation, we may recall, is false information put forth by someone who knows it to be false, and it is a hallmark of Trump's communications.

Any analysis of the riots must therefore reckon with the power of social media not just to organize and document the events of the day but also to shape the way those events are influenced *a priori* by misinformation, disinformation, conspiracy theories, and fake news.

The Rise of Populism, White Supremacy, and the Alt-Right

This disinformation mediascape might help to explain the recent rise of QAnon, the Proud Boys, Oath Keepers, Three Percenters, and other white supremacist, alt-right, or populist ideologies and groups—all of which were present at the riots. However, alt-right ideologies in the US and Europe are nothing new. Trump's famous 'Make America Great Again,' slogan is hardly original. Rather, it replicates Margaret Thatcher's attempts to put the 'Great' back into Great Britain while infamously declaring, 'There's no such thing as society' (Thatcher, 1987, cited in

McLachlan, 2020). A complex set of overlapping factors and events can indeed be traced back to the spectacle under the Thatcher government of what Stuart Hall (1979, p. 14) called 'the moving right show,' which signaled a political and economic shift toward neoliberal capitalism and white supremacy that has continued unabated through to the present moment (Sim, 2000; Danewid, 2021). Thatcher used a defense of whiteness combined with appeals to economic and social class worries to deflect attention away from a massive restructuring of the British state consisting predominantly of a reduction in the social safety net. This is all echoed in Trump's neoliberal capitalist strategies, which include deregulation, privatization, and the responsibilization of the sovereign individual, which together contribute to the erosion of a sense of the common good and the requisite practices of collective solidarity that might support the creation of collective goals, hopes, actions, and social justice movements. Instead, we see the rise of an individualist populism that, following the lead of alt-right leaders and pundits, has intensified neoliberal class warfare (waged by those in dominant groups) across all of its intersections: gender, sexuality, race, housing, and immigration status, among others.

We must be careful, however, not to believe that right-wing populism is a strictly ideological hand-waving argument with no basis in people's material lives:

> Populism is operating on genuine contradictions, and it has a rational and material core. Its success and effectivity does not lie in its capacity to dupe unsuspecting folk but in the way it addresses real problems, real and lived experiences, real contradictions—and yet is able to represent them within a logic of discourse which pulls them systematically into line with policies and class strategies of the Right.
>
> *(Hall, 1979, p. 20)*

By aligning individualist concerns with a reactionary political project, the right gains support for politicians and policies that directly go against the very interests of the populace supporting them. This explains how, for example, the working poor may support alt-right politicians and parties that undermine minimum wage and other labor rights, or why, to take a case in point, a good many white women support the openly misogynist Trump. At the same time, left media have inadvertently amplified the messages of white supremacy in attempts to decry their reactionary, problematic politics (Mondon and Winter, 2020).

The alt-right has also achieved ascendancy because, in the United States at least, the right has structural advantages within the political system. The redistribution or gerrymandering of the electoral colleges by Republicans has benefited less densely populated, white-dominated rural regions that have historically voted Republican, and at the same time, disenfranchised Black voters through concerted efforts to restrict their voting rights. The right also has financial clout through belonging to an elite class that influences economic and social policy to support an intensifying neoliberal capitalism from which they, in a cyclical pattern, then continue to benefit from economically. Power is also exercised by the right in spreading propaganda through mainstream media, including the burgeoning alt-right mediasphere and so-called 'alt-light' outlets such as *Rebel Media* and *Breitbart* (Mondon and Winter, 2020, p. 49). Further, the right controls a range of generously funded think tanks and astroturfed capitalist initiatives—corporate fronts posing as grassroots campaigns (Fisher, 2009; Hvistendahl, 2020; Vogel et al., 2020; Miller, 2021). These and many other hierarchical political, economic, and social structures have been mobilized to benefit the right.

In light of the rise of the right, many events in the recent past have foreshadowed the Capitol riots, but two stand out in their eerie parallels. First, the 2017 'Unite the Right' march in Charlottesville has several parallels with the riots; consisting of white supremacist violence, police non-intervention, and the enduring symbol of a rabble-raising crowd of white men marching with tiki torches, the march led Trump to express admiration for its white supremacist participants, saying there were 'some very fine people on both sides' (Trump, 2017, cited in Gray, 2017). Second, in April 2020, there was a heavily armed incursion into the Michigan Legislature of anti-lockdown protestors who found their way to the main hall and legislature viewing gallery, with minimal pushback from police, as it is not against the law to bear arms in the Michigan state capitol building (Beckett, 2020). These two events and others like them, including Trump's affirming responses, seem to have emboldened white supremacist groups to similar actions at the Capitol riots with an expectation of impunity.

Empowering a combination of right-wing, misogynist, white supremacists has been part of Trump's populist playbook from the start. Taking it on the road to his base in energetic rallies, he has built a following who chant along with him in his simplistic three-word slogans: 'lock her up!' [Hillary Clinton]; 'build the wall!' [on the US/Mexico border]; 'send her back!' [Ilhan Omar]; and 'four more years!' [of Trump as POTUS]. Alongside his hortatory politics, in his term as president, he has followed a transparent divide-and-rule approach to race and migration. Three notable examples include the construction of a militarized wall on the US-Mexico Border alluded to in the chant above, along with the caging of child migrants separated from their parents in detention; the so-called Muslim Ban of 2017 that restricted travel to the US from seven predominantly Muslim countries, with the state detaining travelers and revoking visas; and Trump's refusal to condemn white supremacy in the Presidential debates, saying the Proud Boys (a group Canada has named a terrorist organization), should 'stand back and stand by,' which they immediately took as a call to action (see Chapter 8).

The era of Trump's Presidency has—perhaps unsurprisingly, given the outpouring of overt racism—also seen the rise of anti-racist movements contesting systemic racism and police violence. In May 2020, the murder by police of an African American man named George Floyd led to a new wave of Black Lives Matter (BLM) protests, met with a violent local and federal police response. This included the kidnapping of protesters into unmarked vans in Portland, OR by unidentified teams wearing camo gear, only later discovered to be Federal officers (Levinson et al., 2020).

There is ample evidence that fear of the racialized and gendered 'Other' animates much of right-wing populism today (Chicago Project on Security and Threats, 2021), understood within the intersections of an intensification of hyper-capitalist neoliberal democracy and cries for a renewed white ethnostate (Stern, 2020). There is an ever-tightening belt around the American public, exerting pressure on the body politic, made up of a growing sense of erosion of economic, social, and ecological security, which, as it tightens, appears to make more pronounced the latent bigotry embedded within the founding myths of a racist colonial settler state, which spews forth into problematic public discourse. As America moves into a new era, with widening divides of inequality, the space in which the American dream may be dreamed becomes increasingly imperiled. There are those clinging by their fingernails to the last vestiges of this dream, attempting to align themselves with mythic champions of past glory, but instead becoming complicit in the active oppression of marginalized groups and the deterioration of social solidarity through the selective, aggressive scapegoating of racialized, gendered, religious, and cultural groups.

This, in turn, points to the contestation by the alt-right of critical race theory, yet another ideological or double-think frame in which the plain truth of racial discrimination is actively suppressed. Despite ample research-based evidence revealing ongoing systemic racism in the United States, many legislators on the right continue to question the existence of a racial divide, insisting on the myth of equality long promoted as an existing condition already achieved by American democracy. The Trump presidency has fanned the flames of a populist movement that trades in both a denial of racism and an overt expression of it, mobilizing racialized tropes, such as the allegation that immigrants are stealing American jobs, that Mexicans are all 'rapists and criminals,' (Trump, 2015, cited in Ye Hee Lee, 2015), or that immigrants come from 'shithole countries' (Trump, 2018, cited in Watkins and Phillip, 2018). According to the alt-right, US policies that open borders to racialized immigrants would allegedly make the US both 'poorer and dirtier' (Giroux, 2021), despite the fact that immigrants have greater labor participation in the US compared to their American-born counterparts (US Bureau of Labor Statistics, 2020).

Joe Biden Wins the Election: #stopthesteal

The fourth and final influence and indeed the inciting incident in the drama of the Capitol riots was the Biden defeat of Trump in the November 2020 Presidential election—a win still denied by Trump and his acolytes. The election was characterized by a struggle over the disenfranchisement of predominantly Black voters and included a series of unusual televised presidential and vice-presidential debates within the context of COVID. In what seemed like a predictable move, Trump claimed his loss had been fraudulently orchestrated by the Democrats, a claim he stridently tested in court cases across a number of states—and lost. Despite this, Trump refused to concede or congratulate Biden and

Harris for their win, instead claiming that the technology used by the voting machines had been hacked (for which he now faces a defamation lawsuit) and dragging his heels in providing access for the incoming Administration to documents, funds, and other materials necessary to facilitate the peaceful transition of power. Petulantly mobilizing—and some would say dishonestly manipulating—his massive Twitter following to repeatedly denounce the election results as corrupt through the hashtag #stopthesteal would eventually result in his account being banned from Twitter for the spread of false information. But not until the Capitol riots were over.

One might be tempted to attribute rioter motivations to the overall conditions of precarity that preceded the pandemic, exacerbated by massive losses in secure employment and housing, hand in hand with the loss of access to affordable healthcare. These forms of continued hyper-capitalist exploitation, unprotected by a viable social safety net, must be understood as the backdrop to the disenfranchisement of an ever-increasing proportion of the American public, Trump supporters among them. However, those who participated in the Capitol riots, in terms of social class and economic experience, are not who we might think. Robert Pape (2021) has found in a study of the backgrounds of the first 377 arrestees (now numbering well over 700), a good proportion are middle-aged, well-employed middle managers, business owners, and CEOs, rather than the expected disenfranchised youth who typically make up the predominant demographic of rioters. While claims that Biden somehow stole the election are, even on the surface, factually inaccurate—the result of an orchestrated disinformation campaign spread by the then-POTUS himself—they herald a deepening sense that

FIGURE 1.1 Supporters film the projected image of Trump speaking at the 'March to Save America,' Washington DC, January 6, 2021

*Source: Voice of America, Wikimedia Commons, Public Domain*https://commons.wikimedia.org/wiki/File:2021_United_States_Capitol_VOA_1.jpg.

democracy itself is under attack, a feeling increasingly shared by people all along the political spectrum.

Trump's followers, in this complex cascading-crisis context, mobilized to participate in the 'March to Save America' at the Capitol (see Figure 1.1). The crowd was comprised of participants who had traveled to Washington to participate in what promised to be a historical protest, some as parts of well-organized militia or other right-wing groups and others as atomized or unorganized individuals, ardent Trump supporters willing to put themselves on the line for a Presidency they had wholly invested in, and whose many falsehoods they believed to be true.

Thus, we can understand the Capitol riots to be an outpouring of outrage at the alleged stealing of the election. This perception is evidenced by the massive number of 'tweets' and 'parleys' (messages on Twitter and Parler, respectively) using the #stopthesteal hashtag. This (mis)perception of a democracy under attack is what was at stake in the minds of many Trump supporters as they marched on The Capitol on January 6, 2021, in turn putting the very seat of democracy under attack.

The Context of Global Unrest and Riots

In addition to the specific context of politics and social struggles in the US mapped above, recently riots have unfolded increasingly on the global stage. Indeed, Clover (2016, p. 16) has argued that 'riots have achieved an intransigent social centrality' in today's world, perhaps precisely because of their disruptive and confrontational character. We are living in a particularly fertile era for rioting, it turns out. A cursory look at the daily news shows riots to be an increasingly prevalent tactic in the social protest toolbox. From the Arab Spring in Tahrir Square to the Occupy movement in Oakland, CA, from Black Lives Matter protests in Ferguson, MO to the pro-democracy movement in Hong Kong, and from the Greek Indignados in Athens, Greece, to uprisings in Buenos Aires, Argentina, the world is witnessing a rise in broad-based protests, civil unrest, and uprisings that often culminate in riots. The global citizenry, it appears, is fighting hard for its political, cultural, and economic survival, hotly contesting the intensified precarity of austerity measures, neoliberal capitalism, deteriorating minimum wages, escalating rents and food costs, and also crying out for justice, whether racial, gendered, anti-colonial, LGBTQ+, etc. Rioting, under these conditions, becomes a cathartic conduit for an excess of repressed energies. However, the riots of January 6, 2021, do not take place amidst valiant cries for social justice; rather, they are an attempt to retrench and support existing status quo structures of race, class and gender domination.

Not all riots, one might therefore say, are created equal. Not all riots, moreover, share the foundations of an anti-capitalist framework—the Capitol riots certainly did not—but the context of global neoliberal capitalism must be understood to be a factor, as the ground making up the material preconditions for widespread global uprisings, including the Capitol riots. Not all riots, moreover, share the same reading of these conditions nor present the same demands to change them.

Increasing corruption in democratic states and the consequent leash between state power and capitalist imperatives had long put downward economic pressure on those in the lowest income brackets well before the arrival of COVID. However, interestingly, according to the analysis of the Capitol riot arrestees mentioned above, most did not share an economically marginalized subject position. If not oppressed under the boot of capitalism or racism—rioters we are familiar with and may even feel an affinity for regarding their cries for racial and economic justice—what did these rioters want?

The Fragmented Prolific Messaging of the Rioters

This question is difficult to answer. There is the superficial or obvious statement that they were there to stop what they believed was a stolen election. But even this messaging was not always consistent. The Capitol riots generated a proliferation of messaging: images, videos, selfie media, affective narration, celebratory chanting, and so on, yet a coherent message remains elusive. Comprised of surplus value rather than use value, the Capitol riots may be emblematic of our time—the hyper-spectacle amped up beyond the society of the spectacle or even the falsified simulacrum, the copy without originals, it becomes the hyper-spectacle of surplus media and affective expression with effectively no political coherence or desired outcome. It is the dérive of riots, an aimless wandering through the halls of power. It is hyper-communication of social media and smartphones in the extreme, to which everyone is tuned-in but to which the political and capitalist elite feel little need to listen nor respond, the ultimate exemplar of what Jodi Dean (2005) calls communicative capitalism. A moment in which everything changes—and precisely nothing changes.

Some of the expressed motivations behind the Capitol riots strain the limits of credulity. Simultaneously stoked by and promoting (echoing, retweeting, liking, favoriting, and so on) incoherent or inconsistent messaging from competing media ecologies and flows, including social media, traditional media, alt-right media, and right-wing platforms such as Parler, protesters converged in a collective determination to restore Donald Trump to an allegedly usurped Presidency. Some had the tangential objective, it seems, to take down the corrupt core of a governmental elite, represented, perhaps arbitrarily, by the figures of Mike Pence and Nancy Pelosi. A hangman's noose and scaffold were erected outside the Capitol perimeter, with chants of 'Hang Mike Pence!' ringing out (see Figure 1.2). Moreover, rioters explicitly sought out Pelosi's office in the Capitol building, if only to put their feet up on her desk, read her mail, make off with her sign and laptop, and shoot self-incriminating photos and videos of themselves doing so (see Chapter 8).

The Capitol riots will thus stand as a chronotope (Bakhtin, 1981)—a narrative construction that both defies and defines the nature of a particular place and time—a political moment at the close of the Trump presidency, a political protest whose face was white, angry, and male, a few notable exceptions to that demographic notwithstanding. While it might be characterized as a failed

FIGURE 1.2 Full-scale scaffold erected by Trump supporters outside the Capitol building
Source: Copyright iowyth hezel ulthiin.

insurrection—the breached perimeter led to little more than rampaging and pillaging rather than the direct seizing of power—it might also be characterized as a successfully mediatized event, documented extensively from within the ranks of the Capitol's stormers, climbers, performers, and occupiers. With many mainstream reporters in retreat, forced by protesters back to a distant position from which to observe the unfolding events, the partisans of the riot named themselves citizen journalists, tracking and documenting their own actions from within, posing for snapshots and selfies along the way, contributing hours of livestreaming to social media. There are as many competing theories of what their intentions would be once inside as there were competing intentions brought to the Capitol that day; their objectives have not become clearer in reviewing the many disparate discourses and actions represented in the visual evidence; yet said video footage abounds and analysis of the visual and discursive semiotics does provide some insight (see Chapter 6).

The performative actions depicted in early mainstream media bear mention. A video of Dominic Pezzola smashing a window with a police riot shield, followed by rioters climbing through the broken window and others streaming after them (see Chapter 8, Figure 8.5). A video features a crowd attempting to storm the Senate chambers, with the first person to climb through a smashed window being shot by Capitol police—this event appearing from several POVs. Images of the self-anointed QAnon Shaman, photographed by protesters and professional photo-journalists alike, wearing a fur hat with horns, face painted red, white, and blue, shirtless Norse-tattooed torso, carrying a pointed scepter to which an American flag has been zip-tied—hovering over the Senate dais, head tipped back, chest up, mouth wide open in a guttural scream. An image of Richard Barnett—a Trump supporter and middle-aged married man from Arkansas with a day job—sitting in Nancy Pelosi's aide's chair, an American flag draped over the cabinet, his left foot up on the desk, and later, another shot of him carrying away her mail wearing a look of mischief (see Figure 8.4), discussed further in Chapter 8. A photograph of a rioter carrying away the Speaker's lectern laughing like a child with a loot bag at a birthday party (see Figure 6.3), analyzed in detail in Chapter 6. The early visual evidence from mainstream media shows the bravado of trophy hunters and the naiveté of inexperienced lawbreakers engaged in performance crime, documenting their activities as a crucial component of the riot, although, whether to their credit or not, many did not actually understand that they were committing crimes (see Chapter 8). 'This is our house,' they chanted in awe of the Capitol building itself. 'We've paid for this place.' These images and videos, and many more, will be analyzed in detail in the pages that follow.

Every actionable event was streamed, photographed, commented, tweeted, parleyed, documented, posted online, shared, re-tweeted, echoed, liked, favorited, memed, and otherwise circulated via social media. Yet, these photos would soon be posted on an FBI wanted page, marking the beginning of a large-scale information gathering process of crowd-sourced self-surveillant evidence used in rolling charges laid against the insurrectionists.

State Actions from President to Police

Trump's speech that day, culminating in an exhortation to 'fight like hell,' (Trump, 2021), might be inferred to make him at least partially responsible for the riots, the evidence of which was laid out during two impeachment trials, only escaping prosecution due to partisan rifts, while also surprisingly swaying seven Republican candidates to vote against their own party interests (Cowan et al., 2021). The breaching of the Capitol might easily have led to a coup. Lawmakers were ushered away within a hair's breadth of the rioters breaching the Senate floor. Vice President Mike Pence was purportedly in a safe room just meters away from where a stream of protesters rushed the stairs in pursuit of a Capitol police officer. Alexandria Ocasio-Cortez has said that she nearly lost her life. Ultimately five people died that day, with subsequent losses of life following.

The storming of the US Capitol was a major rupture, a successful if ephemeral occupation of the seat of American democracy. It was indeed the first time in over two hundred years that the Capitol had been besieged, the previous being an 1814 British attack during the War of 1812. The 2021 riot, however, was a domestic attack, an attack by a contingent of disaffected citizens from within a divided nation, the divide perpetuated and deepened by the outgoing POTUS himself.

In an equally ambivalent response, the storming of the Capitol was emboldened by the seeming restraint shown by Capitol police, who appeared to act more like security guards at a moderately out-of-control rock concert than the security detail standing between lawmakers and those storming the seat of democracy, during what is typically heralded as the peaceful transition of power from one US President to the next. The police response was demonstrably light-handed when considered against the well-documented and much more brutal response of increasingly militarized police forces across the country to the Black Lives Matter protests and, indeed, riots. In Ferguson, MO in 2014, the National Guard was called out, the full wrath of the state, mobilized against citizens contesting systemic anti-Black racism evidenced by the ongoing systematized murder of Black people by police and white supremacists. However, a closer look at the oral histories and other emerging evidence shows that there were hundreds of police inside the Capitol, from a range of police forces, including the Capitol Police, the Secret Service, the FBI, and more, working to secure the premises and safeguard lawmakers (Tumulty, 2021). Moreover, a politics of defunding the police and abolitionism, called for by Black Lives Matter activists, might be at odds with calls for increased policing or locking up the protesters, regardless of the fact that BLM and white supremacist politics are at odds (see Chapter 11).

Yet, participants in the Capitol riots included white supremacists, who instead faced a torpid police response with surprisingly few arrests on site. Rather than getting kettled or contained by police, admitting their phones and backpack contents to evidence, rioters at the Capitol were simply allowed to walk away. The police have used the outpouring of videos, images, communications, and social media posts to arrest more than 700 participants through new crowdsourced investigation techniques of the self-surveillant subject (see Chapter 8).

While we want to be clear regarding the dangers of the rise of fascism and white supremacy in the US and globally, with a particular focus on this flashpoint event where it seems to be the dominant organizing factor, at the same time, we want to be careful not to use these arguments to revert to a new authoritarianism of the state or to support neoliberal capitalist agendas (see Chapter 11).

The Capitol Riots as Surplus and Incursion

The Capitol riots, like all riots, were grounded in a surplus (Clover, 2016), not necessarily an economic surplus, but a surplus nonetheless. Clover (2016, pp. 14–15) argues that a 'Riot is itself the experience of surplus. Surplus danger. Surplus information. Surplus military gear.' The surplus danger in this instance is the threat to lawmakers, the danger of policing, which resulted in injuries, arrests, and several deaths, the danger of physical risks leading to injury and death, the dangers inherent in violent insurrection—dangers that did not end after the riots. The surplus information, much of it disinformation, was evident in the mainstream media, alternative media, and social media, in the communications leading up to the 'March to Save America,' in Trump's speech itself, and in the self-surveillant documentation and journalistic reporting on events as they unfolded. In this outpouring of media images, the surplus of military gear is also evident: gear-stuffed backpacks, zip ties, cargo pants, camo, combat boots, and flak jackets abound (see Chapter 9).

With the surplus of danger, information, affect, and gear, the riot itself occupies the space of incursion, taking place when the perimeter is breached. The crowd crosses a boundary, transgressing a socially accepted line: the line of the Capitol premises demarcated by the barricades and the line of the police mobilized there to protect the barricades. When the barricades are attacked by the protesters, this flimsy line is moved, removed, erased. The perimeter is breached through a surplus of misinformation, emotion, affect, anger, and even of gear. The rioters are paradoxically anti-authoritarians 'fighting like hell' for democracy, under the aegis of what some would call an authoritarian President. Drawing a line in the sand, 'The moment when the partisans of riot exceed the police capacity for management, when the cops make their first retreat, is the moment when the riot becomes fully itself, slides loose from the grim continuity of daily life' (Clover, 2016, p. 15). It is in the breach of a space, a barrier, an idea that the riot forms its identity, as a force, a mob, a movement, an unorganized army. When the protesters on January 6th breached the perimeter, pulling down the flimsy metal barricades as the police retreated, they became rioters; when the rioters stormed onto the Capitol premises, turning its walls into a rock-climbing gym (see Figure 1.3), bashing through its windows with two-by-twos and stolen police riot gear, the alienation of a failed hyper-capitalism exceeded the bounds of everyday life, erupting into a surplus of alienation, protest, insurrection, and uprising—the riot fully becoming itself.

FIGURE 1.3 Trump supporters scale the walls of the Capitol building
Source: Copyright iowith hezel ulthiin, ulthiin's impression of an amalgamation of several images.

The Capitol Riots as 'Immediate Riot'

What kind of riot unfolded that day? For Badiou (2012, p. 22), there are three types of riots: 'immediate riot, latent riot and historical riot.' The Capitol riots fall within the first category, being defined as 'unrest among a section of the population, nearly always in the wake of a violent episode of state coercion' (Badiou, 2012, p. 22), in this case, perceived rather than real. Badiou (2012) argues that the leaders of an immediate riot are often youth, and this is one of the surprising elements of the Capitol riots—in the visual imagery, it is evident that participants are predominantly men of an older demographic, boomers and Gen Xers, middle-aged men. They are not alienated youth but disenfranchised retirees, veterans, and family men and some women. Several had heart attacks due to their advanced age and sadly died on-site or were carried off by ambulance. Many carried gear, having received training in the military or police. To Badiou's (2012, p. 22) rhetorical question, 'who has ever seen a riot whose front ranks were made up of the elderly?' we can respond—we have. He suggests that the capacities of youth to be mobile, to assemble, pivot on tactics, and transcend moderation form the foundations of mass riotous action. In the Capitol riots, these same capacities are on display in an older cohort.

The Greek riots of 2008 were also comprised of older generations joined by younger ones to contest austerity measures as well as the shooting death by police of a teenager (Treré et al., 2017). Similarly, in the Spanish Indignados of 2011, a multi-generational mobilization brought together disenfranchised youth, the middle-aged generation of anti-globalization activists, and the older generation who had survived the military junta (Fuster Morell, 2012). Thus, multi-generational riots are nothing new but perhaps also not commonplace.

The Capitol riots might be considered a historical riot, a riot that lays siege to a key city or town, or the seat of power itself, for a period of time and with political objectives (Badiou, 2012). Certainly, the location of the riots was a key seat of power, and the timing was connected to the transition of power, turning around the very question of who would hold the power of the Presidency. However, those who took the Capitol on January 6, 2021, did not lay siege to it with the intention of claiming political power, installing a new leader, or reaffirming an existing leader (Trump did not enter the building with them, rendering this impossible), neither were they making any political proclamations or actions such as burning the Constitution, reading a manifesto, and so forth. Some may have loudly proclaimed 'freedom' among other basic expressions of political ideologies, but without any coordinated plan or strategy to collectively seize power. Or so it would seem. There was no formulated coup nor siege, and thus, following Badiou (2012), no historical riot. After the spectacle, the participants left as quickly as they had arrived, some under arrest, others under their own steam, or pushed back by the National Guard.

However, another level of organization and objectives is starting to emerge through deeper investigations of the mediatization of the day. Four leaders of the Proud Boys have been arrested, indicted on felony conspiracy charges:

> All four men are facing six counts in the indictment, including four felony charges for conspiracy; obstruction of an official proceeding and aiding and abetting others in the obstruction; obstructing law enforcement during civil disorder and aiding and abetting; and destruction of government property valued at more than $1,000.
>
> *(Tillman, 2021)*

They are alleged to have used encrypted communications and attended the march incognito, not wanting to show their affiliation; to have coordinated leadership in organizing several chapters of Proud Boys to travel to Washington and participate in the march, to have raised funds to finance gear and travel, carried paramilitary gear to the protest, used handheld radios to communicate among themselves, and violently forced their way into the Capitol, past the police barricade (Tillman, 2021). Some leaders of the Oath Keepers have also been under investigation for similar actions, with eleven arrested and charged with seditious conspiracy.

These varying forms of participation and intent bear further investigation, as not all participants came to the Capitol with the same idea regarding what might transpire and what their role might be. In addition, we want to pay attention to the power structures and political economy of mainstream and right-wing media reporting on the riots in terms of their specific framing of events and, post-event, the attempts of some media outlets, following Trump, to erase the riots from history altogether (Tumulty, 2021).

These observations beg the question of whether this might be considered something more long-term or ongoing, a kind of unfinished business, a 'historical riot'? A historical riot occurs 'when an immediate riot extends to sectors of the population which, by virtue of their status, social composition, sex or age, are remote from its constitutive core that a genuine historical dimension is on the agenda' (Badiou, 2012, p. 31). In other words, have more people joined in support of the Capitol rioters who don't share their identities?

This does not seem to be the case. The rioters remained in one isolated location for a short period of time, and the riot was not taken up by the broader society to become a riot of historical dimensions, according to Badiou's (2012) criteria. This is not to say that it lacks historical importance, rather, that it exists in a kind of liminal place among riots, limited somewhat in scope due to its lack of coherence, its combination of extreme violence and grade school hooliganism, its cries for freedom without a clear object, goal, or directive, and its failure to achieve any political transformation. The riots thus seem to exist as an homage, a farewell to Trump's Presidency, one last gasp of chaos and cruelty.

What is particularly strange about this particularly strange riot is its tenuous position both in and out of alignment with state power: participants are in alignment with the power of an outgoing President crying foul, and out of alignment with the power of the democratic process that the state was attempting to carry out in good faith. Participants are in alignment with a sense of outrage and fear within a world facing multiple crises, calling these corrupt mechanisms of power into question, and out of alignment with attempts to right the systemic injustices and oppressions of unequal power that fuel these cascading crises along axes of race, class, and gender.

A critical analysis of power is crucial to the unfolding of this book, as we cannot simply denounce the violence of rioters without being attentive to the notion of the casual everyday violence of the powerful, including state violence, police violence, and structural violence. Furthermore, analysis of media representations must also pose the question of who has the power to shape the dominant interpretations of visual and textual framings of events, whether they circulate in mainstream media, alternative media, alt-right media, social media, or the complex interplay of all of these within the global media ecologies of our time.

In understanding the riot through its proliferation of performances, costumes, messages, media, communication, videos, texts, discourses, and images—as pure spectacle—we may understand the rioters' aims as incredibly significant in their discursive and semiotic signals and much less so in their material, political, and social outcomes. Perhaps it was not through an achieved change in the material conditions of everyday life that these rioters made their aims manifest, but rather through a rattling of the rafters, a shaking of the trees, in a symbolic display of civil unrest. Yet, the affective surplus of an incoherent and inchoate fear and rage should not be explained away simply because of its incoherence. Instead, it must be teased apart to attempt to comprehend what drives it.

The Capitol Riots signaled a troubling affective surplus or excess seeking—and finding—expression. If not addressed, the risk is that this excess will continue to manifest in ways that threaten to violently disrupt society. This book, therefore, attempts to make sense of the riots as a discursive, rhetorical, theatrical, symbolic, ideological, and political set of performances embedded in a nostalgic (racist, misogynist, colonial) view of a divided and violent US. We can only hope that this contribution can move us through and past this moment where authoritarianism and divide-and-rule politics have renewed purchase for a large percentage of the US population, as in some other countries around the world.

Our aim with this book is to play a small role in moving us forward into new imagined futures, not limited by the constraints of neoliberal democracy whose inequalities have been laid bare by the COVID pandemic, but rather exploring new imaginaries of a collective intelligence in post-pandemic and post-Capitol-riots futures built beyond the falsely constructed media-framed polarizations of a nation divided, and contesting the everyday realities of isolation, misinformation, and rampant self-absorbed individualism.

Methods by Chapter

To make sense of this event for the annals of history, we ask ourselves not just *what happened* (although certainly that question garners attention here) but also *how* it was documented. To do so, we examine how the events were mediatized and rendered into history through the continuous image-stream produced not just by mainstream media but also by the massive outpouring of text, images, and videos by participatory self-surveillant subjects on social media. Approaching this data stream, we engage a range of multi-disciplinary methods from the social sciences and humanities to provide context and analyses of both the visual and textual content and the big datasets produced and captured that day. In analyzing the digital media and data streams, we attempt to understand the many different media uses and outputs of a range of social actors before, during, and after the riots, to propagate information, including disinformation and fake news, as well as to coordinate and organize their participation, and finally, to document the actions of the day. The question we set out to answer is: how can we critically think through the media and data streams produced at the Capitol riots in ways that allow us to imagine better futures, including more fruitful solutions to the problems of alienation, disinformation, populism, and individualism that permeate American society today?

To respond to this question, we provide a textured analysis, drawing upon interdisciplinary frameworks and methods from the related fields of Communications, Data Science, Sociology, Visual Media, Political Economy, and Cultural Studies. In this book, we first situate the riots in their political, economic, and social context, including pedagogical issues at stake in contested knowledge production (Chapter 2), and the context of misinformation, disinformation, and fake news (Chapter 3), providing a basic narrative, timeline, and mapping of the events of the day (Chapter 4). The methodologies of subsequent chapters engage data science and semiotic approaches: data scraping and analysis of text-based data from Parler, a social media site predominantly used by alt-right groups (Chapter 5); and a comparative cultural semiotic analysis of photography produced by citizens and journalists (Chapter 6). Finally, we explore several thematic interventions, first regarding QAnon conspiracies through a Bakhtinian framework (Chapter 7); second, a cultural criminology approach to performance crime (Chapter 8); third, analysis of gender in terms of white masculinities (Chapter 9) and fourth, women in the riots (Chapter 10); and finally, a consideration of policing, racism, and the state (Chapter 11), looking to prospects for the future of democracy in America.

References

Badiou, A (2012) *The rebirth of history: Times of riots and uprisings*. London UK: Verso.

Bakhtin, MM (1981) *The dialogic imagination*. Austin: University of Texas Press.

Barstow, D, Craig, S and Buettner, R (2018) 'Trump Engaged in Suspect Tax Scheme as He Reaped Riches from His Father,' *New York Times*, 2 October [Online]. Available at: www.nytimes.com/interactive/2018/10/02/us/politics/donald-trump-tax-schemes-fred-trump.html?mtrref=t.co&auth=login-email (Accessed: 19 September 2021).

Beckett, L (2020) 'Armed Protesters Demonstrate Against Covid-19 Lockdown at Michigan Capitol,' *The Guardian*, 30 April [Online]. Available at: www.theguardian.com/us-news/2020/apr/30/michigan-protests-coronavirus-lockdown-armed-capitol (Accessed: 20 September 2021).

Bhambra, S (2019) 'The Montreal experiments: Brainwashing and the ethics of psychiatric experimentation,' *Hektoen International: A Journal of Medical Humanities*, spring.

Black, KA, Rich, R and Felske-Durksen, C (2021) 'Forced and coerced sterilization of Indigenous peoples: Considerations for health care providers,' *Journal of Obstetrics and Gynaecology Canada*, 43(9), pp. 1090–1093.

Blass, T (ed.) (2009) *Obedience to authority: Current perspectives on the Milgram paradigm*. New Jersey: Lawrence Erlbaum.

Chait, J (2021) 'GOP Congresswoman Blamed Wildfires on Secret Jewish Space Laser,' *Intelligencer*, 28 January [Online]. Available at: https://nymag.com/intelligencer/article/marjorie-taylor-greene-qanon-wildfires-space-laser-rothschild-execute.html (Accessed: 20 September 2021).

Chicago Project on Security and Threats (2021) *The face of American insurrection: Right-wing organizations evolving into a violent mass movement*. University of Chicago. https://d3qi0qp55mx5f5.cloudfront.net/cpost/i/docs/americas_insurrectionists_online_2021_01_29.pdf?mtime=1611966204.

Cinelli, M, Quattrociocchi, W, Galeazzi, A, Valensise, CM, Brugnoli, E, Schmidt, AL, Zola, P, Zollo, F and Scala, A (2020) 'The COVID-19 social media infodemic,' *Scientific Reports*, 10 doi:10.1038/s41598-020-73510-5.

Clover, J (2016) *Riot. strike. riot: The new era of uprisings*. London, UK: Verso.

Cowan, R, Morgan, D and Brice, M (2021) 'US Senate Acquits Trump as Republicans Save Him in Impeachment Again,' *Reuters*, 13 February [Online]. Available at: www.reuters.com/article/us-usa-trump-impeachment-idUSKBN2AD0AE (Accessed: 20 September 2021).

Danewid, I (2021) 'Policing the (migrant) crisis: Stuart Hall and the defence of whiteness,' *Security Dialogue* doi:10.1177/0967010621994074.

Dean, J (2005) 'Communicative capitalism: Circulation and the foreclosure of politics,' *Cultural Politics*, 1 (1). doi:10.2752/174321905778054845.

Fisher, M (2009) 'The Politics of Astroturf,' *The Atlantic*, 5 August [Online]. Available at: www.theatlantic.com/politics/archive/2009/08/the-politics-of-astroturf/348484/ (Accessed: 21 September 2021).

Frenkel, S (2020) 'The Rise and Fall of the "Stop the Steal" Facebook Group,' *The New York Times*, 5 November, sec. Technology [Online]. Available at: www.nytimes.com/2020/11/05/technology/stop-the-steal-facebook-group.html (Accessed: 21 September 2021).

Friedberg, B (2020) 'The Dark Virality of a Hollywood Blood-Harvesting Conspiracy,' *Wired*, 31 July [Online]. Available at: www.wired.com/story/opinion-the-dark-virality-of-a-hollywood-blood-harvesting-conspiracy/ (Accessed: 21 September 2021).

Fuster Morell, M (2012) 'The free culture and 15M movements in Spain,' *Social Movement Studies*, 11(3–4) doi:10.1080/14742837.2012.710323.

Giroux, HA (2021) 'Tucker Carlson Is Just the Tip of the Iceberg in Right-Wing Media's War on Truth,' *TruthOut*, 27 May [Online]. Available at: https://truthout.org/articles/tucker-carlson-is-just-the-tip-of-the-iceberg-in-right-wing-medias-war-on-truth/ (Accessed: 21 September 2021).

Gray, R (2017) 'Trump Defends White-Nationalist Protesters: "Some Very Fine People on Both Sides",' *The Atlantic*, 15 August [Online]. Available at:www.theatlantic.com/politics/archive/2017/08/trump-defends-white-nationalist-protesters-some-very-fine-people-on-both-sides/537012/ (Accessed: 21 September 2021).

Hall, S (1979) 'The Great Moving Right Show', *Marxism Today*, January. Available at: http://banmarchive.org.uk/collections/mt/pdf/79_01_hall.pdf (Accessed: 22 September 2021).

Hvistendahl, M (2020) 'Masks Off: How the Brothers who Fueled the Reopen Protests Built a Volatile Far-right Network', *The Intercept*, July 17. Available at: https://theintercept.com/2020/07/17/dorr-brothers-coronavirus-protests/ (Accessed: 22 September 2021).

Jones, JH (2008) 'The Tuskegee syphilis experiment,' in Emanual, EJ, Grady, C, Crouch, RA, Lie, RK, Miller, FG and Wendler, D (eds.) *The Oxford textbook of clinical research ethics*. Oxford, UK: Oxford University Press, pp. 86–96.

Kessler, G, Rizzo, S and Kelly, M (2021) 'Trump's False or Misleading Claims Total 30,573 over 4 Years,' *Washington Post*, 24 January [Online]. Available at: www.washingtonpost.com/politics/2021/01/24/trumps-false-or-misleading-claims-total-30573-over-four-years/ (Accessed: 21 September 2021).

Klein, N (2008) *The shock doctrine: The rise of disaster capitalism*. Toronto: Vintage.

Klein, N (2020) 'The Great Reset Conspiracy Smoothie,' *The Intercept*, 8 December [Online]. Available at: https://theintercept.com/2020/12/08/great-reset-conspiracy/ (Accessed: 21 September 2021).

Levinson, J, Wilson, C, Doubek, J and Nuyen, S (2020) 'Federal Officers Use Unmarked Vehicles to Grab People in Portland, DHS Confirms,' *NPR*, 17 July [Online]. Available at: www.npr.org/2020/07/17/892277592/federal-officers-use-unmarked-vehicles-to-grab-protesters-in-portland (Accessed: 21 September 2021).

Lewis, H (2020) 'The Coronavirus Is a Disaster for Feminism,' *The Atlantic*, 19 March [Online]. Available at: www.theatlantic.com/international/archive/2020/03/feminism-womens-rights-coronavirus-covid19/608302/ (Accessed: 21 September 2021).

Lewis, NM, Friedrichs, M, Wagstaff, S et al. (2020) 'Disparities in COVID-19 Incidence, Hospitalizations, and Testing, by Area-Level Deprivation,' *Morb Mortal Wkly Rep.*, 69: 1369–1373. doi:10.15585/mmwr.mm6938a4.

McLachlan, H (2020) 'Why "There's No Such Thing as Society" Should Not Be Regarded with Moral Revulsion,' *The Conversation Canada*, 24 April [Online]. Available at: https://theconversation.com/why-theres-no-such-thing-as-society-should-not-be-regarded-with-moral-revulsion-136008 (Accessed: 21 September 2021).

Miller, T (2021) *The Covid charter: A better world.* New Brunswick, NJ: Rutgers University Press.

Miller, T and Ahluwalia, P (2020) 'The Covid conjuncture,' *Social Identities*, 26 (5). doi:10.1080/13504630.2020.1824359.

Millet, GA, Jones, AT, Benkeser, D et al. (2020) 'Assessing Differential Impacts of COVID-19 on Black Communities', *Ann Epidemiol.*, 47: 37–44. doi:10.1016/j.annepidem.2020.05.003.

Mondon, A and Winter, A (2020) *Reactionary democracy: How racism and the populist far right became mainstream.* London, UK: Verso.

Pape, R (2021) 'What an Analysis of 377 Americans Arrested or Charged in the Capitol Insurrection Tells Us,' *The Washington Post*, 6 April [Online]. Available at: https://perma.cc/B5L9-2KVV (Accessed: 22 September 2021).

Program on Extremism (2021) 'This is our house: A preliminary assessment of the Capitol Hill siege participants.' George Washington University [Online]. Available at: https://extremism.gwu.edu/sites/g/files/zaxdzs2191/f/This-Is-Our-House.pdf (Accessed: 22 September, 2021).

Schwartz, B (2021) 'Pro-Trump Dark Money Groups Organized the Rally That Led to Deadly Capitol Hill Riot,' *CNBC*, 9 January [Online]. Available at: www.cnbc.com/2021/01/09/pro-trump-dark-money-groups-organized-the-rally-that-led-to-deadly-capitol-hill-riot.html (Accessed: 22 September 2021).

Sim, J (2000) 'Against the punitive wind: Stuart Hall, the state and the lessons of the great moving right show,' in Gilroy, P, Grossberg, L and McRobbie, A (eds.) *Without guarantees: In honour of Stuart Hall.* London, UK: Verso, pp. 318–334.

Stern, AM (2020) *Proud Boys and the white ethnostate: How the alt-right is warping the American imagination.* Boston: Beacon.

Tillman, Z (2021) 'Two Proud Boys Leaders Indicted In a Capitol Riot Conspiracy Are Going to Jail,' *BuzzFeed News*, 19 April [Online]. Available at: www.buzzfeednews.com/article/zoetillman/proud-boys-leaders-jailed-capitol-riot-conspiracy (Accessed: 22 September 2021).

Treré, E, Jeppesen, S and Mattoni, A (2017) 'Comparing digital protest media imaginaries: Anti-austerity movements in Greece, Italy & Spain,' *tripleC: Communication, Capitalism & Critique*, 15(2). doi:10.31269/triplec.v15i2.772.

Trump, D (2021) 'Read Trump's Jan. 6 Speech, A Key Part of Impeachment Trial,' *NPR*, 10 February [Online]. Available at: www.npr.org/2021/02/10/966396848/read-trumps-jan-6-speech-a-key-part-of-impeachment-trial (Accessed: 22 September 2021).

Tumulty, K (2021) 'The Shameless Revisionism of the Capitol Attack Cannot Be Allowed to Take Root,' *The Washington Post*, 3 April [Online]. Available at: www.washingtonpost.com/opinions/2021/04/03/shameless-revisionism-capitol-attack-cannot-be-allowed-take-root/ (Accessed: 22 September 2021).

US Bureau of Labor Statistics (2020) 'Employment status of the foreign-born and native-born populations by selected characteristics, 2019–2020 annual averages' [Online]. Available at: www.bls.gov/news.release/forbrn.t01.htm (Accessed: 22 September 2021).

Vogel, KP, Rutenberg, J and Lerer, L (2020) 'The Quiet Hand of Conservative Groups in the Anti-Lockdown Protests,' *The New York Times*, 21 April [Online]. Available at: www.nytimes.com/2020/04/21/us/politics/coronavirus-protests-trump.html (Accessed: 22 September 2021).

Voice of America (2021) 'Trump speaking at the "Stop the Steal" rally on January 6, 2021.' Available at: https://commons.wikimedia.org/wiki/File:2021_United_States_Capitol_VOA_1.jpg.

Watkins, E and Phillip, A (2018) 'Trump Decries Immigrants from "Shithole Countries" Coming to US,' *CNN*, 12 January [Online]. Available at: www.cnn.com/2018/01/11/politics/immigrants-shithole-countries-trump/index.html (Accessed: 22 September 2021).

Ye Hee Lee, M (2015) 'Donald Trump's False Comments Connecting Mexican Immigrants and Crime,' *The Washington Post*, 8 July [Online]. Available at: www.washingtonpost.com/news/fact-checker/wp/2015/07/08/donald-trumps-false-comments-connecting-mexican-immigrants-and-crime/ (Accessed: 22 September 2021).

2

AGAINST APARTHEID PEDAGOGY IN THE AGE OF WHITE SUPREMACY[1]

Henry Giroux

The toxic thrust of white supremacy runs through American culture like an electric current. Jim Crow is back without apology, suffocating American society in a wave of voter suppression laws, the elevation of racist discourse to the centers of power, and the ongoing attempt by right-wing politicians to implement a form of apartheid pedagogy that makes important social issues that challenge the racial and economic status quo disappear. The cult of manufactured ignorance now works through disimagination machines engaged in a politics of falsehoods and erasure. Matters of justice, ethics, equality, and historical memory now vanish from the classrooms of public and higher education and from powerful cultural apparatuses and social media platforms that have become the new teaching machines.

In the current era of white supremacy, the most obvious version of apartheid pedagogy is present in attempts by Republican Party politicians to rewrite the narrative regarding who counts as an American. This whitening of collective identity is largely reproduced by right-wing attacks on diversity and race sensitivity training, critical race programs in government, and social justice and racial issues in the schools. These bogus assaults are all too familiar and include widespread and coordinated ideological and pedagogical attacks against both historical memory and critical forms of education.

The fight to censor critical, truth telling versions of American history and the current persistence of systemic racism is part of a larger conservative project to prevent teachers, students, journalists, and others from speaking openly about crucial social issues that undermine a viable democracy. Such attacks are increasingly waged by conservative foundations, anti-public intellectuals, politicians, and media outlets. These include right-wing think tanks such as Heritage Foundation and Manhattan Institute, conservative scholars such as Thomas Sowell, right-wing politicians such as Mitch McConnell, and far-right media outlets such as *City Journal, The Daily Caller, The Federalist,* and *Fox News.* The threat of teaching

DOI: 10.4324/9781003246862-3

children about the history and systemic nature of racism appears particularly dangerous to *Fox News,* which since June 5, 2020 has posited 'critical race theory' as a threat in over 150 different broadcasts (Harris, 2021). What is shared by all of these individuals and cultural apparatuses is the claim that critical race theory and other 'anti-racist' programs constitute forms of indoctrination that threaten to undermine the alleged foundations of Western Civilization.

The nature of this moral panic is evident in the fact that 15 state legislatures across the country have introduced bills to prevent or limit teachers from teaching about the history of slavery and racism in American society. In doing so, they are making a claim for what one Texas legislator called 'traditional history,' which allegedly should focus on 'ideas that make the country great' (McGee, 2021). Idaho's lieutenant governor, Janice McGeachin, is more forthright in revealing the underlying ideological craze behind censoring any talk by teachers and students about race in Idaho public schools. She has introduced a taskforce to protect young people from what she calls, with no pun intended, 'the scourge of critical race theory, socialism, communism, and Marxism' (Wong, 2021).

Such attacks are about more than censorship and racial cleansing. They make the political more pedagogical in that they use education and the power of persuasion as weapons to discredit any critical approach to grappling with the history of racism and white supremacy. In doing so, they attempt to undermine and discredit the critical faculties necessary for students and others to examine history as a resource in order to 'investigate the core conflict between a nation founded on radical notions of liberty, freedom, and equality, and a nation built on slavery, exploitation, and exclusion' (Sanchez and English, 2020). The current attacks on critical race theory, if not critical thinking itself, are but one instance of the rise of apartheid pedagogy. This is a pedagogy in which education is used in the service of dominant power in order to both normalize racism, class inequities, and economic inequality while safeguarding the interests of those who benefit from such inequities the most. In pursuit of such a project, they impose a pedagogy of oppression, complacency, and mindless discipline. They ignore or downplay matters of injustice and the common good, and rarely embrace notions of community as part of a pedagogy that engages pressing social, economic and civic problems. Instead of an education of civic practice that enriches the public imagination, they endorse all the elements of indoctrination central to formalizing and updating a mode of fascist politics.

The conservative wrath waged against critical race theory is not only about white ignorance being a form of bliss but is also central to a struggle over power—the power of the moral and political imagination. White ignorance is crucial to upholding the poison of white supremacy. Apartheid pedagogy is about denial and disappearance–a manufactured ignorance that attempts to whitewash history and rewrite the narrative of American exceptionalism as it might have been framed in the 1920s and 30s when members of a resurgent Ku Klux Klan shaped the policies of some school boards. Apartheid pedagogy uses education as a disimagination machine to convince students and others that racism does not exist, that teaching about racial justice is a form of indoctrination, and that understanding history is more an exercise in blind reverence than critical analysis. Apartheid pedagogy aims to reproduce current systems of racism rather than end them. Organizations such as *No Left Turn in Education* (2021) not only oppose teaching about racism in schools, but also comprehensive sex education, and teaching children about climate change, which they view as forms of indoctrination. Without irony, they label themselves an organization of 'patriotic Americans who believe that a fair and just society can only be achieved when malleable young minds are free from indoctrination that suppresses their independent thought' (No Left Turn in Education, 2021). This is the power of ignorance in the service of civic death and a flight from ethical and social responsibility. Kali Holloway (2021), citing the NYU philosopher Charles W. Mills, succinctly sums up the selective memory and calculated forgetting at the heart of white ignorance. She writes:

> While white ignorance is related to the anti-intellectualism that defines the white Republican brand, it should be regarded as yet more specific. According to Mills, white ignorance demands a purposeful misunderstanding of reality—both present and historical—and then treats that fictitious worldview as the singular, de-politicized, unbiased, "objective" truth.

New York Times columnist Michelle Goldberg (2021a) reports that right-wing legislators have taken up the cause to ban critical race theory from not only public schools but also higher education. She highlights the case of Boise State University, which has banned dozens of classes dealing with diversity. She notes that soon afterwards, 'the Idaho State Senate voted to cut $409,000 from the school's budget, an amount meant to reflect what Boise State spends on social justice programs' (Goldberg, 2021a). Such attacks are happening across the United States and are not only meant to curtail teaching about racism, sexism, and other controversial issues in the schools, but also to impose strict restrictions on what non-tenured assistant professors can teach and to what degree they can be pushed to accept being both deskilled and giving up control over the conditions of their labor.

In an egregious example of an attack on free speech and tenure itself, the Board of Trustees at the University of North Carolina denied a tenure position to Pulitzer Prize-winning journalist, Nikole Hannah-Jones, because of her work on the *New York Times Magazine*'s 1619 project, 'which examined the legacy of slavery in America' (Robertson, 2021). The failure to provide tenure to Hannah-Jones, who is also the recipient of a MacArthur Foundation 'Genius Grant,' and an inductee into the North Carolina Media and Journalism Hall of Fame, is a blatant act of racism and a gross violation of academic freedom. Let's be clear. Hannah-Jones was denied tenure by the North Carolina Board of Trustees because she brings to the university a critical concern with racism that clashes with the strident political conservatism of the board. It is also another example of a racist backlash by conservatives who wish to deny that racism even exists in the United States, never mind that it should even by acknowledged in the classrooms of public and higher education.

This is a form of 'patriotic education' being put in place by a resurgence of those who support Jim Crow power relations and want to impose pedagogies of repression on students in the classroom. This type of retribution is part of a long-standing politics of fear, censorship and academic repression that has been waged by conservatives since the student revolts of the 1960s (Goldberg, 2021b). It is also part of the ongoing corporatization of the university in which business models now define how the university is governed, faculty are reduced to part-time workers, and students are viewed as customers and consumers (Giroux, 2020).

Equally important, Hannah-Jones' case is an updated and blatant attack on the ability and power of faculty rather than Boards of Trustees to make decisions regarding both faculty hiring and the crucial question of who decides how tenure is handled in a university (Weineck, 2021). Keith E. Whittington and Sean Wilentz (2021) are right in stating that the Board's actions to deny Hannah-Jones a tenured professorship are about more than a singular violation of faculty rights, academic freedom, and an attack on associated discourses relating to critical race theory. They write:

> The perception and reality of political intervention in matters of faculty hiring will do lasting damage to the reputation of higher education in North Car-olina—and will embolden boards across the country similarly to interfere with academic operations of the universities that they oversee.

Holding critical ideas has become a liability in the contemporary neoliberal uni-versity. Also at risk here is the relationship between critical thinking, civic values, and historical remembrance in the current attempts to suppress not just voting rights but also dangerous memories, especially regarding the attack on Critical Race Theory. David Theo Goldberg (2021) has brilliantly outlined how the war on Critical Race Theory and other anti-racist programs is designed largely to eliminate the legacy and persistent effects of systemic racial injustice and its underlying structural, ideological, and pedagogical fundamentals and components. This is apartheid pedagogy with a vengeance. As David Theo Goldberg (2021) writes, the

> conservative attack on CRT is largely meant to distract from the Right's own paucity of ideas. The strategy is to create a straw house to set aflame in order to draw attention away from not just its incapacity but its outright refusal to address issues of cumulative, especially racial, injustice.

The public imagination is now in crisis. Radical uncertainty has turned lethal. In the current historical moment, tyranny, fear, and hatred have become defining modes of governance and education. Right-wing politicians bolstered by the power of corporate controlled media now construct ways of thinking and feeling that prey on the anxieties of the isolated, disenfranchised, and powerless. This is a form of apartheid pedagogy engineered to substitute disillusionment and incoherence for a sense of comforting ignorance, the thrill of hyper-masculinity, and the security that comes with the militarized unity of the accommodating masses waging a war on democracy. The public imagination is formed through habits of daily life, but only for the better when such experiences are filtered through the ideals and promises of a democracy. This is no longer true. Under neoliberal fascism, the concentration of power in the hands of a ruling elite has ensured that any notion of change regarding equality and justice is now tainted, if not destroyed, as a result of what Theodor Adorno called a retreat into apocalyptic bombast marked by 'an organized flight of ideas' (Weiss, 2020, p. 61).

Violence in the United States has become a form of domestic terrorism; it is omnipresent and works through complex systems of symbolic and institutional control. It extends from the prison and school to the normalizing efforts of cultural apparatus that saturate an image-based culture. Violence registers itself in repressive policies, police brutality, and in an ongoing process of exclusion and disposability. It is also present in the weaponization of ideas and the institutions that produce them through forms of apartheid pedagogy. Fear now comes in the form of both armed police and repressive modes of education. As the famed artist Isaac Cordal (2020) observes, 'We live in societies … that use fear in order to make people submissive…. Fear bends us [and makes us]vulnerable to its desires…. Our societies have been built on violence, and that heritage, that colonial hangover which is capitalism today still remains' (Evans and Cordal, 2020). Under gangster capitalism's system of power, the poverty of the civic and political imagination is taking its last breath.

Authoritarian societies do more than censor and subvert the truth, they also shape collective consciousness and punish those who engage in dangerous thinking (Giroux, 2015). For instance, the current plague of white supremacy fueling neoliberal fascism is rooted not only in structural and economic forms of domination, but also intellectual and pedagogical forces, making clear that education is central to politics. It also points to the urgency of understanding that white supremacy is first and foremost a struggle over agency, assigned meanings, and identity—over what lives count and whose don't. This is a politics and pedagogy that often leaves few historical traces in a culture of immediacy and manufactured ignorance.

The emergent and expanding presence of white supremacy and fascist politics disappear easily in a culture dominated by the endless images of spectacularized violence that fill screen culture with mass shootings, police violence, and racist attacks on Blacks and Asian Americans in the post-Trump era. Disconnected and decontextualized, such images vanish in an image-based culture of shock, entertainment, and organized forgetting. When critical ideas come to the surface, right-wing politicians and pundits attack dissidents as un-American and the oppositional press as 'an enemy of the American people.' They also attempt to impose a totalitarian notion of 'patriotic education' on public schools and higher education and censor academics who criticize systemic abuses (Klein, 2021; Crowley, 2020).

As is well known, former President Trump waged a relentless attack on the media and in ways too similar to ignore echoed written and spoken sentiments that Hitler used in his rise to power (Las Vegas Sun, 2017). In this instance, culture, increasingly shaped by an apartheid pedagogy, has turned oppressive and must be addressed as a site of struggle while working in tandem with the development of an ongoing massive resistance movement. This suggests the need for a more comprehensive understanding of politics and the power of the educational force of the culture. Such connections necessitate closer attention be given to the educational and cultural power of a neoliberal corporate elite who use their mainstream and social media platforms to shape pedagogically the collective consciousness of a nation in the discourse and relations of hate, bigotry, ignorance, and conformity.

America's slide into a fascist politics demands a revitalized understanding of the historical moment in which we find ourselves, along with a systemic critical analysis of the new political formations that mark this period. Part of this challenge is to create a new language and mass social movement to address and construct empowering terrains of education, politics, justice, culture, and power that challenge existing systems of racist violence and economic oppression. The beginning of such a political and pedagogical strategy can be found in the Black Lives Matter movement and its alignment with other movements fighting against authoritarianism. The Black Lives Matter movement teaches us 'that eradicating racial oppression ultimately requires struggle against oppression in all of its forms … [especially] restructuring America's economic system' (Hamilton, 2017). This is especially important as those groups marginalized by class, race, ethnicity, and religion have become aware of how much in this new era of fascist politics they have lost control over the economic, political, pedagogical, and social conditions that bear down on their lives. Visions have become dystopian, devolving into a sense of being left out, abandoned, and subject to increasing systems of terror and violence. These issues can no longer be viewed as individual problems but as manifestations of a broader failure of politics. Moreover, what is needed is not a series of stopgap reforms limited to particular institutions or groups, but a radical restructuring of the entirety of US society.

The call for a socialist democracy demands the creation of visions, ideals, institutions, social relations, and pedagogies of resistance that enable the public to imagine a life beyond a social order in which racial, class, gender, and other forms of violence produce endless assaults on the environment, systemic police violence, a culture of ignorance and cruelty. Such challenges must also address the assault on the public and civic imagination, mediated through the elevation of war, militarization, violent masculinity, and the politics of disposability to the highest levels of power. Capitalism is a death driven machine that infantilizes, exploits, and devalues human life and the planet itself. As market mentalities and moralities tighten their grip on all aspects of society, democratic institutions and public spheres are being downsized, if not altogether disappearing, along with the informed citizens without which there is no democracy.

Any viable pedagogy of resistance needs to create the educational and pedagogical tools to produce a radical shift in consciousness, capable of both recognizing the scorched earth policies of neoliberal capitalism, and the twisted ideologies that support it. This shift in consciousness cannot take place without pedagogical interventions that speak to people in ways in which they can recognize themselves, identify with the issues being addressed, and place the privatization of their troubles in a broader systemic context (Latham, Kingsmith, Von Bargen, and Block, 2020). Nico Block (2020) gets it right in arguing for a 'radical recasting of the leftist imagination,' in which the concrete needs of people are addressed and elevated to the forefront of public discussion in order to confront and get ahead of the crises of our times. He writes that this involves

> building bridges between the real and the imaginary, so that the path to achieving political goals is plain to see. Accordingly, the articulation of leftist goals must resonate with people in concrete ways, so that it becomes obvious how the achievement of those goals would improve their day-to-day lives.

A pedagogy of resistance must be on the side of hope and civic courage in order to fight against a paralyzing indifference, grave social injustices, and mind deadening attacks on the public imagination. At stake here is the struggle for a new world based on the notion that capitalism and democracy are not the same, and that we need to understand the world, how we think about it and how it functions, in order to change it. In the spirt of Martin Luther King, Jr's call for a more comprehensive view of oppression and political struggle, it is crucial to address his call to radically interrelate and restructure consciousness, values, and society itself. In this instance, King and other theorists, such as Saskia Sassen, call for a language that bridges ideological ruptures and changes the nature of the debate. This suggests more than simply a rhetorical challenge to the economic conditions that fuel neoliberal capitalism. There is also the need to move beyond abstract notions of structural violence and identify and connect the visceral elements of violence that bear down on and 'constrain agency through the hard surfaces of [everyday] life' (Graeber, 2012, p. 105).

We live in an era in which the distinction between the truth and misinformation is under attack. Ignorance has become a virtue, and education has become a tool of repression that elevates self-interest and privatization to central organizing principles of both economics and politics. The socio-historical conditions that enable racism, systemic inequality, anti-intellectualism, mass incarceration, the war on youth, poverty, state violence, and domestic terrorism must be remembered in the fight against that which now parades as ideologically normal. Historical memory and the demands of moral witnessing must become part of a deep grammar of political and pedagogical resistance in the fight against neoliberal capitalism and other forms of authoritarianism.

A pedagogy of resistance necessitates a language that connects the problems of systemic racism, poverty, militarism, mass incarceration, and other injustices as part of a totalizing structural, pedagogical, and ideological set of condition endemic to capitalism in its updated merging of neoliberalism and fascist politics. Audre Lorde was right in her insistence that 'There is no such thing as a single-issue struggle because we do not live single-issue lives.'

We don't need master narratives, but we do need a recognition that politics can only be grasped as part of a social totality, a struggle rooted in overlapping differences that bleed into each other. We need relational narratives that bring together different struggles for emancipation and social equality.

Central to any viable notion of pedagogical resistance is the courage to think about what kind of world we want—what kind of future we want to build for our children. These are questions that can only be addressed when we address politics and capitalism as part of a general crisis of democracy. This challenge demands the willingness to develop an anti-capitalist consciousness as the basis for a call to action, one willing to dismantle the present structure of neoliberal capitalism. Chantal Mouffe (2018, p. 37) is correct in arguing that 'before being able to radicalize democracy, it is first necessary to recover it,' which means first rejecting the commonsense assumptions that capitalism and democracy are synonymous.

Clearly, such a project cannot combat poverty, militarism, the threat of nuclear war, ecological devastation, economic inequality, and racism by leaving capitalism's system of power in place. Nor can resistance be successful if it limits itself to the terrain of critique, criticism, and the undoing of specific oppressive systems of representation. Pedagogies of resistance can teach people to say no, become civically literate, and create the conditions for individuals to develop a critical political consciousness. The challenge here is to make the political more pedagogical. This suggests analyzing how the forces of gangster capitalism impact consciousness, shape agency, and normalize the internalization of oppression. Such a project suggests a politics willing to transcend the fragmentation and politicized sectarianism all too characteristic of left politics in order to embrace a Gramscian notion of 'solidarity in a wider sense' (Institute for Critical Social Analysis, 2020). There is ample evidence of such solidarity in the policies advocated by the progressive Black Lives Matter protest, the call for green socialism, movements for health as a global right, growing resistance against police violence, emerging ecological movements such as the youth-based Sunrise movement, the Poor People's Campaign, the massive ongoing strikes waged by students and teachers against the defunding and corporatizing of public education, and the call for resistance from women across the globe fighting for reproductive rights.

What must be resisted at all costs, is an 'apartheid pedagogy,' rooted in the notion that a particular mode of oppression, and those who bear its weight, offers political guarantees (Shatz, 2021, p. 28). Identifying different modes of oppression is important, but it is only the first step in moving from addressing the history and existing mechanisms that produce such trauma to developing and embracing a politics that unites different identities, individuals, and social movements under the larger banner of democratic socialism. This is a politics that refuses the easy appeals of ideological silos which 'limits access to the world of ideas and contracts the range of tools available to would-be activists' (Kelley, 2016).

The only language provided by neoliberalism is the all-encompassing discourse of the market and the false rhetoric of unencumbered individualism, making it difficult for individuals to translate private issues into broader systemic considerations. Mark Fisher (2009, p. 2) was right in claiming that capitalist realism not only attempts to normalize the notion that there is not only no alternative to capitalism, but also makes it 'impossible even to imagine a coherent alternative to it.' This is a formula for losing hope because it insists that the world cannot change. It also has the hollow ring of slow death.

The urgency of the historical moment demands new visions of social change, an inspired and energized sense of social hope, and the necessity for diverse social movements to unite under the collective struggle for democratic socialism. The debilitating political pessimism of neoliberal gangster capitalism must be challenged as a starting point for believing that rather than being exhausted, the future along with history is open and now is the time to act. It is time to make possible what has for too long been declared as impossible.

Note

1 A version of this chapter first appeared on CounterPunch,org on May 28, 2021 at: www. counterpunch.org/2021/05/28/againstapartheid-pedagogy-in-the-age-of-white-suprema cy/#post-202972-endnote-3.

References

Block, N (2020) 'Augmenting the Left: Challenging the Right, Reimagining Transformation,' *Socialist Project: The Bullet*, 31 August [Online]. Available at: https://socialistp roject.ca/2020/08/augmenting-the-left-challenging-the-right-reimagining-transformation/ (Accessed: 28 September 2021).

Crowley, M (2020) 'Trump Calls for "Patriotic Education" to Defend American History from the Left,' *New York Times*, 17 September [Online]. Available at: www.nytimes.com/2020/ 09/17/us/politics/trump-patriotic-education.html (Accessed: 28 September 2021).

Evans, B and Cordal, I (2020) 'Histories of Violence: Look Closer at the World, There You Will See,' *Los Angeles Review of Books*, 28 December [Online]. Available at: https://larev iewofbooks.org/article/histories-of-violence-look-closer-at-the-world-there-you-will-see/ (Accessed: 28 September 2021).

Fisher, M (2009) *Capitalist realism: Is there no alternative?* Winchester, UK: Zero Books.

Giroux, HA (2015) *Dangerous thinking in the age of the new authoritarianism*. New York, NY: Routledge.

Giroux, HA (2020) *Neoliberalism's war on higher education*. Chicago, IL: Haymarket Press.

Goldberg, DT (2021) 'The War on Critical Race Theory,' *Boston Review*, 7 May [Online]. Available at: https://bostonreview.net/race-politics/david-theo-goldberg-war-critical-ra ce-theory (Accessed: 28 September 2021).

Goldberg, M (2021a) 'The Social Justice Purge at Idaho College,' *New York Times*, 26 March [Online]. Available at: www.nytimes.com/2021/03/26/opinion/free-speech-ida ho.html (Accessed: 28 September 2021).

Goldberg, M (2021b) 'The Campaign to Cancel Wokeness,' *New York Times*, 26 February [Online]. Available at: www.nytimes.com/2021/02/26/opinion/speech-racism-academ ia.html (Accessed: 28 September 2021).

Graeber, D (2012) 'Dead zones of the imagination,' *HAU: Journal of Ethnographic Theory*, 2(2). https://doi.org/10.14318/hau2.2.007.

Hamilton, L (2017) 'This Is Going to Hurt: Serious Challenges to the Status Quo Will Be Met with Panic and Repression,' *The New Inquiry*, 11 April [Online]. Available at: http s://thenewinquiry.com/this-is-going-to-hurt/ (Accessed: 28 September 2021).

Harris, A (2021) 'The GOP's 'Critical Race Theory' Obsession,' *The Atlantic*, 7 May [Online]. Available at: www.theatlantic.com/politics/archive/2021/05/gops-critical-ra ce-theory-fixation-explained/618828/ (Accessed: 27 September 2021).

Holloway, K (2021) 'White Ignorance Is Bliss—and Power,' *Yahoo! News*, 24 May [Online]. Available at: https://news.yahoo.com/white-ignorance-bliss-power-08023202 5.html (Accessed: 28 September 2021).

Institute for Critical Social Analysis (2020) 'A Window of Opportunity for Leftist Politics?,' *Socialist Project: The Bullet*, 3 August [Online]. Available at: https://socialistproject.ca/ 2020/08/window-of-opportunity-for-leftist-politics/ (Accessed: 28 September 2021).

Kelley, RDG (2016) 'Black Study, Black Struggle,' *Boston Review*, 7 March [Online]. Available at: https://bostonreview.net/forum/black-study-black-struggle/robin-d-g-kel ley-robin-d-g-kelleys-final-response (Accessed: 28 September 2021).

Klein, C (2021) 'Mitch McConnell: Don't Teach Our Kids That America Is Racist,' *Vanity Fair*, 4 May [Online]. Available at: www.vanityfair.com/news/2021/05/mitch-mccon nell-dont-teach-our-kids-that-america-is-racist (Accessed: 28 September 2021).

Las Vegas Sun (2017) 'Trump's Crusade Against the Media Is a Chilling Echo of Hitler's Rise,' *Las Vegas Sun*, 14 August [Online]. Available at: https://lasvegassun.com/news/20 17/aug/14/trumps-crusade-against-the-media-is-a-chilling-ech/ (Accessed: 28 September 2021).

Latham, R, Kingsmith, AT, Von Bargen, J and Block, N (eds.) (2020) *Challenging the right, augmenting the left: Recasting leftist imagination*. Winnipeg, MN: Fernwood Publishing.

McGee, K (2021) 'Texas' Divisive Bill Limiting How Students Learn About Current Events and Historic Racism Passed by Senate,' *Texas Public Radio*, 23 May [Online]. Available at: www.tpr.org/education/2021-05-23/texas-divisive-bill-limiting-how-students-learn-about-current-events-and-historic-racism-passed-by-senate (Accessed: 27 September 2021).

Mouffe, C (2018) *For a left populism*. London, UK: Verso.

No Left Turn in Education (2021) 'Mission goals and objectives' [Online]. Available at: www.noleftturn.us/mission-goals-objectives/ (Accessed: 28 September 2021).

Robertson, K (2021) 'Nikole Hannah-Jones Denied Tenure at University of North Car-olina,' *New York Times*, 19 May [Online]. Available at: www.nytimes.com/2021/05/19/ business/media/nikole-hannah-jones-unc.html (Accessed: 28 September 2021).

Sanchez, G and English, B (2020) 'OAH Statement on White House Conference on American History,' *Organization of American Historians*, 25 September [Online]. Available at: www.oah.org/insights/posts/2020/september/oah-statement-on-white-house-confer ence-on-american-history/ (Accessed: 27 September 2021).

Shatz, A (2021) 'Palestinianism,' *London Review of Books*, 43(9) [Online]. Available at: www. lrb.co.uk/the-paper/v43/n09/adam-shatz/palestinianism (Accessed: 28 September 2021).

Weineck, SM (2021) 'The Tenure Denial of Nikole Hannah-Jones Is Craven and Dangerous,' *The Chronicle of Higher Education*, 20 May [Online]. Available at: www.chronicle.com/a rticle/the-tenure-denial-of-nikole-hannah-jones-is-craven-and-dangerous (Accessed: 28 September 2021).

Weiss, V (2020) 'Afterword,' in Adorno, TW (ed.) *Aspects of the new right-wing extremism.* London, UK: Polity, p. 61.

Whittington, KE and Wilentz, S (2021) 'We Have Criticized Nikole Hannah-Jones. Her Tenure Denial Is a Travesty,' *The Chronicle of Higher Education*, 24 May [Online]. Available at: www.chronicle.com/article/we-have-criticized-nikole-hannah-jones-her-tenure-denial-is-a-travesty? (Accessed: 28 September 2021).

Wong, JC (2021) 'The Fight to Whitewash US History: "A Drop of Poison Is All You Need",' *The Guardian*, 25 May [Online]. Available at: www.theguardian.com/world/2021/may/25/critical-race-theory-us-history-1619-project (Accessed: 27 September 2021).

3

MEDIATIZED VISIONS OF A NATION ON FIRE

Negotiating Truth Under Shifting Epistemic Conditions

Michael Hoechsmann

It is easier said than done to produce a crisp narrative that provides context for what happened at the US Capitol on January 6th, 2021. Yes, rioters from across the US traveled to Washington D.C., attended a Trump rally to protest what was falsely considered a stolen election and then marched upon the Capitol where legislators, in the process of certifying the election results, were disrupted by the incursion of angry and violent rioters. That is an accurate account of a series of cascading events that took place at the Capitol on January 6th.

However, it does not help to explain the historical conditions upon which the events unfolded, nor does it unpack the overlapping narratives and experiences the rioters carried in their backpacks that stoked the flames of this insurrection. Under the surface, there are far more complex and sometimes contradictory stories that sparked the ardor of various protestors. A spirit of rebellion fueled the transgressions of the day. Regardless of what others may think, the Capitol rioters came to the event as self-stylized outsiders fighting for their constitutional rights as US citizens. The decision by thousands of people to attend the 'March to Save America' rally, the subsequent march to the Capitol grounds, and the forced entrance into the Capitol building were not spontaneous acts but rather an orchestrated event involving many moving parts and decisions made by militants and protestors. The grievances of the actors are discussed throughout this book, but here we take up the impact of historical factors on the actions of the day, with respect to economic, social, technological, digital, and media conditions.

Daniel Boorstin's historic analysis in *The Image: A Guide to Pseudo-Events in America* (1961) is instructive here. Writing 60 years ago, at a time when the art of propaganda had been honed over more than four decades by the public relations and advertising industries, and polished on audio (radio) and audiovisual (film and TV) media, Boorstin claims that 'not truth but credibility is the test.... All American citizen-consumers are daily *less interested if something is a fact than in whether it is*

DOI: 10.4324/9781003246862-4

convenient that it should be believed' (as cited in Carey, 1987; emphasis added). This statement puts a lie to the idea that the concepts of 'post truth' and 'alternative facts' are new in the US, and suggests rather that they are elements of a long history of propaganda and media manipulation. Generations have been nurtured and raised on a steady diet of easily digested forms of culture that distract attention from the dark underbelly of this late imperial global power that is the US. This, combined with an incessant patriotic pageantry and boosterism scaffolds the notion that the 'City upon the Hill'—in the oft-repeated words of American pilgrim John Winthrop—is the greatest nation on Earth. The fears of immanent decline which seemed to fuel the events of January 6th were based on real concern for an America that both was and never was, a simulacrum of a past that is representative of some of these protestors' experiences but also a nostalgia for some prelapsarian past, elements of the zeitgeist that Donald Trump tapped into and amplified. A slogan such as Trump's *Make America Great Again* can thus be read quite differently depending on the reader's social location and historical understanding of the past, but it clearly resonates strongly for thousands of Americans.

What Past Were They Fighting For?

The period of relative prosperity and growth of the middle classes in the post-World War II economic boom, though long gone, continues to resonate in the collective memory of US citizens. The benevolent state and relative labor peace that emerged in stages in the early part of the 20th century and flourished for about a quarter of a century in the post-war period was dependent on a number of relations that began to unravel with the exhaustion of the first world Fordist, mass production period in about 1973 (cotemporaneous with the OPEC oil crisis which put a sudden stress on national economies). The post-war period was characterized by a relatively harmonious set of relations existing among finance capital, an organized workforce, and national state apparatuses that together supported the economic and social status quo. This harmony resulted from a domestic economic order of relatively symbiotic mass production and consumption cycles. In short, markets and production sites were in geographic proximity to one another and the interests of capital required a compliant workforce with the economic means to consume the very products it produced and the requisite state-provided social supports to maintain its physical and social health (Harvey, 1989). The beneficiaries in the US of this domestic economic harmony tended to be the white, predominantly male, working and middle classes, with working class wages for unionized laborers allowing them access to the comforts and consumerism of the middle class, often including home ownership.

Since the 1980s, neoliberal strategies for minimizing state interference in the smooth machinations and flows of global capital have intensified (Harvey, 2005; Monbiot, 2016). Neoliberalism has had broad impacts on the societies, economies, polities, public institutions and environments of low-income and high-income countries alike, creating global extremes of rich and poor, mirrored domestically in the US. Some of the objectives and impacts of neoliberal policy include: deregulation of domestic and global economies through free trade; promotion of the rhetoric of small government invisibly at the service of big corporations; pressure to privatize state functions putting them outside citizen control; tax cuts, particularly to corporations and individuals in higher income tax brackets; cutbacks to essential services such as hospitals, education, and welfare; a punishing state law with law and order rhetoric driving increased investments and incarcerations in prisons; and deregulating environmental protection, with environmental concerns relegated to unaccountable corporate externalities (Roy, 2004).

In this context, two key economic innovations of the neoliberal era, with key impacts on Trump-era economics, were the offshoring of production and the financialization of the economy (Chomsky, 1999). First, in the post-Fordist period, not only was production increasingly sent overseas, but new, developing technologies enabled inventory control that favored small-batch niche-market goods, often produced in sweat shop conditions, to replace the mass-produced items of the typical Fordist factories (Harvey, 1989; Hoechsmann, 1997). For global capital, these combined circumstances threatened the post-war harmony, as workers were seen as increasingly 'flexible' or disposable (Giroux, 2008), and state-supported institutions and services costly and unnecessary. In this breach, neoliberal economic and social policy was applied, with on-going negative impacts on those who would go on to participate in the Capitol riots. This is somewhat ironic, one might observe, as the Republicans have long supported and driven neoliberal policy in the US, while the negative impacts are most egregiously felt by Republican supporters, who tend to be lower income and less educated, but who participate in a long-standing phenomenon of voting against their own best interests.

Despite its prominence as an ideological force in countries such as the US, neoliberalism is largely unnamed and ignored by media pundits and ordinary citizens alike, yet relentlessly promoted by prominent think tanks (Monbiot, 2016), critiqued by academics and grassroots movements (Springer, 2021), but nonetheless imposed by the 'shock troops' of conservative and liberal democratic governments alike (Klein, 2007). Coupled with the Reagan-era myth of trickle-down economics is the neoliberal faith in laissez-faire market fundamentalism, the problematic and widely-critiqued idea that the flow of private capital unimpeded by state regulation is in the best interest of societies (Springer, 2021).

Alongside the offshoring of production, a second key feature of neoliberal economic policy is the financialization of the economy (Chomsky, 1999; Harvey, 2005; Klein, 2007; Giroux, 2011). This stage of late capitalism involves the further abstraction of material production from financial processes, and the growth of speculative, 'casino capitalism' (Giroux, 2011). The financialization of the economy involves the movement of investment funds from the industrial production of material goods towards finance capital, insurance and real estate. The influence of the banking and securities sectors in the US (and many other high-income countries) grows exponentially in this period. Whereas in 1970, 90% of economic activity centered on production and trade, and 10% on finance speculation, twenty-five years later, those figures had reversed (Chomsky, 2002). The money in circulation is more likely inherited inter-generationally than earned through the wage economy (Piketty, 2014), thus the neoliberal era enables a growing divide between rich and poor, with concomitant racial and gender inequalities, as well as the consolidation of the financial elite now known as the 1% (Sayer, 2015). The movement to speculative capitalism parallels other postmodern processes of abstraction as 'all that is solid melts into air' (Berman, 1982), now even increasingly more rapidly.

Neoliberalism and the New Culture Wars

The possibility of a vibrant, informed democratic polity, in particular, is under-mined in this period by the ubiquity of the image and the immersive nature of contemporary media, corporate media concentration, the ongoing transformation of politics into public relations, the new forms of authoritarian populism (Hall, 1988) exemplified today in characters such as Boris Johnson and Donald Trump, and the inculcation through education and the media of an erasure of a sense of history (Hall, 1991) in what quickly is becoming a culture of forgetting (Giroux, 2014). Hall (1991) argues that objective answers rooted in structural analyses are eclipsed by a more dynamic interplay of subjective, cultural, relativist, and ideo-logical factors. Civil society, on the bright side, becomes a much more contested space of power, politics and possibility, with social change agendas dependent on the flattening of the vertical axes of class relations (Ross, 1989), and identitarian social movements investing in the meta-political framing of a post-Marxist era (Laclau and Mouffe, 1985; Fraser, 2012).

   While the neoliberal era hinges on economic stagnation for the working and middle classes and a growing divide between rich and poor, the same historical period sees the rise of feminism and a massive influx of women in to the work force; the consolidation of the gains of the civil rights movement and a gradual increase of racialized workers in to white collar professions; the mainstreaming, advanced edu-cation, and increased economic contributions of second-generation immigrants; the integration of human rights for LGBTQ+ communities through marriage equality legislation in some states; and the ongoing immigration of economic migrants and refugees from low-income countries in economic and political crisis. Globally, widespread economic expansion occurs in what are now called the BRICS coun-tries—Brazil, Russia, India, China, and South Africa—enabling millions of formerly impoverished people to join the middle classes in those countries. Yet, as subject positions become more contested, liquid and dynamic, and global capital becomes more mobile while also less transparent and accountable, the social space of struggle remains rooted in the territoriality of physical space, whether that be city, region or nation, with an increasing uptake of digital media as a new space of contestation.

   The social and economic improvements of women, racialized and LGBTQ+ people in this period forms the core of the popular response to neoliberal policies in the wake of the 2008 financial crash followed closely on its heels by the impo-sition of austerity measures in high-income countries. Protest movements such as Occupy, the Indignados, the Arab Spring, Idle No More, Black Lives Matter, and #MeToo all reignited interest in left political movements, evidence of active resistance to neoliberalism (Jeppesen, 2021). While some racialized groups achieve social and economic advances, many more remain in poverty, as blue collar and other labor opportunities stagnate, labor turns flexible and governments focus on creative cities that benefit the new creative upper-middle class knowledge worker (Leslie and Catungal, 2012), and the brutality of the state towards Black and Indigenous peoples continues unabated though increasingly contested. Meanwhile, the ongoing criminalization of poverty paired with the stigmatization of immigration and immigrants becomes more acute as housing and shelter become commoditized in the new global city, and political, economic, and climate refugees from Latin America, Syria, and Afghanistan, among others, stream into Europe and the US.

Conservative governments have proven adept at encouraging formerly privi-leged groups to channel their economic frustrations, born of historical changes to economic models, at liberal and social-democratic political parties, accusing them of being poor economic managers. This vitriol is also channeled toward the poor and newly-arrived members of a society who collectively are constructed by lea-ders on the right as somehow posing a threat to the security of the middle and working classes, as these groups are discursively chastised in public discourse for taking too much from the state in handouts for which they are undeserving, or stealing the dwindling remainder of well-paid working-class jobs from their rightful entitled candidates.

Donald Trump came into power playing this 'blame game.' It could be argued that this is his most persistent refrain, alongside uncoupling the state from any type of function of care and stripping away any encumbrance to financial capital in terms of regulation and taxation. That Trump held onto the grip he has over his coalition despite running roughshod over the economic interests of most of his followers demonstrates the hegemonic swing in the US towards a late neoliberal state potentially moving towards unbridled authoritarianism. The emergence of militia groups on the political stage, as exemplified in the armed incursion into the Michigan Legislature on April 29, 2020, and the 2017 Charlottesville protests, among many other public protest events, sets the stage for the insurrection on January 6th.

2020 Vision of a Nation at Odds

The circumstances of 2020, outlined in Chapter 1, are preceded by events over the four years of the Trump presidency that gave the impression that the US was under siege from within, particularly with respect to knowledge production and epistemic ideological interventions. These Trump denouncements and pronouncements were many and widespread. A widespread demonization of educators and journalists took place, including the politicized ousting of progressive university faculty members who were deridingly labelled Marxists and communists, and the dismissive labelling of critical fact-based reporting as 'fake news.' A growing disdain and suspicion towards climate scientists, medical professionals, and research-based evidence was offset by permanent political campaigning featuring fact-free political rallies as the ongoing celebrity spectacle featuring Trump as TV star. Institutionally, this was bolstered by the stacking of the US Supreme Court with Republican far-right appointees and a constant and ongoing push to divide and polarize the American public through sowing division and disrespect in the halls of power.

The push to divide and polarize is evident on January 6th and numerous other occasions when Donald Trump exhorts his supporters to protect an imaginary shared understanding of the once-glorious white-dominated United States that is now alarmingly, for Trump and his supporters, allowing women, people of color, and LGBTQ+ groups to gain power and access human rights. Trump claimed that he would 'drain the swamp' of an elite political establishment and positioned himself as an ally of those who distrust government, except of course that element of government with the legitimate right to violence, the military and police forces, and as a supporter of the right to bear arms in public in order ostensibly to keep these same violent state forces, of which they are uncritical, in check.

Trump links his political ambitions therefore with a longer history of distrust for federal authority that picks up steam in the 1990s after two incidents of government killings of armed militia or gun rights' civilian groups at Ruby Ridge, Idaho and Waco, Texas, as well as armed standoffs on federal land with supporters of the Bundy family in Oregon in 2014 and 2016. Second amendment gun rights figure prominently in his supporters' politics, which he also defends vehemently. Protestors who assembled at the Capitol on January 6th came to defend a President seen as sympathetic to the complaints of those who felt the government was a threat to a romanticized and non-existent prelapsarian and economically successful America that did not have to make space for immigrants nor Black and Indigenous people, and where women existed only in their traditional gender roles of subservient mother and wife (see Chapter 10).

The Space of 21st Century Media

This was a protest and riot undertaken just beyond the crossroads of two media epochs, the outgoing hierarchical mass media model of the 20th century and the mobile, interactive, ubiquitous, algorithm-driven, participatory media model of the 21st. On the one hand, newspapers, television and radio stations covered the Capitol riots extensively as they unfolded, and on the other hand, cameras and microphones in the hands of thousands of 'citizen journalists'—protestors, rioters and those commenting from home—recorded, shared, re-posted, and commented on almost every moment of the day. To evaluate the role that media played in the Capitol riots, it is necessary to examine not only media activity and representations, but also broader questions around 21st century media including media ecologies and mediascapes.

First, shifting media ecologies are very much part of the story here, different ecosystems with distinct strategies and tactics for how media is made and understood. Media ecologies, the study of the ways in which media and technologies are embedded in social constructions of reality, today see ever-shifting permutations and combinations of mainstream, alternative and social media discourses and political economies. This provides fertile ground in which, we argue, the discourses of post-truth and alternative facts are not just rhetorical ruses of the Trump presidency, but part of the cultural conditions of a post-literacy epoch. It is not enough to claim that 'fake news' is in circulation, but rather we must also acknowledge that the epistemic conditions upon which truth is negotiated have changed profoundly. The emergent and increasingly complex media ecologies of the 21st century forms part of the epistemological quicksand which enveloped many of the riot's participants, some of whom later expressed bewilderment at the irrational foundations of their own motives, going so far as to apologize and denounce the groups in which they were deeply ideologically, personally, and politically involved only days earlier (Billeaud and Tarm, 2021).

Second, we must also consider contemporary mediascapes, loosely understood as the representations constructed of the world and societies within the aforementioned global media ecologies. Mediascapes behind the events of January 6th included the right-wing alt-right digital media sphere, social media discourses, and rogue, increasingly ideological elements of the mainstream media such as Rupert Murdoch's Fox News Channel (FNC). Despite the ongoing influence of some TV networks, social media and its datafied audiences have changed the delivery, impact and shape of contemporary mediascapes. We live in a digital environment which offers extraordinary support for the sharing of collective intelligence, but which also absorbs us into a spider's web of distraction, obsession and trivialization. Among the impacts of 21st century mediascapes are people everywhere hunched over small, mobile screens; the wisdom—or lack thereof—of crowdsourcing; increasingly divided publics; narcissism and hostility bred in socially divided echo chambers; information overload and the apparent gullibility of end users; and a massive-scale provision of big data by online individuals to Internet and data strategy corporations.

The propagation of misinformation, disinformation, and fake news

It is not a new finding that new technologies often simultaneously offer many positive affordances and result in negative unintended consequences (Ellul, 1964). Many previously existing communication technologies are now available digitally through a process of technological convergence, to be offered today on mobile devices. This has provoked a profound transformation that we are still struggling to reconcile, yoking together older forms of hierarchical point-to-many mass media and communications with the participatory Web 2.0 and data-driven Web 3.0 media frameworks that offer many-to-many communication affordances with the lines now fully blurred between news media producers and consumers. This fragmented media ecology provides the space—notwithstanding the digital divide of haves and have-nots—for participatory democratic access to the tools to produce and circulate media, where citizen journalists and marginalized communities can have their say, all of which is very positive for democracy. Yet, this radical process of decentralization also results in a complex mediascape where representation and messaging become exceedingly chaotic, diffuse, unreliable, and unaccountable. Where news media editors once served as fact-checkers to verify the veracity of stories, this task now falls to the audience, many of whom are ill-equipped or cannot be bothered to do so. This has resulted in a mediascape beset by mountains of undifferentiated misinformation, disinformation, and fake news.

Let's start with fake news. From the moment of Trump's inauguration, which supposedly had 'the largest crowds ever,' despite visible evidence to the contrary, fake news was weaponized by Donald Trump in two ways. First, Trump dismissed any analysis that differed from his own personal sense of things as 'fake news,' including reporting by the well-respected, agenda-setting *New York Times* and *Washington Post* newspapers. Agree with the content of their reporting or not, we can rest assured that these newspapers are not producing fake news. Second, Trump created his own set of 'alternative facts,' which actually amounted to 'fake news,' on any given issue, ideas that had only a tangential relationship to the truth, deviating and wandering from it in specific self-serving ways, as Trump attended more to his own image and fan base than to good governance and political leadership. As mentioned in Chapter 1, The *Washington Post* fact-checking team found that Trump lied or made misleading claims a total of 30,573 times during his four years as President (Kessler et al., 2021). This created a complicated and contradictory mediascape in which citizens scrambled to sift the truth out of the lies, and to make sense of what was actually happening. Many Trump supporters simply took lies and half truths at face value—as the reliable and undisputed truth.

Without reviewing upwards of thirty-thousand speech acts, we can fast forward to the biggest disinformation campaign of Trump's Presidency—Stop The Steal. To pause a moment on terminology, disinformation can be defined as 'falsehoods that are spread deliberately' (Bergstrom and West, 2021, p. 29), while misinformation is perhaps less intentional, understood as 'claims that are false but not deliberately designed to deceive' (Bergstrom and West, 2021, p. 29). Stop The Steal was clearly a campaign of disinformation, spreading false claims that those sharing knew or ought reasonably to have known were false. Moreover, the claims were deliberately designed to deceive the US public, persuading them that Donald Trump had actually won the election, and to take insurrectionary action in his defense—and at his call—which very directly and explicitly led to and culminated in the Capitol riots of January 6th.

The ideological polarization of mainstream media content

Trump himself is, of course, not the only person responsible for this disinformation campaign which he could not have carried out on his own. Contemporary mediascapes have changed alongside media ecologies in the 21st century. The slow transformation, erosion, and digitization of the hegemonic mass media apparatus have afforded space for a burgeoning right-wing media sphere consumed both directly and through its amplification by circulation on social media networks. Bergstrom and West (2021, p. 26) argue that since the turn of the millennium, mainstream media outlets have become increasingly polarized, with Fox News Channel slanting to the right, CNN holding more or less center-left, and MSNBC slanting leftward. This has shifted the news mediascape from one where reliable, fact-checked journalism—albeit often biased—was the industry norm, to a mediascape fraught with thinly-disguised hyper-partisan news that might be based in actual events and stories, but 'so strongly filtered through an ideological lens that they often include significant elements of untruth' (Bergstrom and West, 2021, p. 26). This results in fragmented national dialogues, a lack of national imagined communities rooted in shared values and beliefs, and partisan epistemologies in which the truth must be negotiated in a mediascape of epistemic contestation. Thus, we no longer know if some exemplars of the mainstream news media are telling us the actual truth, and journalistic ethics are regularly called into question.

We also see, in the past decade or so, the rise of an 'alt-right' and 'alt-light' stable of news producers such as Breitbart, Joe Rogan's podcast, and so on. As Benkler et al. (2017) explain:

> A right-wing media network anchored around Breitbart developed as a distinct and insulated media system, using social media as a backbone to transmit a hyper-partisan perspective to the world. This pro-Trump media sphere appears to have not only successfully set the agenda for the conservative media sphere, but also strongly influenced the broader media agenda.

What Benkler et al. go on to describe is two asymmetric media spheres, a liberal sphere that orbits around traditional news media such as the *New York Times, The Washington Post,* and CNN, and a right-wing sphere that draws more heavily on newly emerged right-wing media channels heavily dependent on social media for audiences and circulation. The right-wing media sphere is a closed loop that can put forward any sort of 'alternative facts' without significant challenge, and which is wholeheartedly believed by its followers:

> The right-wing media system [has developed] into an internally coherent, relatively insulated knowledge community, reinforcing the shared worldview of readers and shielding them from journalism that challenged it. The prevalence of such material has created an environment in which the President can tell supporters about events in Sweden that never happened, or a presidential advisor can reference a non-existent Bowling Green massacre.
>
> *(Benkler et al., 2017)*

And this separated audience believes it. Labeling mainstream traditional sources as fake news has been weaponized by Trump to close down debate and repudiate critical responses to misrepresentations, distortions and outright disinformation. At the same time, the right-wing sphere is replete with a sort of privileged-victim complex where pundits regularly regale their audiences with accounts of the dangers of cancel culture, political correctness, and social justice warriors to the audience's own established positions of (heterosexual, white, cis-gendered, middle class, etc.) privilege in society. Such is the dissemination of the threat of left-wing mobs that people in a number of small towns across the US believed the lie in the summer of 2020 that Antifa was coming to attack their cities, and these right-wing audience members prepared small brigades of armed civilians in their town squares for alleged threats that never materialized—because they consisted entirely of disinformation.

Nonetheless, when distinguishing between the influence of 20th and 21st century media, it is important not to draw the lines too coarsely. The ability to attract audiences for Fox pundits Sean Hannity, Laura Ingraham, and Tucker Carlson is another powerful and almost unbridled influence of right-wing media. A latecomer to the 20th century mediascape in 1996, Fox News Channel has risen to become the right-wing cornerstone of the television news universe. Carlson has an outsize influence as a newscaster willing to go the distance to stretch the truth beyond recognition and engage in media spectacle through outlandish claims, all 'by encouraging his audiences to suspend their critical faculties' (Giroux, 2021). Carlson is a proponent of the 'great replacement theory' that fueled much of the outrage both at the 'Unite the Right' rally in Charlottesville in 2017 and at the Capitol riots of 2021. Carlson has developed his following based on his ability to spin almost any story to match the outcomes that make right-wing listeners tune in, dialing up their feelings as the alleged victims of a 'deep state' intent on disrupting their communities and dismantling their rights. In the aftermath of the Capitol riots, Carlson has been busy deflecting any blame from the perpetrators—both in the Republican leadership and in the streets—and developing conspiracies such as the FBI having orchestrated the riots (Rupar, 2021). When claims are made on screen by Carlson, they are amplified and circulated on social media networks where they develop a life of their own, regardless of any eventual retraction of the original story.

Algorithms, filter bubbles, and echo chambers

The unhinging of truth from opinion and spin has hit a new gear in the era of Web 3.0 with its infinitely participatory, ubiquitous and datafied media, all driven by algorithms, the computer programs that underlie, drive, determine, and decide what appears in all internet searches and social media posts. These are black box proprietary programs and codes that are so complex today that not even their designers and coders claim to understand how they work any longer. Web 3.0 algorithms are not designed for participatory democratic citizenship, but rather they are designed to maximize the profits of corporations such as Google and Facebook. They are coded to capture the attention of the public for as long as possible, increasing clicks and eyeballs on pages, through techniques that include the fomentation of rumor and outrage, which add emotional heat to any news event. The more angering a post, and the more provocative a story, the more likely audience members are to respond and stay on the site, sending dollars directly to the coffers of the big tech giants. Thus, we can easily argue that algorithms are not neutral. They have also been shown by many researchers in a variety of fields and disciplines—from data science to math, and from computer science to social sciences—to be racist, sexist, ableist, ageist, and more. Despite collective attempts by social media sites such as Facebook and Twitter—those used extensively by Trump and his acolytes, many of whom are also middle-aged—to curtail the dissemination of false information, 'alternative facts' continue to thrive in a media ecosystem which mirrors the broader body politic, where public trust in authority is low and where political actors stoke this distrust for their own ends.

As Trump fanned the flames of disinformation, his fans and admirers happily followed suit, demonstrating remarkable allegiance to his presidency while exhibiting all of the characteristics of confirmation bias in their echo chamber or filter bubble in-groups. In these spaces, posts fed to audiences are designed to reinforce what users have demonstrated, through big-data-mined clickstreams, that they already feel and believe. Zeynep Tufekci (2018, p. 17) explains filter bubbles and echo chambers this way:

> we encounter opposing views in the age and context of social media … like … fans in a football stadium…. We bond with our team by yelling at fans of the other one…. This is why various projects for fact checking claims in the news, while valuable, don't convince people.

Increasingly, where and how an audience member gets their news is predictive of the views that will be held by those persons and groups. While a few of the participants in the Capitol riots may have drawn upon word of mouth to make plans, the majority of the participants used and produced social media that day, and, arguably, were brought up to speed on the issues of the day in the days, weeks and months previous by right-wing news media broadcasts and social media messages. The proliferation of disinformation was so great that many were kicked off Facebook and Twitter, moving to an alt-right social media site called Parler (see Chapter 5).

Capitol Riots as Media Event

We also saw in the days leading up to the riots, an inexplicable rise in QAnon and other conspiracy theories (see Chapter 7). Douglas Rushkoff (2021) advances the following provocation with respect to conspiracy theory: 'There is no man behind the curtain, no secret cabal controlling our destinies, no marvelous or nefarious plan driving COVID, vote counting, or global affairs. They need to awaken to something way more frightening than politicians eating children: shit just happens, no one is in charge, and chaos reigns.'

Given the role of some corporate mainstream media and the right-wing media sphere in shaping the metanarratives contributing to this rebellion, and the social media in amplifying, circulating, interpreting, and transforming the central tropes and motifs of the prevailing narratives, it is important to examine the role the media played, not as agent but as agenda setter. The media's role in the body-politic of most nations is a powerful agenda-setting one which shapes the public imaginary, and it is particularly accentuated in the US—the laboratory and site of many of the media's innovations over the 20th and 21st century. The American imaginary is well supplied with a reader's digest of facts and distortions most US residents receive in their long schooling in popular culture, sound-bite news casts, advertising slogans, game show hucksterism, television sport fandom and other forms of spectacle. Trump is an embodiment of this culture, a former reality TV star with a gift for spin who is most comfortable in front of an energized audience.

Ultimately, the Capitol riots were a massively documented and disseminated global media event, despite the insufficient just-in-time coverage provided on mainstream media, and the disorganized chaos of social media activity. Most of America and the rest of the world experienced the Capitol riots that day via media of some kind. Some of us turned on the television or opened our laptops to news channels to see it live, only to be disappointed by the paucity of information and the poverty of live footage, much of it shot from a great distance, and with the similar video footage looping as a backdrop to confused reportage.

We learned only later that mainstream journalists were physically excluded from the proceedings with threats of violence, that cameras and other equipment were ripped from media professionals and smashed, leaving them unable to do their jobs effectively. Well after the day's events were done and the crowds dispersed, we learned that the event had been intensely recorded and documented often by those engaged in acts that would see them arrested (See Chapters 5 and 8). Thus, the live television image gave the impression of cheap seats, mainly a long view of the events from afar, with very little in-depth analysis of what was happening. Mean-while, social media was abuzz with queries, and sites such as Twitter and Parler were alive with live updates from those who were there, propagating the sort of speculative ruminations in the comments section typical of the distracted opinions shared regarding live events by those who were elsewhere.

The gulf between what is learned from the media and experienced empirically in everyday life has continued to blur over the many years since Boorstin wrote in 1961 that the illusions propagated in American media are often so realistic that people can live within them. Dramatic social, economic, political and technologi-cal changes since that time have disrupted lifestyles and expectations for indivi-duals, and have transformed communities and the broader national fabric of the US. Media saturation has increased exponentially, and social media and datafica-tion have made it easier to spread disinformation, something which a relatively new right-wing media sphere has unwittingly mobilized. The events at the Capitol on January 6th took place under these material and imaginary—perhaps even imagined—conditions.

References

Benkler, Y, Faris, R, Roberts, H and Zuckerman, E (2017) 'Study: Breitbart-led right-wing media ecosystem altered broader media agenda,' *Columbia Journalism Review*, March 3. doi:www.cjr.org/analysis/breitbart-media-trump-harvard-study.php.

Bergstrom, CT and West, JD (2020) *Calling bullshit: The art of skepticism in a data-driven world* (1st ed.). NY: Random House.

Berman, M (1982) *All that is solid melts in to air: The experience of modernity*. NY: Verso.

Boorstin, D (1961) *The image: A guide to pseudo-events in America*. NY: Harper and Row.

Chomsky, N (1999) *Profit over people: Neoliberalism and the global order*. NY: Seven Stories Press.

Chomsky, N (2002) *Understanding power: The indispensable Chomsky*. NY: New Press.

Ellul, J (1964) *The technological society*. Knopf Doubleday.

Fraser, N (2012) 'On justice', *New Left Review*, 74, 41–51.

Giroux, H (2008) *Against the terror of Neoliberalism: Politics beyond the age of greed*. Boulder, CO: Paradigm.

Giroux, H (2011) *Zombie politics and culture in the age of casino capitalism*. NY: Peter Lang.

Giroux, H (2014) *The violence of organized forgetting: Thinking beyond America's disimagination machine*. San Francisco: City Lights.

Giroux, H (2021) 'Tucker Carlson is just the tip of the iceberg in right-wing media's war on truth,' *TruthOut*, May 27. doi:https://truthout.org/articles/tucker-carlson-is-just-the-tip-of-the-iceberg-in-right-wing-medias-war-on-truth/.

Hall, S (1988) *The hard road to renewal: Thatcherism and the crisis of the left*. London: Verso.

Hall, S (1991) 'Brave new world,' *Socialist Review* 91(1), 57–64.

Harvey, D (1989) *The condition of postmodernity: An enquiry into the origins of cultural change*. Oxford: Blackwell.

Harvey, D (2005) *A brief history of neoliberalism*. Oxford UK: Oxford University Press.

Hoechsmann, M (1997) 'Benetton culture: Marketing difference to the new global consumer.' In Riggins, S (ed.) *The language and politics of exclusion: Others in discourse* (pp. 183–202). Thousand Oaks CA: Sage.

Jeppesen, S (2021) *Transformative media: Intersectional politics from Indymedia to #Black-LivesMatter*. Vancouver: UBC Press.

Kessler, G, Rizzo, S and Kelly, M (2021) 'Trump's false or misleading claims total 30,573 over 4 years,' *Washington Post*, January 24. Available at: www.washingtonpost.com/politics/2021/01/24/trumps-false-or-misleading-claims-total-30573-over-four-years/.

Klein, N (2007) *The shock doctrine: The rise of disaster capitalism*. Toronto: Vintage.

Laclau, E and Mouffe, C (1985) *Hegemony and socialist strategy: Towards a radical democratic politics*. London: Verso.

Leslie, D and Catungal, JP (2012) 'Social justice and the creative city: Class, gender and racial inequalities,' *Geography Compass* 6 (3): 111–122. Available at: https://doi.org/10.1111/j.1749-8198.2011.00472.x.

Monbiot, G (2016) *How did we get into this mess? Politics, equality, nature*. London: Verso.

Piketty, T (2014) *Capitalism in the twenty-first century*. Trans. A Goldhammer. Cambridge MA: Harvard University Press.

Ross, A (1989) *No respect: Intellectuals and popular culture*. NY: Routledge.

Roy, A (2004) *An ordinary person's guide to empire*. South End Press.

Rupar, A (2021) 'The glaring problem with Tucker Carlson's attempt to blame the FBI for the insurrection,' *VOX*, June 23. doi:2021/6/23/22544084/tucker-carlson-january-6-insurrection-fbi.

Rushkoff, D (2021) 'Plunging into the abyss,' *Gen.*, July 21. doi:898faa144.

Sayer, A (2015) *Why we can't afford the rich*. Bristol: Policy Press.

Springer, S (2021) *Fuck neoliberalism: Translating resistance*. Oakland: PM Press.

Tufekci, Z (2018) 'How social media took us from Tahir Square to Donald Trump,' *Technology Review*, August 14. doi:2018/08/14/240325/how-social-media-took-us-from-tahrir-square-to-donald-trump/.

PART 2

Visualizing the Events of January 6, 2021

4

MAPPING THE EVENTS OF THE CAPITOL RIOTS IN TIME AND SPACE

iowyth hezel ulthiin, Miranda McKee and David VanDyke

This chapter builds a chronology and geography of the events of January 6, 2021, synthesizing and critically evaluating existing mappings of the events, including: those produced by reclaimed Parler videos archived in chronological order by ProPublica; a birds-eye-view map of the area surrounding the Capitol building with embedded links to geotagged videos from the rioters, built by Patr10tic; as well as reconstructed mappings produced by mainstream media outlets such as the BBC, the *New York Times*, and *The Washington Post*.

We attempt to locate and narrate the events moment by moment, following particular key participants and actions. These will reference media outputs and spaces that include social media platforms, mainstream news, and niche social media spaces, all of which served to assemble and curate the events of the day for public consumption. This timeline and event mapping therefore articulate the chronological and geospatial events of the riots in relation to the protesters' imaginaries—their imagined relationship to key signifiers such as democracy, freedom, government and the actions they engaged in—and how these imaginaries were prolifically expressed both in real life and in the media that day as the events unfolded.

An infographic timeline (see Figure 4.1) provides an at-a-glance overview of the events of January 6, 2021, from Trump's early morning tweet to the final completion of the vote certification in the wee hours of January 7th.

A 'Stolen' Election

On November 4th, 2020 at 2:21am ET, Donald Trump called his own victory in the 58th US Presidential election to a group of onlookers in the East Room of the White House, saying, 'We'll be going to the US Supreme Court. We want all voting to stop' (Wilkie, 2020). In the days following, Trump and those around

DOI: 10.4324/9781003246862-6

Donald J. Trump ✔
@realDonaldTrump

States want to correct their votes, which they now know were based on irregularities and fraud, plus corrupt process never received legislative approval. All Mike Pence has to do is send them back to the States, AND WE WIN. Do it Mike, this is a time for extreme courage!

ⓘ This claim about election fraud is disputed

8:17am (Trump quotes: Factbase, 2021)

10:50 10:50am Giuliani's speech incites trial by combat

12:00 12:00pm Trump's speech begins

12:40

12:53pm First barricade breach northwest side — **12:50** — 12:58pm USCP Chief Sund asks for MPD assistance

1:00pm Huge crowd from Ellipse reaches Capitol — **1:00** — 1:00pm Congress convenes in House

1:10pm Rioters throw metal polls at police, multiple injuries — **1:10** — 1:10pm Trump urges crowd to 'Fight like hell'

1:59pm Rioters breaking windows to enter building — **1:20** — 1:15pm Police & rioters spray chemicals

1:30pm Pipe bombs found — **1:30**

1:49pm Rioters tear at scaffolding northwest steps — **1:40** — 1:48pm House & Senate debate vote

1:59pm Rioters break window to enter building — **1:50** — 1:50pm MPD Comander declares a riot

2:00pm Riot breaches east barricades — **2:00** — 2:11pm Mob reaches stairs by Senate

2:10pm Northwest barricades breached — **2:10** — 2:13pm Senate is called into recess

2:14pm Rioters chase Officer Goodman — **2:20** — 2:24pm Trump tweets Pence lacks courage

2:41pm Rioters storm Pelosi's offices — **2:30** — 2:30pm Senate evacuates

2:44pm Ashli Babbitt shot entering House lobby window — **2:40** — 2:38pm Trump tweets to support Police

2:50 2:53pm House members fully evacuated

3:00 3:04pm Defense Secretary calls National Guard

3:10 3:13pm Trump tweets 'no violence!'

4:00pm Police regain control of upper levels — **4:00** — 4:05pm Biden calls on Trump to end siege

4:18pm Maryland & Virginia send reinforcement — **4:10** — 4:17pm Trump video '...go home. We love you'

5:00 5:02pm DC National Guard heads to Capitol

6:00pm DC Curfew in effect — **6:00** — 5:45pm Police confirm Babbitt's death

7:00pm Facebook removes Trump's posts — **7:00** — 6:01pm Trump tweets 'Remember this day forever!'

7:02 Twitter shuts down Trump's account — **8:00** — 8:00pm Police declare Capitol building secure

8:36pm Facebook blocks Trump's page 24hrs — **9:00** — 8:06 Pence reopens Senate

3:40am

'Around 3:40 a.m., more than 13 hours after the Capitol was breached, Vice President Pence officially affirmed the election results, declaring Biden the winner.'

(Tan, Shin, Ridler, 2021)

FIGURE 4.1 Approximate timeline of the Capitol riots events, January 6, 2021
Source: Copyright Miranda McKee and David VanDyke.

him took legal action to contest the actual election results, the win of Joe Biden. Trump supporters, and some would argue those very close to the Trump Administration (see Chapter 5) soon began mobilizing his grassroots base under the hashtag #stopthesteal.

Adam Enders, assistant professor of Political Science at the University of Louisville, says that politicians are increasingly using populist unrest as a weapon (Enders, 2020, cited in Stanton, 2020), a phenomenon that plays out in Trump's subsequent campaign of disinformation and mobilization. This campaign, claiming massive voter fraud, is arguably a premeditated maneuver (Swan, 2020) which generated over $280 million dollars in donations for court fees for the Trump leadership Political Action Committee (PAC) (Save America), with the aid of the Republican National Convention (RNC), both bombarding supporters with over 600 emails in the weeks and months that followed the election (Kim and Streakin, 2021). Fundraising was also done on Parler (see Chapter 6) despite rules against it.

Trump's followers eagerly joined the #stopthesteal campaign. A tweet by @willchamberlain on November 3rd, 2020 featuring a video of a poll-watcher prevented from entering a polling station (Chamberlain, 2020), apparently caused by genuine confusion over protocol (Sardarizadeh and Lussenhop, 2021), was opportunistically inculcated into the hashtag #StoptheSteal which went viral shortly after its first use.

The disinformation campaign claimed that illegal voting had taken place on a massive scale, particularly centering out mail-in ballots as suspect. Claims of voter fraud were found to be, in a study by The Brennen Center for Justice, as unlikely as getting struck by lightning (Levitt, 2007). Dominion Voting Machines (DVM), the company that produced and secured the machines that counted the ballots on a national scale, would later sue Trump's lawyer, Rudy Giuliani, for damages of more than $1.3 billion after repeated claims of fraud were levelled at their technology. DVM called the claims 'a viral disinformation campaign,' insinuating that rather than a mistaken apprehension, the claims were intentionally crafted to enrich key actors through legal and speaker fees. Giuliani dismissed this claim, alleging intimidation (Corasaniti, 2021). At the time of writing, this lawsuit is still before the courts. Giuliani would later have his license to practice law suspended by both the New York and Washington DC Courts, based on this attempt to overturn the election via the court system, and the resultant allegations that he had made patently false statements, violating professional ethical standards (Diaz, 2021).

By mid-afternoon on November 4th, 2020, the same day Trump said he would take the election results to the Supreme Court, a newly created 'Stop the Steal' Facebook group had amassed more than 300,000 members, making it one of the fastest growing groups in the platform's history (Sardarizadeh and Lussenhop, 2021). Facebook quickly moved to ban the group under a condition labelled 'exceptional measures,' meant to control misinformation on the platform. This resulted in a whack-a-mole game wherein other Facebook groups sprang up to replace those deleted and were then themselves deleted (Brewster, 2020). Hundreds of groups persisted, however, well after the crackdown. One group advancing the #StoptheSteal agenda called 'Keeping

America Great!' amassed more than 265,000 members (Lyons, 2020). Yet, even when groups were purged from major platforms, other platforms more favorable to the alt-right and less picky about disinformation, such as Parler, Gab, Telegram, and Discord (among others), continued to proliferate false messaging, as did independent forums like those located on TheDonald.win, where supporters were able to freely express their opinions (Dilanian and Collins, 2021).

Parler, branding itself as a 'free-speech' platform, served as a breeding ground for disinformation and violent, insurrectionary messaging leading up to the day of the riots (see Chapter 5). Yet even Parler referred violent content to the FBI over 50 times in the weeks before the riots, including posts by one user who planned to wear body armor, purportedly saying that 'It's no longer a protest.... This is a final stand where we are drawing the red line at Capitol Hill. I trust the American people will take back the USA with force and many are ready to die to take back #USA' (anonymous, 2021, cited in Gurman and Horwitz, 2021).

Others discussed bringing firearms in case the protest escalated to a gun battle, or zip tie handcuffs to detain members of Congress. Police reports would later provide evidence of at least one man in possession of zip ties that were taken from police inside the Capitol building (Shamsian, 2021). Other weapons that rioters brought to DC with them that day included a handgun and semi-automatic rifle (Hsu, 2021), and in the car of one rioter, an AR-15-style rifle, a shotgun, a crossbow, several machetes, smoke grenades, and eleven Molotov cocktails (Johnson, 2021).

Yet the FBI has claimed to have had no credible intelligence leading up to the attack on the Capitol, saying that 'unattributed comments on social media don't always add up to credible intelligence, in part because many people fail to act on the things they say online' (Dilanian and Collins, 2021, para. 8). This response calls into question exactly how seriously these threats should have been taken—and whether they may have been handled differently if the social media users had been supporting BLM, or Antifa (see Chapter 11). One might argue that the threat was made more credible by the volume and scope of posts from across the US, with hundreds of posts discussing concrete plans to engage in violence and to overwhelm police in a move on the Capitol (Dilanian and Collins, 2021).

Finally, after the riots, in response to violent rhetoric proliferating on the Parler platform, on January 8th Google removed Parler from its mobile-app store as did Apple on January 9th; and on January 10th, Amazon removed Parler from their hosting services, effectively shutting the site down (Fung, 2021). Parler was later reinstated by Apple on its mobile-app store on April 19, 2021 but with tightened restrictions against 'violent or inciting content' (Lyons, 2021).

The 'Million MAGA March': Lead-Up to a Riot

On November 17th, 2020, two weeks after the election, the 'Million MAGA March' took place. According to media estimates, and despite the name's claim, marchers numbered in the thousands, with official organizers claiming attendance into the hundreds of thousands (Sadeque, 2020). Gathering to dispute the validity of the US election, with a presidential motorcade briefly making an appearance, protesters and counter-protesters clashed, adherents to 'two irreconcilable versions of America, each refusing to accept what the other considered to be undeniable fact' (Lang et al., 2020, para. 3). Twenty protesters were arrested, two on gun charges. Two officers were injured through conflicts that went on well into the night. Throughout November and December, Atlantic Council's DFRLab (2021, para. 13) reports, 'smaller but escalatory far-right events took place around the country, predominantly in capitals in states with close election results.'

As tensions continued to escalate, on December 19, Trump sent a tweet to his supporters: 'Big Protest in DC on January 6th. Be there, will be wild!' (Trump, 2021, cited in Pazniokas, 2021). Trump's tweets had been marked as 'potentially misleading' by Twitter since as early as May 2020 (Fung, 2021). At the time of the 'will be wild' tweet, Peter Navaro, a senior Trump advisor, had just released a 36-page report which alleged 'more than sufficient' evidence of voting irregularities (Navaro, 2020, cited in Miller, 2020). However, one journalist, quoted as a source in the document, points out that it 'throws out as near-certainties things that are unfounded, misrepresented or unimportant' (Bump, 2020, para. 5). Regardless of this, a narrative of certainty triggered 'inspired believers' into the belief that the US Presidency was illegitimately stolen by those seeking to destroy the American way of life. This narrative was circulated by, among others, Sean Hannity, a pundit at Fox News who said, 'Don't think for a second that Joe Biden is going to be sworn in on January 20th' (Hannity, 2020, cited in Wemple, 2020).

Early in the new year, on January 2nd, 2021, Louis Gohmert, a lawyer and member of the US House of Representatives—who sought to file a lawsuit to overthrow the election results—stated publicly on the online news site Newsmax, that a court ruling denying his case meant that 'you gotta go to the streets and be as violent as Antifa and BLM' (Gohmert, 2021, cited in Wade, 2021).

Three days later, following his speech at a warmup event on the night of January 5th, conspiracy theorist Alex Jones posted a video on his website Info-Wars.com of a live speech given at Freedom Plaza, saying, 'We have only begun to resist the globalists. We have only begun to fight against their tyranny. They have tried to steal this election in front of everyone' (Jones, 2021, cited in Frontline, 2021). Jones would later be seen at the Capitol building on January 6th with bullhorn in hand (Frontline, 2021). Rhetorical flourishes of this nature were not outliers, but rather the norm in the corners of the online and television news likely to be watched by those who would later attend the 'March to Save America,' some of whom would go on to participate in the protest, riots or insurrection that day.

The phenomenon of disinformation is nothing new, but rather an intensification of pre-existing patterns. Preston Padden (2021, para. 11), a former Fox News executive, wrote in an essay for the *Daily Beast* that 'Fox News has caused many millions of Americans—most of them Republicans— … to believe things that simply are not true.' Padden (2021, para. 9) also articulates that 'over the past nine months I have tried, with increasing bluntness, to get Rupert (Murdoch) to understand the real damage that Fox News is doing to America,' ending by saying, rather fatalistically, 'I failed and it was arrogant and naïve to ever have thought that I could succeed.'

By January 6th, a certain broad segment of the American population had been primed to coalesce around a media stream actively promoting this newly constructed 'reality' based on 'alternative facts,' while also paving the way for more extreme channels such as One America News (OAN), who were shown preference at press conferences under the Trump Administration (Ellefson, 2020).

The protest on January 6th, which would foment into insurrection, was organized by two competing groups, one of which was called 'Women for America First,' led by Tea Party founding member Amy Kremer, whose initial plan was to allow speakers to present arguments in a public forum that day. However, another group under the name 'Stop the Steal,' allegedly linked with 'pro-Trump super PACs and allies of Trump advisor Roger Stone' (Nguyen, 2021, para. 4) wanted to push the envelope with President Trump speaking alongside other more radical pundits, among the likes of Alex Jones. Yet, despite omissions, 12 other speakers were represented on January 6th, many of whom held institutional credentials which lent credibility to their claims, but nonetheless all echoing the false narratives[1].

A ProPublica report, reviewing months of personal correspondence, found that Trump aides were warned 'events could turn chaotic, with tens of thousands of people potentially overwhelming ill prepared law enforcement officials' (Sapien and Kaplan, 2021, para. 6). Despite warnings and tasked with organizing for the march, these same aides arranged for speakers considered too inflammatory for the rally itself—speakers such as InfoWars' Alex Jones, and the leader of Stop the Steal, Ali Alexander—to speak to speak near the Ellipse at Freedom Plaza on the evening of January 5th. This event culminated with alt-right organizer Ali Alexander leading a chant of 'Victory or Death!' (Alexander, 2021, cited in Sapien and Kaplan, 2021).

The next day, an anonymous protester is shown—in a video segment later compiled by *The New York Times* entitled 'Day of Rage: An In-Depth Look at How a Mob Stormed the Capitol'—saying, 'It's so much more than just rallying for President Trump. It's really rallying for our way of life, the American dream, against fake news' (anonymous, 2021, cited in Dmitriy et al., 2021). The stage is set, the disinformation tinder gathered; all that remains is to light the spark.

January 6th, the Protest Begins

Trump followers started the day of January 6, 2021 reading the following tweet, posted by @realDonaldTrump at 8:17am ET:

> States want to correct their votes, which they now know were based on irregularities and fraud, plus corrupt processes never received legislative approval. All Mike Pence has to do is send them back to the States, AND WE WIN. Do it Mike, this is a time for extreme courage!
>
> *(Trump, 2021, cited in BBC News, 2021)*

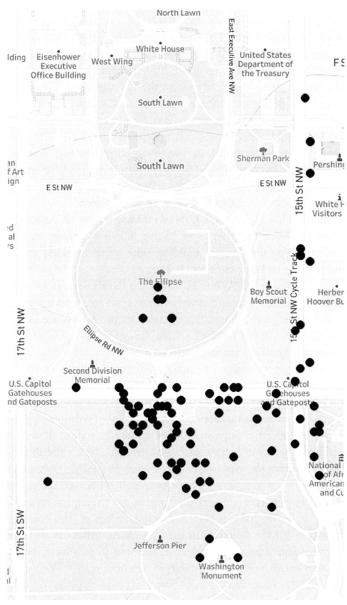

FIGURE 4.2 Aerial map, Ellipse, Washington DC. Black dots represent location of Parler post activity 10:30am–12:30pm ET on January 6, 2021. Location and time details extracted from metadata of Parler posts scraped by @donk_enby and others, published by David Zumbach (2021)

Source: Copyright David VanDyke, map created with © Mapbox, © OpenStreetMap.

Trump's lawyer and staunch supporter Rudy Giuliani spoke at the rally before Trump, using the rousing line, 'Let's have trial by combat. I'm willing to stake my reputation, the President is willing to stake his reputation on the fact that we're going to find criminality there' (Giuliani, 2021, cited in Taylor, 2021, para. 6).

At noon, the outgoing President took to the podium at the Ellipse to deliver a historic speech, in which he exclaims, 'We fight. We fight like hell and if you don't fight like hell, you're not going to have a country anymore!' (Trump, 2021, cited in Naylor, 2021).

This speech, many have argued, lit a relatively short fuse to a powder keg assiduously put in place over months of incessant posturing, media messaging, disinformation, and political maneuvering. Speeches took place starting that morning from 10:30am–12:30pm (see Figure 4.2), with large crowds gathering both at the Ellipse for the speeches and near the Capitol building in protest. As early as 9:00am the Park Police radioed that they were having difficulty dealing with over three hundred protesters at the Capitol building who were breaking through fence barriers and refusing to leave (Sinclair, 2021).

Supporters amassing at the White House begin their march down the National Mall, Constitution Avenue, and Pennsylvania Avenue in a planned and permitted demonstration under the banner #stopthesteal to meet with supporters already gathering at the US Capitol building where the certification of the US Electoral College Votes was gradually getting underway.

It would seem that there was a glimmer of historicity shared by those in attendance, many of whom were drawn into participation by conversations on online platforms. This was not just a march or a demonstration for many, but an opportunity to act in support of an outgoing President whose claims of corruption, if true, would have been anti-democratic. Supporters were quoted as saying, 'If we occupy the Capitol building, there will be no vote' (anonymous, 2021, cited in Dilanian and Collins, 2021), showing the explicit aim of blocking the peaceful transition of power.

At the time of the protest, 29% of Americans polled believed the allegations of a stolen election and another 4% said they would be willing to engage in violent protest to stop it (Pape, 2021, p. 44). A research report in *The Atlantic* states that 89% of those arrested for their role in the Capitol riots that day were unaffiliated citizens, coming from across the country in response to calls from their President. Another 10% in attendance were members of a militia, with 1% being members of gangs (Pape, 2021). Organized groups were cited as the 'tips of the spear' in breaching both the barricades and the Capitol building itself (Program on Extremism, 2021, p. 52). These were the attitudes, beliefs, and imaginaries held by the thousands of Americans from across the country amassing themselves at the gates of their democracy.

Gathering at the Capitol

Large numbers of protesters had already begun to arrive at the Capitol building when, at 12:35pm ET, Senator Josh Hawley greeted the crowd with a raised fist as

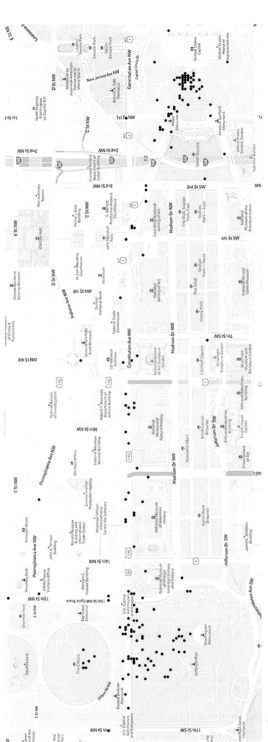

FIGURE 4.3 Aerial map, Ellipse to US Capitol. Black dots represent Parler post locations 1:00pm–3:00pm ET on January 6, 2021. Location and time details extracted from metadata of Parler posts scraped by @donk_enby and others, published by David Zumbach (2021)

Source: Copyright David VanDyke, map created with © Mapbox, © OpenStreetMap.

he entered the Capitol building, captured in a photograph by Francis Chung, reporter for *EandE News* (Allred, Olmos, and Clancy, 2021).

By 12:53pm ET, protesters had amassed around the west perimeter, spurred on, supported by, and some would say, led by organized groups like The Proud Boys and the Three Percenters (see Figure 4.3). This mob breached the first barricades, which were staffed by only a few dozen police, all lacking riot gear or any kind of protective equipment (Dmitriy et al., 2021), and was now well on its way to becoming a riot.

Around the same time, two pipe bombs were reported to have been found nearby, one at the Republican National Committee Headquarters (Leatherby et al., 2021) and a second at the Democratic National Committee Headquarters, the perpetrator of which remains at large, despite a compilation of surveillance footage tracking their actions in placing the bombs the previous night (Mallin, 2021).

The initial breach of the barricades was the inciting incident in a fight that would go on into the evening, rioters clashing with officers on multiple fronts, both outside and within the building. US Capitol Police (USCP) Chief Steven Sund had earlier asked for the National Guard to be on-call, however the Pentagon had held off on their deployment due in part to concerns about bad 'optics' (Wamsley, 2021). Therefore, when the US Capitol Police were overrun, they had no back-up on site.

Breaking Through the Barricades

By 12:50pm ET, hundreds of protesters had broken through the barricades, and despite the Capitol Police radioing for the Washington DC Metropolitan Police and the National Guard to provide support, they themselves were ill prepared, showing up with neither riot shields nor helmets as they were unable to access their equipment locker. The National Guard would not show up for another three to four hours after eventually being called, not by outgoing-President Trump himself, but by Mike Pence from his sequestered location (Dmitriy et al., 2021).

USCP and Metro DC police officers there to protect the Capitol were met with a rabble-rousing force who came equipped with military gear, chemical sprays, baseball bats, walkie talkies, and more (Driesbach and Mak, 2021). Those riot participants with military and police training were able to detect and exploit weaknesses in the police lines. One such incident involving the Proud Boys and others resulted in a brutal fight with police, wherein protesters were able to reach the upper levels of the Capitol building, which led to the decisive breach of the Capitol building itself.

Riot Declared: 1:50pm ET

Outside the building, protesters erected a makeshift gallows scaffold replete with hangman's noose, chanting 'Fight for Trump,' 'Hang Mike Pence,' and 'Whose House? Our House' (Groeger et al., 2021). About the same time, in the Senate,

House of Representatives Speaker Nancy Pelosi and Vice President Mike Pence began the certification process. Outside, US Capitol Police officers had already called for backup.

At 1:10pm ET, rioters begin to engage police on the steps of the Capitol. An evacuation warning was sent to the Library of Congress, Madison Building, and Cannon House office Building as of 1:26pm ET.

At 1:39pm ET a riot was declared by the police dispatcher after protesters overran police at the west steps and police radioed that they had lost the line. The House of Congress would not actually be evacuated until 2:20pm ET, as rioters began to force their way deeper into the building. Despite it being clear that clashes were occurring, officials were anxious to complete their mission and delayed evacuation until rioters breached the Capitol building itself (Talbot, 2021).

From this moment forward, events unfolded quickly. Rioters breached the Capitol building at 2:11pm ET by smashing in a window and climbing through (see Chapter 8, Figure 8.5).

At 2:15pm ET, the Senate was called to an emergency recess. In the rush to Senators to get to safety, some came within 30 meters of armed rioters, with no door secured between them, escaping disaster only through the actions of a lone security officer, Eugene Goodman, who drew attention away from the fleeing Senators and the undefended Senate doorway, instead leading the pro-testers to a location where police reinforcements were available (Dmitriy et al., 2021).

Rioters inside the building caused a general sense of chaos. A photograph of Adam Johnson walking away with the lectern of the Speaker of the House went viral (see Chapter 6, Figure 6.3). Some rioters smoked cigarettes in an act of teenage rebellion, while one claimed to have used a toilet without flushing (Tavernise and Rosenberg, 2021). Another photo that went viral was that of a self-styled 'QAnon Shaman' wielding an American flag attached to a spear, his shirtless body adorned with furs and symbols of Norse Heathenism (see Chapter 6, Figure 6.1). A panoply of costumes, theatrical scenes, songs, prayers, and chants were deployed by the rioters in the Rotunda and in the Senate which they quickly took over in a visual and aural display of patriotic zeal.

While the rioters partied, sang, and danced, Nancy Pelosi's staff huddled under a conference room table. Some rioters searched for Pelosi herself, shouting her name while banging on doors. The outer door to the conference room where they were huddled, was broken down by one rioter, with only the second locked and barricaded door saving them from the hands of the rioters.

Pelosi and Pence became powerful symbols of the day, standing in for a system the rioters believed had betrayed them. Mike Pence, once their hero, was cast as a traitor for failing to take a stand against the alleged miscarriage of justice. In relation to Mike Pence, his own Vice President, at 2:24pm ET @realDonaldTrump tweeted:

Mike Pence didn't have the courage to do what should have been done to protect our Country and our Constitution, giving States a chance to certify a corrected set of facts, not the fraudulent or inaccurate ones which they were asked to previously certify. USA demands the truth!

(Trump, 2021)

All the while, Pence was being spirited away to a secure location, carrying the country's nuclear launch codes (Dmitriy et al., 2021). As rioters spread throughout the building, opening the Rotunda doors to allow more to enter, officers inside the building were soon overwhelmed.

Yet, despite the evacuation orders and hundreds of rioters overrunning the building, the House would remain in session even at 2:30pm ET, as representative Jim McGovern said that he wanted to hear objections about the election results from Representative Paul Gosar.

Rioters were swarming into the Capitol building, which had been breached in eight different locations, with hundreds of people inside and thousands outside, engaging in festive celebrations and some in ongoing clashes with police. These escalated in violence, with several officers at the Inauguration door being dragged into the crowd, one by his helmet, suffering serious injuries including head trauma, broken bones, and more. At this same location, Trump supporter Roseanne Boyland would be trampled by the crowd after collapsing, later dying in hospital.

Inside, rioters were able to circumvent security personnel, coming within sight of fleeing representatives and continuing to post on Parler (see Figure 4.4). Three officers in basic uniforms were protecting a door to the House lobby that was being repeatedly punched between their heads. During a brief moment of confusion, as they were being replaced by police in riot gear, the punching rioter finally broke the glass of the door. One of the rioters noticed and articulated out loud, 'He's got a gun' observing a drawn weapon on the other side of the door. At 2:44pm ET, the first person to attempt to climb through the window and into the House was Ashli Babbitt. Clad in an American flag tied around her neck like a cape, Babbitt was boosted by several other rioters through the broken window and was shot in the shoulder and killed by a member of the US Capitol Police (Dmitriy et al., 2021).

This officer was later cleared of wrongdoing, said to have saved many more lives that day through his actions. Ashli Babbitt's actions were recorded by citizen journalist John Sullivan, who had found his way to the front lines of the riots, and this and other videos of that moment spread virally on social media, with Babbitt almost instantaneously being declared a martyr (see Chapter 10).

For another four hours, rioters would rage against police in skirmishes on various fronts, with a particularly intense skirmish taking place at the entrance to a tunnel leading to the secret location where lawmakers were sequestered.

By 4:00pm ET, when reinforcements arrived, including the belated National Guard, protesters and rioters alike were finally being pushed off the Capitol grounds by tight lines of military and police in full riot gear with linked riot shields.

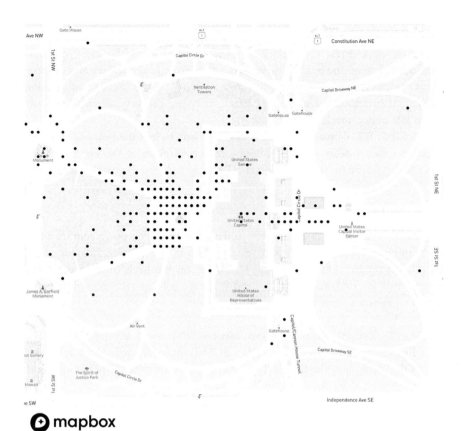

FIGURE 4.4 Aerial map of US Capitol Building. Black dots represent Parler post locations 3:00pm–5:00pm ET on January 6, 2021. Location and time details extracted from metadata of Parler posts scraped by @donk_enby and others, published by David Zumbach (2021)

Source: Copyright David VanDyke, map created with © Mapbox, © OpenStreetMap.

In a fitting denouement, at 6:01pm ET, facing increasing pressure to speak publicly and denounce the rioters, Donald Trump finally tweeted to his base:

> These are the things and events that happen when a sacred landslide election victory is so unceremoniously and viciously stripped away from great patriots who have been badly and unfairly treated for so long. Go home with love and in peace. Remember this day forever!
>
> *(Trump, 2021, cited in Dmitriy et al., 2021)*

Thus ended the first breach of the US Capitol building since 1814, an ingress by rioters seeking redress for an alleged stolen election, believing in a disinformation and fake-news fueled imaginary wherein a mass injustice had been perpetrated against the American people. Responding to what they had misinterpreted as a threat to democracy itself, rioters successfully interrupted the democratic process through violent acts of insurrection, themselves becoming that very threat. In other words, through digital media and disinformation, believing that democracy was under attack, they put the very seat of democracy in the US under attack.

At 6:27pm ET, despite the rioters' valiant efforts to halt the peaceful transition of power, after a delay of several hours, the certification of the election would begin again, finally finishing at 3:39am ET the next day, on January 7th, 2021.

After the Riots

On Friday, January 8th, 2021, Twitter initiated a purge of accounts culminating in the banning of @realDonaldTrump, 'due to the risk of further incitement of violence' (Twitter Inc., 2021, para. 1). This came on the heels of a Trump tweet, replete with his exclamation marks and emphatic all-cap sections signifying his increasing agitation, that read:

> The 75,000,000 great American Patriots who voted for me, AMERICA FIRST, and MAKE AMERICA GREAT AGAIN, will have a GIANT VOICE long into the future. They will not be disrespected or treated unfairly in any way, share (sic) or form!!!
>
> *(Trump, 2021, cited in Twitter Inc., 2021, para. 6)*

Trump continues to spread disinformation about election fraud, and is now embroiled in a disinformation campaign to deny that any violence took place at the Capitol that day.

Extrapolating an analysis from the identity of those arrested over their involvement in the Capitol riots—which in itself is a method subject to debate—we can infer that a majority of the rioters were 35 years of age and older, predominantly white, male, and employed, and hailed from pro-Biden and battleground counties (Pape, 2021). They were members of a dominant class, who expressed narratives of being wronged by an illegitimate or 'stolen election,' and were thereby emboldened to push back against what they alleged was an anti-democratic power grab by the Democrats. The socio-cultural dynamics of the time provided them with ample reason to believe that they were entitled to do so, with a frenzied storm of media attention from both online and traditional outlets.

Although the media clearly documented the presence of right-wing militia, gangs, and white supremacist groups, and it is evident from online interactions leading up to January 6th that these groups played an influential role in the organization, encouragement and perhaps even incitement of rioters, the power and brute force of the attacks emerged from the all-American citizen, ordinary people concerned by what they were hearing and inflamed by a desire to support a President they believed to be sincere.

Why did these individuals ultimately answer the call to arms? What was the key to convincing them to violently overtake the symbolic center of their own country's democracy? What made them willing to betray stated allegiances, attacking officers while simultaneously waving pro-police flags (Lang and Jamison, 2021)?

It is crucial to acknowledge the loss of life of at least five people at the Capitol riots, and several subsequent suicides, to absorb the horrific experience of staffers, press, law enforcement, Senators, and House representatives who truly feared for their lives as an armed mob violently tore through the Capitol building, and to understand the on-going repercussions for those more than seven hundred people who participated and have subsequently been arrested.

Knowing how close rioters came to confronting and possibly even capturing their 'enemies'—including Mike Pence, who carried with him the nuclear launch apparatus, and Nancy Pelosi who was forced to shelter in place—all the while emboldened by an outgoing President's inflammatory tweets, should compel the American and global public to call into question the present and future of American democracy.

While we do not attempt to provide a political forecast of potential American futures, it is clear that the media—social, alt-right, mainstream, and otherwise—will continue to play a crucial role in any emerging narrative. It is from this perspective that we approach our analysis in these pages.

Note

1 Represented on the day were: Mo Brooks (Representative, Alabama's 5th Congressional District), Katrina Pierson (Former Trump Campaign Adviser), Amy Kremer (Chair, Women for American First), Vernon Jones (Former Member, Georgia House of Representatives), Ken Paxton (Texan Attorney General), Lara and Eric Trump (Daughter-in-law and son of Former President Trump), Kimberley Guilfoyle (Former Trump Campaign Adviser), Donald Trump Jr. (Son of Former President Trump), Madison Cawthorn (Representative, North Carolina's 11th Congressional District), Rudy Giuliani (Trump's Personal Attorney), and John Eastman (Constitutional Lawyer) (Choi, 2021).

References

Allred, A, Olmos, D and Clancy, S (2021) 'Photo Shows Hawley Giving Fist Pump to Trump Supporters Before Capitol Violence,' *KSDK*, 7 January [Online]. Available at: www.ksdk. com/article/news/politics/national-politics/senator-josh-hawley-photo-capitol-trump-sup porters/63-3b5d7611-9d07-41bd-8113-a9ccf74ebb68 (Accessed: 27 September 2021).

Al Jazeera (2021) '"Call it an Insurrection": Oath Keepers Charged for Capitol Riot,' *Al Jazeera*, 31 May [Online]. Available at: www.aljazeera.com/news/2021/5/31/call-it-a n-insurrection-oath-keepers-charged-for-jan-6-riot (Accessed: 27 September 2021).

Atlantic Council's DFRLab (2021) '#StopTheSteal: Timeline of Social Media and Extremist Activities Leading to 1/6 Insurrection,' *Just Security*, 10 February [Online]. Available at: www.justsecurity.org/74622/stopthesteal-timeline-of-social-media-and-extremist-acti vities-leading-to-1-6-insurrection/ (Accessed: 27 September 2021).

BBC News (2021) 'Capitol riots timeline: The Evidence Presented Against Trump,' *BBC News*, 13 February [Online]. Available at: www.bbc.com/news/world-us-canada -56004916 (Accessed: 27 September 2021).

Brewster, J (2020) 'Facebook Banned "Stop The Steal"—Then Other Groups Popped Up In Its Place.' *Forbes*, 6 November [Online]. Available at: www.forbes.com/sites/jackbrewster/2020/11/06/facebook-banned-stop-the-steal-then-other-groups-popped-up-in-its-place/ (Accessed: 27 September 2021).

Bump, P (2020) 'This Might Be the Most Embarrassing Document Created by a White House Staffer,' *The Washington Post*, 18 December [Online]. Available at: www.washingtonpost.com/politics/2020/12/18/this-might-be-most-embarrassing-document-created-by-white-house-staffer/ (Accessed: 27 September 2021).

Chamberlain, W (2020) 'A Poll Watcher in Philly Was Just Wrongfully Prevented from Entering the Polling Place #StopTheSteal,' *@willchamberlain*, 3 November [Online]. Available at: https://twitter.com/willchamberlain/status/1323615834455994373 (Accessed: 27 September 2021).

Choi, M (2021) 'Trump Is on Trial for Inciting an Insurrection. What About The 12 People Who Spoke Before Him?,' *Politico*, 10 February [Online]. Available at: www.politico.com/news/2021/02/10/trump-impeachment-stop-the-steal-speakers-467554 (Accessed: 27 September 2021).

Corasaniti, N (2021) 'Rudy Giuliani Sued by Dominion Voting Systems Over False Election Claims,' *The New York Times*, 25 January [Online]. Available at: www.nytimes.com/2021/01/25/us/politics/rudy-giuliani-dominion-trump.html≥ (Accessed: 27 September 2021).

Diaz, J (2021) 'An Appeals Court Has Suspended Rudy Giuliani's Ability to Practice Law in DC,' *NPR*, 8 July [Online]. Available at: www.npr.org/2021/07/08/1014047881/an-appeals-court-has-suspended-rudy-giulianis-ability-to-practice-law-in-d-c≥ (Accessed: 27 September 2021).

Dilanian, K and Collins, B (2021) 'Feds Aren't Using Posts About Plans to Attack the Capitol as Evidence,' *NBC News*, 20 April [Online]. Available at: www.nbcnews.com/politics/justice-department/we-found-hundreds-posts-about-plans-attack-capitol-why-are-n-n1264291 (Accessed: 27 September 2021).

Dmitriy, K, Willis, H, Hill, E, Reneau, N, Jordan, D, Engelbrecht, C, Triebert, C, Cooper, S, Browne, M and Botti, D (2021) 'Day of Rage: An In-Depth Look at How a Mob Stormed the Capitol,' *The New York Times*, 30 June [Online]. Available at: www.nytimes.com/video/us/politics/100000007606996/capitol-riot-trump-supporters.html (Accessed: 27 September 2021).

Dreisbach, T and Mak, T (2021) 'Capitol Riot Weapons Include Bear Spray, Fire Extinguishers and Baseball Bats,' *NPR*, 19 March [Online]. Available at: www.npr.org/2021/03/19/977879589/yes-capitol-rioters-were-armed-here-are-the-weapons-prosecutors-say-they-used (Accessed: 27 September 2021).

Ellefson, L (2020) 'OANN's Chanel Rion Says White House Press Secretary Stephanie Grisham Invited Her Back to Briefing Room,' *The Wrap*, 2 April [Online]. Available at: www.thewrap.com/oanns-chanel-rion-says-white-house-press-secretary-stephanie-grisham-invited-her-back-to-briefing-room/ (Accessed: 27 September 2021).

Factbase (2021) 'Donald Trump. Speeches. Tweets. Policy. Unedited. Unfiltered. Instantly.' *Factbase*, [Online]. Available at: https://factba.se/trump/ (Accessed: 4 October 2021).

Frontline (2021) 'What Conspiracy Theorist Alex Jones Said in The Lead Up to the Capitol Riot,' *Frontline*, 12 January [Online]. Available at: www.pbs.org/wgbh/frontline/article/what-conspiracy-theorist-alex-jones-said-in-the-lead-up-to-the-capitol-riot/ (Accessed: 27 September 2021).

Fung, B (2021) 'Parler App Has Now Been Booted by Amazon, Apple and Google,' *CNN*, 11 January [Online]. Available at: www.cnn.com/2021/01/09/tech/parler-suspended-apple-app-store/index.html (Accessed: 27 September 2021).

Groeger, LV, Jeff, K, Shaw, A, Syed, M and Eliahou, M (2021) 'What Parler Saw During the Attack on the Capitol,' *ProPublica*, 17 January [Online]. Available at: https://projects.propublica.org/parler-capitol-videos/ (Accessed: 27 September 2021).

Gurman, S and Horwitz, J (2021) 'Parler Says it Informed FBI of Violent Content Before Capitol Riot,' *Wall Street Journal*, 25 March [Online]. Available at: www.wsj.com/articles/parler-says-it-informed-fbi-of-violent-content-before-capitol-riot-11616702400 (Accessed: 27 September 2021).

Hsu, SS (2021) 'In first, US Charges Jan. 6 Defendant with Bringing Firearms to Capitol Under Controversial Federal Rioting Law,' *The Washington Post*, 17 June [Online]. Available at: www.washingtonpost.com/local/legal-issues/rare-weapons-charge-capitol-riot/2021/06/17/9abef4ec-cf94-11eb-8cd2-4e95230cfac2_story.html (Accessed: 27 September 2021).

Johnson, R (2021) 'Yes, Jan. 6 Capitol Assault was an "Armed Insurrection",' *PolitiFact*, 15 February [Online]. Available at: www.politifact.com/factchecks/2021/feb/15/ron-johnson/yes-jan-6-capitol-assault-was-armed-insurrection/ (Accessed: 27 September 2021).

Kim, SR and Streakin, W (2021) 'How Trump, RNC Raised Hundreds of Millions Pushing Baseless Election Fraud Claims,' *ABC News*, 2 February [Online]. Available at: https://abcnews.go.com/US/trump-rnc-raised-hundreds-millions-pushing-baseless-election/story?id=75633798 (Accessed: 27 September 2021).

Lang, MJ and Jamison, P (2021) 'Attitudes Toward Police Officers Among Far Right Are Changing, Experts Warn,' *The Washington Post*, 8 January [Online]. Available at: www.washingtonpost.com/local/capitol-police-officers-support/2021/01/08/a16e07a2-51da-11eb-83e3-322644d82356_story.html (Accessed: 27 September 2021).

Lang, MJ, Miller, ME, Jamison, P, Moyer, JW, Williams, C, Hermann, P, Kunkle, F and Woodrow Cox, J (2020) 'After Thousands of Trump Supporters Rally in DC, Violence Erupts When Night Falls,' *The Washington Post*, 14 November [Online]. Available at: www.washingtonpost.com/dc-md-va/2020/11/14/million-maga-march-dc-protests/ (Accessed: 27 September 2021).

Leatherby, L, Ray, A, Sighvi, A, Triebert, C, Watkins, D and Willis, H (2021) 'Insurrection at the Capitol: A Timeline of How It Happened,' *The New York Times*, 12 January [Online]. Available at: www.nytimes.com/interactive/2021/01/12/us/capitol-mob-timeline.html (Accessed: 27 September 2021).

Levitt, J (2007) 'The Truth About Voter Fraud,' Brennan Center for Justice, 9 November [Online]. Available at: www.brennancenter.org/our-work/research-reports/truth-about-voter-fraud (Accessed: 27 September 2021).

Lyons, K (2020) 'Facebook Still has Hundreds of "Stop the Steal" Groups Despite Earlier Crackdown,' *The Verge*, 20 November [Online]. Available at: www.theverge.com/2020/11/20/21579293/facebook-stop-the-steal-groups-election-trump-disinformation (Accessed: 27 September 2021).

Lyons, K (2021) 'Parler Returns to Apple App Store with Some Content Excluded,' *The Verge*, 17 May [Online]. Available at: www.theverge.com/2021/5/17/22440005/parler-apple-app-store-return-amazon-google-capitol (Accessed: 27 September 2021).

Mallin, A (2021) 'FBI Releases New Video of Suspect Who Placed Pipe Bombs Outside RNC, DNC Before Jan. 6 Riot,' *ABC News*, 8 September [Online]. Available at: https://abcnews.go.com/Politics/fbi-releases-video-suspect-pipe-bombs-rnc-dnc/story?id=79898344 (Accessed: 27 September 2021).

Mapbox (n.d.) 'Maps, Geocoding, and Navigation APIs and SDKs,' *Mapbox* [Online]. Available at: www.mapbox.com/ (Accessed: 27 September 2021).

Miller, AM (2020) 'Peter Navarro Releases 36-Page Report Alleging Election Fraud "More Than Sufficient" to Swing Victory to Trump,' *The Washington Examiner*, 17 December

[Online]. Available at: www.washingtonexaminer.com/news/wh-adviser-navarro-relea ses-report-election-fraud-swing-victory-to-trump (Accessed: 27 September 2021).

Naylor, B (2021) 'Read Trump's Jan. 6 Speech, A Key Part of Impeachment Trial,' *NPR*, 10 February [Online]. Available at: www.npr.org/2021/02/10/966396848/read-trump s-jan-6-speech-a-key-part-of-impeachment-trial (Accessed: 27 September 2021).

Nguyen, T (2021) 'MAGA Marchers Plot Final DC Stand on Jan. 6,' *Politico*, 4 January [Online]. Available at: www.politico.com/news/2021/01/04/maga-marchers-trump-la st-stand-454382 (Accessed: 27 September 2021).

Padden, P (2021) 'Former Murdoch Exec: Fox News is Poison for America,' *The Daily Beast*, 5 July [Online]. Available at: www.thedailybeast.com/former-murdoch-exec-sa ys-fox-news-is-poison-for-america (Accessed: 27 September 2021).

Pape, RA (2021) 'Understanding American domestic terrorism: Mobilization potential and risk factors of a new threat trajectory,' The University of Chicago [Online]. Available at: https://d3qi0qp55mx5f5.cloudfront.net/cpost/i/docs/americas_insurrectionists_online_2 021_04_06.pdf?mtime=1617807009 (Accessed: 27 September 2021).

Pazniokas, M (2021) 'Trump Admits Loss as Democrats Push Long-Shot Removal,' *The CT Mirror*, 7 January [Online]. Available at: https://ctmirror.org/2021/01/07/trump -admits-loss-as-democrats-push-long-shot-removal/ (Accessed: 27 September 2021).

Pengelly, M (2021) '"Hang Mike Pence": Twitter Stops Phrase Trending After Capitol Riot,' *The Guardian*, 10 January [Online]. Available at: www.theguardian.com/us-news/ 2021/jan/10/hang-mike-pence-twitter-stops-phrase-trending-capitol-breach (Accessed: 27 September 2021).

Program on Extremism (2021) 'This is our house: A preliminary assessment of the Capitol Hill siege participants,' The George Washington University [Online]. Available at: http s://extremism.gwu.edu/sites/g/files/zaxdzs2191/f/This-Is-Our-House.pdf (Accessed: 27 September 2021).

Ruby, RA and Pape, K (2021) 'The Capitol Rioters Aren't Like Other Extremists,' *The Atlantic*, February [Online]. Available at: www.theatlantic.com/ideas/archive/ 2021/02/the-capitol-rioters-arent-like-other-extremists/617895/ (Accessed: 27 September 2021).

Sadeque, S (2020) 'Million Maga March: Trump Fans Rage Against Dying of the Light,' *The Guardian*, 15 November [Online]. Available at: www.theguardian.com/us-news/ 2020/nov/15/million-maga-march-trump-supporters (Accessed: 27 September 2021).

Sapien, J and Kaplan, J (2021) 'New Details Suggest Senior Trump Aides Knew Jan. 6 Rally Could Get Chaotic,' *ProPublica*, 25 June [Online]. Available at: www.propublica.org/art icle/new-details-suggest-senior-trump-aides-knew-jan-6-rally-could-get-chaotic?token= NeFLGIpiIWUgGa61DRsO5KqljQI-2YWT (Accessed: 27 September 2021).

Sardarizadeh, S and Lussenhop, J (2021) 'The 65 Days That Led to Chaos at the Capitol,' *BBC News*, 10 January [Online]. Available at: www.bbc.com/news/world-us-canada -55592332 (Accessed: 27 September 2021).

Semones, E (2021) 'Man Shown Carrying Nancy Pelosi's Lectern at Capitol Riots Arres- ted,' *Politico*, 9 January [Online]. Available at: www.politico.com/news/2021/01/09/p elosi-lectern-capitol-riots-arrest-456830 (Accessed: 27 September 2021).

Shamsian, J (2021) 'Munchel Zip Tie Guy Detention Memo,' *Insider*, 20 January [Online]. Available at: www.documentcloud.org/documents/20461405-munchel-zip-tie-guy-de tention-memo (Accessed: 27 September 2021).

Sinclair, H (2021) 'Bombshell Recordings Show Police Overwhelmed by Protesters before Trump Speech,' *The Independent*, October 1 [Online]. Available at: www.independent.co. uk/news/world/americas/us-politics/capitol-riot-park-police-new-recordings-b1930757. html (Accessed: 4 October 2021).

Stanton, Z (2020) 'You're Living in the Golden Age of Conspiracy Theories,' *Politico*, 17 June [Online]. Available at: www.politico.com/news/magazine/2020/06/17/conspiracy-theor ies-pandemic-trump-2020-election-coronavirus-326530 (Accessed: 27 September 2021).

Swan, J (2020) 'Trump Plans to Declare Premature Victory if He Appears "Ahead" On Election Night,' *Axios*, 1 November [Online]. Available at: www.axios.com/trump-claim-election-vic tory-ballots-97eb12b9-5e35-402f-9ea3-0ccfb47f613f.html (Accessed: 27 September 2021).

Talbot, H (2021) 'Inside the House Chamber as the Capitol was Overrun by an Angry Mob,' *NBC News*, 9 January [Online]. Available at: www.nbcnews.com/politics/congress/inside-house-chamber-capitol-was-overrun-angry-mob-n1253640 (Accessed: 27 September 2021).

Tan, S, Shin, Y and Rindler, D (2021) 'How one of America's ugliest days unraveled inside and outside the Capitol,' *Washington Post*, 9 January [Online]. Available at: https://www.washingtonpost.com/nation/interactive/2021/capitol-insurrection-visual-timeline/ (Accessed: 4 October 2021).

Tavernise, S and Rosenberg, M (2021) 'These Are the Rioters Who Stormed the Nation's Capitol,' *The New York Times*, 7 January [Online]. Available at: www.nytimes.com/2021/01/07/us/names-of-rioters-capitol.html (Accessed: 27 September 2021).

Taylor, R (2021) 'Rudy Giuliani Speech Transcript at Trump's Washington, DC Rally: Wants "Trial by Combat",' *Rev*, 6 January [Online]. Available at: www.rev.com/blog/transcripts/rudy-giuliani-speech-transcript-at-trumps-washington-d-c-rally-wants-trial-by -combat (Accessed: 27 September 2021).

Trump, D (2021) 'Mike Pence Didn't Have the Courage …,' *Facebook*, 6 January [Online]. Available at: www.facebook.com/DonaldTrump/posts/mike-pence-didnt-have-the-coura ge-to-do-what-should-have-been-done-to-protect-ou/10166091123235725/ (Accessed: 27 September 2021).

Twitter Inc. (2021) 'Permanent Suspension of @realDonaldTrump,' *Twitter Blog*, 8 January [Online]. Available at: https://blog.twitter.com/en_us/topics/company/2020/suspension (Accessed: 27 September 2021).

Wade, P (2021) 'Louie Gohmert Suggests People "Go to the Streets" and Be "Violent" After Judge Throws Out Baseless Election Suit,' *Rolling Stone*, 3 December [Online]. Available at: www.rollingstone.com/politics/politics-news/louie-gohmert-suggests-vio lent-response-after-judge-rejects-election-suit-1109175/ (Accessed: 27 September 2021).

Wamsley, L (2021) 'What We Know So Far: A Timeline of Security Response at the Capitol on Jan. 6,' *NPR*, 15 January [Online]. Available at: www.npr.org/2021/01/15/956842958/what-we-know-so-far-a-timeline-of-security-at-the-capitol-on-january-6 (Accessed: 27 September 2021).

Wemple, E (2020) 'Fox News host Hannity Continues Denying Biden's Win Over Trump,' *The Washington Post*, 14 December [Online]. Available at: www.washingtonpost.com/op inions/2020/12/14/sean-hannity-americas-no-2-threat-democracy-an-a-to-z-guide/?itid= lk_inline_manual_9 (Accessed: 27 September 2021).

Wilkie, C (2020) 'Trump Tries to Claim Victory Even as Ballots Are Being Counted in Several States—NBC Has Not Made a Call,' *CNBC*, 4 November [Online]. Available at: www.cnbc.com/2020/11/04/trump-tries-to-claim-victory-even-as-ballots-are-being-counted-in-several-states-nbc-has-not-made-a-call.html (Accessed: 27 September 2021).

Zumbach, D (n.d.) 'Zumbov2—Overview,' *GitHub* [Online]. Available at: https://github.com/zumbov2 (Accessed: 27 September 2021).

5

CODED DATA

Tracking Discursive Trends in the January 6 Parler Data

David VanDyke

Parler is a social media platform founded by John Matze in 2018. The platform advertises itself as 'the world's premier free speech platform' and only two rules govern users: (1) Parler is not to be used for illegal acts and (2) No use of bots or posting of spam.

Parler's name is derived from the French word *'parler'* meaning *to speak.* However, the platform's creator, users and the media pronounce Parler as *'par-ler'* (sounds like parlor). Parler might best be described as alt-right Twitter meets alt-right Instagram.

The Parler platform advertises itself as 'unbiased social media.' However, Parler was started with funding from conservative donor Rebekah Mercer and is actively advertised to members of the political right (Trump Team, 2020).

While Parler's rules forbid the use of bots and spam, an exception appears to have been made for Donald Trump's campaign account @TeamTrump which

TABLE 5.1 Twitter and Parler Terminologies

Platform			Description
Generic	**Twitter**	**Parler**	
user	user	citizen	a user of the Parler platform
post	tweet	parley	a post (character limits, Parler: 1000; Twitter: 280)
repost	retweet	echo	a reposting of existing content
reply	reply	comment	a text-based response to a post
upvote	like	vote	posts are scored based on the votes they receive
Verified User	Blue Badge	Parler Citizen	Parler users who upload photo-id can become verified users and a Parler badge is displayed below their photo

Source: Copyright David VanDyke.

DOI: 10.4324/9781003246862-7

posts a message asking new Parler accounts for campaign contributions: 'Welcome to Parler! Help us MAKE AMERICA GREAT AGAIN by clicking the link below. Be sure to text TRUMP to 88022!' (Trump Team, 2020). Within the Parler dataset, this message appears over 880,000 times.

As a result of Parler's small size in comparison to other social networks, combined with its conservative beginnings and advertising that predominantly targets the Republican base, Parler users demonstrate a high level of political homophily. This reduces the proíbability of politically diverse interaction, as any parleys that oppose alt-right views are aggressively downvoted (Halberstam and Knight, 2016). Examples of both upvoted and downvoted comments will be provided later in the chapter. The notion that Parler is unbiased must be called into question when prominent conservative politicians use the platform as a marketing tool and its userbase skews so far to the right. The term 'free speech' is used by Parler as a marketing slogan which Parler uses to justify the free circulation of fake news, disinformation, misinformation, hate speech and baseless opinions that are fact-free.

While Parler and Twitter provide much of the same functionality, Parler is a far more political platform and makes greater use of embedded media such as photos and videos. Parler also uses its own terminology with parallels to Twitter (see Table 5.1).

The Archived Parler Data

The Parler data used in this analysis is available thanks to donk_enby, a researcher and self-described 'hacktivist' (hacker activist) from Austria. donk_enby began archiving the data from the Parler platform after the January 6, 2021 Capitol riots with the goal of archiving all Parler data from that day (Dixit, 2021) (see Figure 5.1). When she realized the importance of the January 6 data and learned that Amazon would soon stop hosting Parler content, donk_enby worked with Archive Team, a group of data archival hobbyists, to download an estimated 99%

FIGURE 5.1 Word Cloud of all Parleys January 6, 2021
Source: Copyright David VanDyke (background image from https://pixabay.com/photos/us-capitol-building-washington-dc-4077168/).

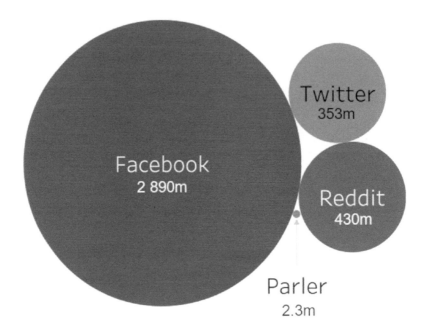

FIGURE 5.2 Size Comparison of Active Users on Social Media Platforms. Area of bubbles indicates number of monthly active users (millions). Based on self-reported figures of platform providers

Source: Copyright David VanDyke.

of the publicly available Parler content (Nally, 2021). The primary dataset used in this analysis contains 13 million users and 119 million Parler posts and comments spanning from August 2018 to January 2021 (adatascienti.st, 2021). For those who are interested in doing their own research, Twitter user @anonymousdata_ has shared observations and has made the Parler dataset accessible to those without a data science background through a searchable database publicly available at https://adatascienti.st/ (2021).

When comparing the size of social networks, Parler is much smaller than its more mainstream social media peers. Parler's peak monthly active user count of 2.3 million users makes the platform about 150 times smaller than Twitter and 1,000 times smaller than Facebook (see Figure 5.2).

The Most Popular Parler Hashtags

Within Parler, hashtags are manually added by users, resulting in many versions of the same hashtag e.g., #Trump2020 and #TRUMP2020. For the purpose of data analysis, all hashtags are converted to lowercase and similar hashtags have been combined (see Figure 5.3).

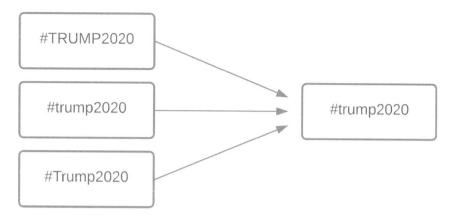

FIGURE 5.3 Hashtag Conversion
Source: Copyright David VanDyke.

Several of the most popular hashtags used on Parler are analyzed here and depicted in a data visualization (see Figure 5.4).

Welcome to Parler: #parlerconcierge, #truefreespeech

The most commonly used Parler hashtag is #parlerconcierge. This hashtag is used to welcome new users to the Parler network, providing introductory information and the rules and guidelines that govern the site. Similarly, new users tend to make use of #newuser and #truefreespeech when joining the platform.

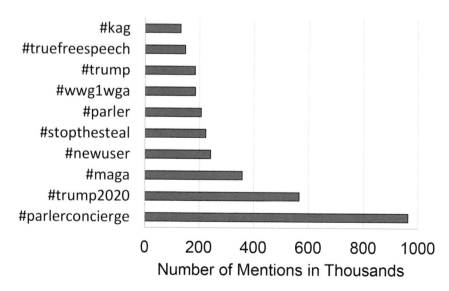

FIGURE 5.4 Top Parler Hashtags based on 119 million Parler posts and comments
Source: Copyright David VanDyke.

Hashtags supporting Donald Trump: #trump2020, #trump, #maga, #kag, #stopthesteal,

Hashtags supporting Donald Trump are also extremely prevalent across the Parler network.

#trump2020 and #trump are hashtags used in posts to show support for Donald Trump, to endorse the notion that Trump should be re-elected president in 2020, and after Trump's 2020 election loss, to support the disproven allegations that Trump won the election, but it was stolen due to voter fraud.

#maga and #kag are two hashtags that represent Trump's presidential campaign slogans, 'Make America Great Again' and 'Keep America Great.'

#stopthesteal is included in posts alleging that the election was rigged against Trump, posts claiming election fraud occurred, and posts endorsing the 'stop the steal' rallies and marches, up to and including the Capitol riots.

QAnon: #wwg1wga

#wwg1wga is an acronym for 'where we go one, we go all,' a slogan used by the 'inspired believers' of QAnon conspiracy theories (see Chapter 7). QAnon conspiracy theorists on Parler also make use of the hashtags #QAnon #q #qarmy and #deepstate.

Network Diagrams

Network diagrams are a way to explore the conversations occurring in Parler comments. The network diagram plots visualized here illustrate the relationship between the most commonly occurring word pairs or 'bigrams.' The bigram network plots were created based on the 500 highest-ranked and 500 lowest-ranked comments on Parler. Duplicate posts were removed from the dataset along with 'stop words' (e.g., articles, pronouns, prepositions, etc.) as well as the non-signifying words (for our purposes), 'enjoy', 'echo', 'please', 'like', 'share', 'follow' and 'back'.

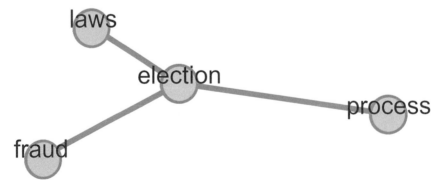

FIGURE 5.5 Network Diagram of bigrams 'election laws,' 'election fraud,' and 'election process'

Source: Copyright David VanDyke.

The Network Diagrams for Parler comments do not indicate directionality, and multiple word pairs can be derived from the connections. Three key bigrams that arose in the analysis related to the election include 'election + laws,' 'election + fraud,' and 'election + process' (see Figure 5.5).

Most Upvoted Comments

By examining network diagram plots for the most upvoted and most downvoted comments, we can identify the primary topics of conversation occurring on the Parler network. We can also determine which views are being promoted through upvoting, and which views are being silenced by downvoting.

The upvoted Parler comments (see Figure 5.6, Table 5.2) show unequivocal support for Trump. They use the term 'patriot' to refer to their presumed in-group ('thank you for being a true patriot,' 'American Patriots' and 'Keep fighting Patriots'), a term that has been co-opted by militia and other alt-right groups to signify allegiance to their interpretation of the Constitution and a willingness to fight against anyone who opposes them. Many parleys allege election fraud, voter fraud, anti-Trump media bias, and at the same time call now-President Joe Biden a 'traitor.' Moreover, the use of war-like discourse in

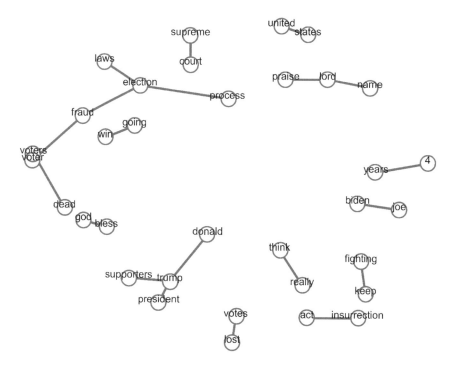

FIGURE 5.6 Network Diagram of Most Upvoted Parler Comments based on > 80 million comments
Source: Copyright David VanDyke.

TABLE 5.2 Examples of Most Upvoted Parler Comments based on > 80 million comments

Examples of Most Upvoted Comments	Score
Thank you for being a true patriot and supporting our president and our country!	4,500
Help me out to understand. the DOJ won't take action against election fraud because …	3,600
The media have dropped all pretence now. They're openly anti–Trump. They don't want him …	3,500
He told us what his plan was when he said 'we have created the most extensive voter fraud …'	3,300
I really can't believe and can't accept that a traitor with Alzheimer's is about to become …	3,300
Blow up Amazon with complaints American Patriots! Cancel culture works in many ways …	3,000
If we turn our heads to the fraudulence that we have seen we will never have a voice	3,000
TRUMP NEVER CONCEDED TO BIDEN, TRUMP SAID THERE WILL BE A 'SMOOTH PEACEFUL …'	2,800
It's not even close to over. Keep fighting Patriots.	2,700
We love you, Lin, thanks for fighting for us	2,600
If you're okay with someone cheating and stealing from you … you're also the problem	2,500
He's NOT responsible nor is Trump. The Left is fully responsible.	2,500

Source: Copyright David VanDyke.

terms such as 'blow up' and 'fighting' demonstrate Parler users' vehemence in contesting the election outcome and foreshadow their predilection for violence in the Capitol riots.

Most Downvoted Comments

The most downvoted comments seem to be diametrically opposed to the upvoted comments (see Figure 5.7, Table 5.3). They are pro-Biden and anti-Republican comments, which are often responded to with personal attacks ('nothing you say is true,' 'you won't be missed,' 'a sucker born every minute'). Several comments focus on Trump's history of telling lies and his promotion of disinformation (see Chapter 3). These comments attempted to some extent to correct the disinformation allegations of the stolen election, so they revert to more factual evidence, but in tone they are just as disrespectful as the upvoted comments. Given Parler's strong political homophily, it is unlikely that perspectives supporting the actual election results or debunking the 'stolen election' allegations are given consideration or viewed by the majority of Parler's citizens.

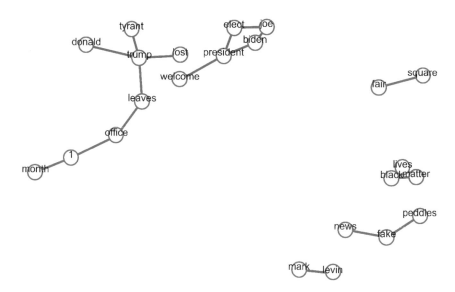

FIGURE 5.7 Network Diagram of Most Downvoted Parler Comments based on > 80 million comments

TABLE 5.3 Examples of Most Downvoted Parler Comments based on > 80 million comments

Examples of Most Downvoted Comments	Score
Lets face it, Trump lost!	–3000
Nothing you say is true. Mad Mark Levin peddles fake news.	–2000
Biden won. Deal with it.	–2000
Trump lied about a birth certificate. He lied about crowd size. He lied about his taxes. He lied…	–2000
Bye, everyone. Most of you won't be missed.	–2000
There's a sucker born every minute—and 90% grow up to be republicans …	–1000
Biden is responsible for the stocks soaring actually	–1000
Trump lied about dominion. Anomalies do not prove voter fraud. They are anomalies that's it …	–1000
Biden is going to be a great President. I'm looking forward to January 20! And Twitter > Parler.	–1000
COME CELEBRATE! FAREWELL TO TRUMP PARTY Come celebrate on PARLER Donald …	–1000
FINISH THE ORANGE-BELLIED COWARD TRUMP OFF. HE LOST. OUT! EVEN ALT-RIGHT …	–1000
Nothing was stolen. Quit crying and man up. Trump lost cause America is sick of his shit.	–1000

Mapping the Most Prominent Members of Parler

Parleys created by the most prominent Parler citizens receive substantially more views and responses than posts made by other more ordinary users. This contradicts the notion of participatory democracy that is presumed to be inherent on the internet and on social media platforms where it is believed by users that their content will be viewed and promoted as much as the next person's. This is simply not true.

Based on post count, average Parler citizens appear to be more engaged in responding to the posts made by prominent users and reacting to the comments than they are in creating original materials or responding to other users' parleys. This increases and amplifies the circulation and prominence of the messages by already-prominent people.

A directed and weighted network diagram has been generated illustrating the connections between the most prominent Parler citizens (see Figure 5.8). The map is based on parleys that have received a minimum of 5,000 views. Mentions (the use of hashtags and handles in posts) have been used to create connections. The direction of the arrow reflects the direction of the conversation and the line thickness represents the number of upvotes the parley has received.

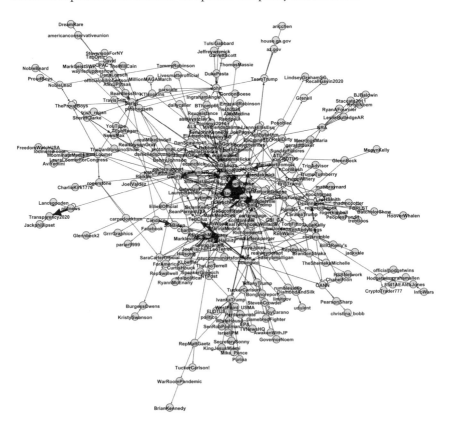

FIGURE 5.8 Parler Network Diagram of posts with >5,000 views
Source: Copyright David VanDyke.

The node representing Donald Trump is located in the center near the triangle (see Figure 5.8). Nodes towards the outside of the diagram include far-right and fringe news organizations such as InfoWars, FreedomWatchUSA, NTD News, and One American News Network.

Donald Trump

Whereas most network diagrams exhibit bidirectionality, Donald Trump's node @realDonaldTrump serves only as a destination of the other nodes (see Figure 5.9). This is because Donald Trump does not have a personal Parler account.

However, that fact notwithstanding, Trump is the central figure of the Parler network. Within the Parler network, Trump-related hashtags are shared more than those referring to any other public figure. On Parler, users refer to Trump through the hashtag #realDonaldTrump over 68,000 times.

Based on the number and strength of connections in the network diagrams, those closest to Donald Trump include Lin Wood, Rudy Giuliani and Scott Presler. Their own network diagrams will be shown later in the chapter.

On December 19, 2020, following his election loss to Joe Biden, Donald Trump tweeted

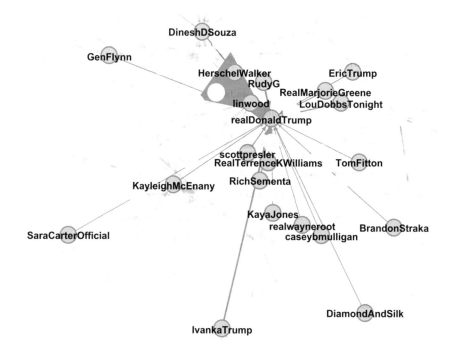

FIGURE 5.9 Donald Trump's Parler Network Connections based on mentions of @realDonaldTrump

Source: Copyright David VanDyke.

Peter Navarro releases 36-page report alleging election fraud 'more than sufficient to swing victory to Trump …' A great report by Peter. Statistically impossible to have lost the 2020 Election. Big protest in D.C. on January 6th. Be there, will be wild!

(Trump, 2020)

Donald Trump's tweet created a ripple effect that resonated through Parler and contributed to 'election fraud' and the 'stolen election' becoming central or trending topics on Parler. The topics of Parler conversations will be explored later in the chapter.

@TeamTrump

On Parler, @TeamTrump is the official Parler account for the Trump campaign. In addition to encouraging donations to the Trump campaign, other roles of the @TeamTrump Parler account include sharing the following message encouraging voters to report election fraud:

Help stop voter suppression, irregularities and fraud! Tell us what you are seeing. Report a case: djt45.co/stopfraud Call: (888) 503–3526.

(Team Trump, 2020)

Along with this text an image was included with every parley (see Figure 5.10). The text and associated image are shared by @TeamTrump repeatedly, receiving over 100 million views, not including reposts from Parler citizens.

FIGURE 5.10 @TeamTrump's Report Election Fraud Parley
Source: Parler, Image shared by @TeamTrump.

Sharing the same message multiple times was clearly an act of political pro-paganda. The illusory 'Truth Effect' describes the phenomenon of a statement becoming more believable the more it is heard (Hasher, Goldstein and Top-pino, 1977). Researchers have found that repetition of a statement will increase the message's believability and also the strength of the belief (Begg, Anas and Farinacci, 1992).

Lin Wood @linwood

Lin Wood is a lawyer, a QAnon conspiracy theorist, and a strong supporter of Donald Trump. Wood's parleys include a wide variety of voter fraud allegations (see Figure 5.11). Wood blames Georgia, *'STOP THE SUNDAY ATTEMPT TO DESTROY EVIDENCE OF VOTING FRAUD IN GEORGIA'* (Wood, 2020c). He also creates parleys alleging fraud by Dominion Voting Machines: 'they [the voting machines] were rigged across the nation. Evidence is overwhelming & conclusive' (Wood, 2020b). Wood's scattershot approach also blames China, as he writes, 'Chinese Communists used computer fraud & mail ballot fraud to interfere with our national election' (Wood, 2020a), alleging they are somehow responsible for voter fraud leading to Trump's election loss.

In relation to the Capitol riots and the 'stop the steal' campaign, Lin encourages Parler users to take action on January 6: 'The time has arrived for each American citizen to take a stand. Patriot or Traitor?' (Wood, 2021), providing evidence again of the discourse of patriots (the Republican base) and traitors (Joe Biden, and eventually also Mike Pence).

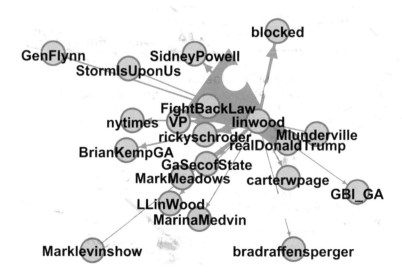

FIGURE 5.11 Lin Wood's Parler Network Connections based on mentions of @linwood
Source: Copyright David VanDyke.

Rudy Giuliani @RudyG

@RudyG is the official Parler account for Rudy Giuliani (see Figure 5.12), a former New York City mayor and Trump's former personal lawyer, who lost his ability to practice law in New York and Washington DC as a result of misconduct that included the finding 'false statements were made to improperly bolster respondent's narrative that due to widespread voter fraud, victory in the 2020 United States presidential election was stolen from his client' (Acosta, 2021, p. 2).

Guiliani is currently the subject of a 1.3-billion-dollar lawsuit from Dominion Voting Systems for false voting fraud claims (see Chapter 4) such as:

> After the last exam of Democrat Dominion machines in Michigan showed 86% of ballots subject to adjudication and 63% inaccuracies, crooked Democrats in Arizona are trying to coverup these vote stealing machines. Criminals coverup.
>
> *(Giuliani, 2020)*

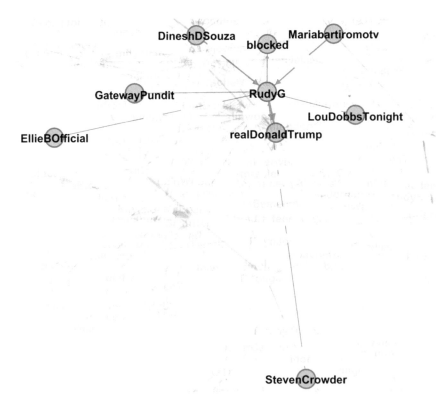

FIGURE 5.12 Rudy Giuliani's Parler Network Connections based on mentions of @RudyG

Source: Copyright David VanDyke.

Rudy Giuliani was a speaker who preceded Donald Trump on stage during the January 6 'March to Save America' rally that was followed by the storming of the Capitol. During Giuliani's speech, he rouses the crowds with election fraud claims and riles up the crowd by saying, 'Let's have trial by combat' (Reuters, 2021).

Scott Presler @scottpresler

Scott Presler is a political activist and a fervent supporter of Donald Trump. Presler's devotion for Trump is evident through his parleys:

> I feel this deeply & intensely within my bones. I promise you & I make a commitment that I will do everything within my power to re-elect President @realDonaldTrump. We are fighting for the soul of our country.
>
> *(Presler, 2020b)*

Presler is also a prominent 'anti-Muslim hatemonger,' QAnon conspiracist, and organizer of the 'stop the steal' events (Goot, 2021).

Additional parleys by Presler provide examples of his involvement in organizing the 'stop the steal' events: 'I'm in DC, preparing for the Stop The Steal rally tomorrow & there are Trumpers everywhere. The best way I can describe it is a "love fest"' (Presler, 2020c).

He also issues this call to action in Pennsylvania in relation to the 'stop the steal' events: 'Calling All Pennsylvanians: Show up TODAY in Gettysburg & bring your

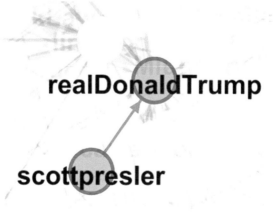

FIGURE 5.13 Scott Presler's Parler Network Connections based on mentions of @scottpresler
Source: Copyright David VanDyke.

stop the steal signs. Wyndham Gettysburg Hotel 95 Presidential Circle @ 12:30 p.m'
(Presler, 2020a).

Marjorie Taylor Greene @RealMarjorieGreene

Marjorie Taylor Greene is a Representative of Georgia's 14th congressional district,
with strong network connections on Parler (see Figure 5.14).

On December 22, 2020, Greene publicly announced her support of the 'stop
the steal' campaign and redeclared her fealty to Trump and his unsubstantiated
voter fraud claims by posting on Parler that she would object to fraudulent votes
on January 6th. In her Parley, Greene states: 'I must have a grassroots army behind
me... call your representative and Senators urging they FIGHT FOR TRUMP
and OBJECT to the voter fraud...' (Greene, 2020). Greene ends her statement by
encouraging her followers to 'FIGHT FOR TRUMP' and 'STOP THE STEAL!'

With 39 million views, 240,000 upvotes and 12,000 comments, Greene's post
quickly became the most viewed, commented and upvoted post in the history of
Parler. The popularity of Greene's post may be the result of astroturfing. Astroturfing is a play on 'artificial grassroots' and is defined by Merriam Webster (2021)
as 'organized activity that is intended to create a false impression of a widespread,
spontaneously arising, grassroots movement in support of or in opposition to

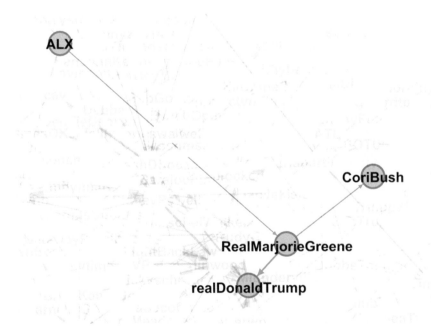

FIGURE 5.14 Marjorie Taylor Greene's Parler Network Connections based on mentions
of @RealMarjorieGreene
Source: Copyright David VanDyke.

something.' Evidence suggests that sponsored advertising was utilized to increase the number of views that Greene's December 22nd post received. As the number of views of Greene's post increased, so did the number of upvotes and comments, creating the appearance of widespread grassroots support for Greene and the election fraud narrative.

Twitter user Bo Gardiner describes being on Parler 'in the weeks before Jan 6th [where] it seemed every 5th post was a promoted post from Greene' (Gardiner, 2021). The timing of the increased popularity of Greene's post coincided with payments made from December 23–29, 2020 by 'Greene for Congress' to 'Parler LLC' with the 'Purpose of disbursement' listed as 'Digital advertising for fundraising' totaling $68,500 (Federal Election Commission, 2021). A likely motivation for Greene's December 22nd post was to exploit the popularity of #stopthesteal to raise money for her own re-election campaign. Following the link in Greene's post and signing the 'Fight for Trump' petition redirected users to a payment page with the message:

> Thank you for signing your petition to FIGHT FOR TRUMP. I MUST rally more support for January 6. Your donation of $15, $25, $50, $100—whatever you can afford —will allow me to reach hundreds of thousands of patriots like you and urge them to take action. Please chip in right away!
>
> *(Greene for Congress, 2021)*

According to the fine print located at the bottom of the page, contributions would be 'designated to the 2022 primary election.' Thus, what seemed like a grassroots movement fuelled by a trending parley on Parler mobilized by Trump's base to #stopthesteal on January 6th was an opportunistic, astroturfed, election fundraising campaign, organized and paid for by Greene herself rather than any grassroots organization.

In reaction to Greene's parley, many side discussions occurred in the comments. Topics of conversation included: sharing examples of election fraud, proclaiming the greatness of President Trump, bashing the left, and discussing the need for a violent uprising.

Some of the more dramatic examples of the need for a violent uprising include 'We will stop it. Forget the courts. forget the electoral college. They are all compromised! We the people's Army will win back freedom,1776 again!' (@Deantolley07, 2020). In this post, 1776 refers to the American Revolution and the Declaration of Independence.

Other Parler citizens, responding to Greene, are more directly violent and militant in their intentions, @Tobia47kills reacts to Greene's post by writing:

> Can we all just march on Washington DC fully armed. With our military backing our [militias] up. Trump won the election. And these people in Washington DC think they have the right to sabotage our election…. I say we march and hang them all.
>
> *(@Tobias47kills, 2021)*

Claims of Election Fraud (30%)	Other Responses (18%)	In Support of President Trump (13%)	
"If you're okay with someone cheating and stealing from you....you're also the problem"	"Call your congressmen and Senators!!!!"	"I will no longer support or vote for any politician who does not stand firmly with President Trump!....The media is trying to stifle our voices, we must speak up to be heard!"	
"God bless you ! My vote was removed with the fraud Millions of votes were removed. The ballot is what makes me equal to the richest person in America and it was taken from me,..."	"Tell us who is threatening you and we can protect you from them. Stand bold and confident. Know you're safe! Unite, Fight and WIN!"	"I that's the problem we always move on thinking it will get better 4yrs ago we voted for Trump and he as blocked at every turn.... We are standing up and saying enough we will not back down we will not shut up we will fight for America"	
"...Insanity is accepting a fraudulent stolen election. Over 40 cases filed and ZERO heard because the courts are afraid the truthful evidence will come out."	"Signed – now fight" "Signed. Emailed Rick Scott and Rubio"	"This is fight for trump..."	
"Cant lose again without losing the first time and that hasn't happened. You are too stupid to know what the constitution says. This is all in there as the process of determining who won. There is no president elect until this is done in the 6th of January. And if y'all are so sure, why hasn't he blow job harris resigned her senate seat yet?"		**Anti-Left, Anti-Biden, Anti-Clinton etc. (11%)**	**Attending the Capitol or Need for an Uprising (9%)**
"Insanity is thinking the election wasn't rigged."		"Majorie, way to go! I immigrated to US in 1993 from a country that had socialist government so I know what will US turn into if we don't stop this! Please keep fighting"	"PLANNING TO BACK YOU AT THE CAPITOL ..."
".... Why would a governor NOT allow all data to be audited and verified?"	**In Support of Marjorie Taylor Greene (14%)**	"I got hairy legs that turned blonde in the sun. And the kids used to come up and reach into the pool and rub my leg down so it was straight and watch the hair come back up again, Joe Biden"	"I signed the petition. I will be in D.C. on the 6th..."
"The time to move on crowd needs to understand that those of us who believe this election was fraudulant need the evidence..If there was no fraud why is everyone blocking the path to the truth? Prove it!"	"Majorie, way to go! I immigrated to US in 1993 from a country that had socialist government so I know what will US turn into if we don't stop this! Please keep fighting" "Thank you for being a true patriot and supporting our president and our country!"	"Kilary is a MURDERER AND A TRAITOROUS FUKN SLUT!!!!"	"There is no moving forward next step is CW (Civil War) so get ready u maggot"
"Patriots are willing to fight the injustices, the Fraud, the Corruption.... When will America push back against the Treasonous Democrat party Anti-American Politicians, the Deep State corrupt swamp in DC, the Domestic Terrorist commie groups of Antifa/BLM..."	"Keep the faith and stay the course regardless of the cowards who won't fight" "Donated and God bless you !" "We need more like you!!"		"And we will be there to have your back. Millions will be coming. ALL OF DC WILL SHIVER IN FEAR AS THEY SHOULD"
		Related to Covid-19 (4%)	
		"You have it do your job We are absolutely tired of being bullied by the Democratic Party and passing this Covid bill..."	

Figure 5.15 Treemap of Top 200 Most Upvoted Responses to Marjorie Taylor Greene's December 22, 2020 Parley
Source: Copyright David VanDyke.

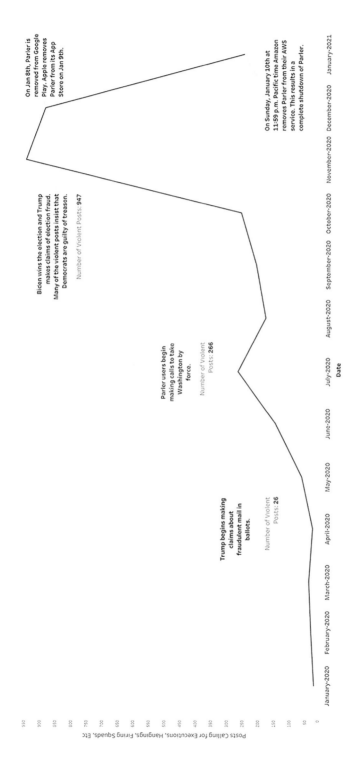

FIGURE 5.16 Line Graph Representing Extremely Violent Parleys including 'hanging,' 'firing squads,' 'lethal injection,' and other calls for death

Source: Copyright David VanDyke.

A Treemap has been created to visually illustrate the 200 most upvoted responses to Marjorie Taylor Greene's December 22, 2020 parley (see Figure 5.15).

Treemaps can be interpreted similarly to pie charts in that the area of each segment of the chart relates to a percentage and all the percentages add up to the whole. Treemaps also avoid many of the negatives related to pie charts including low density and the difficulty that humans have in accurately interpreting angles and relative size of pie chart areas (Tufte, 2001).

Discourses of Violence on Parler

Violent posts appear more commonly on Parler than on any other mainstream social media network. One reason for this is a lack of consistent moderation on the site. On Parler, moderation policies are enforced for impersonating public figures but moderation for violence is rare and applied inconsistently (Aliapoulios et al., 2021). Another reason for the prominence of violent discourses, is that Parler attracts the most extreme users who have often been banned from other platforms such as Facebook and Twitter for participating in abuse, harassment, or threats of violence.

Amy Kremer, conservative political activist and co-founder of 'Women for Trump' provides examples of content that is banned by Twitter but allowed on Parler. Kremer describes being in 'Twitter Jail' after receiving a 12-hour ban for posting that 'The Nashville Mayor should be "tarred and feathered" in the town square and then charged criminally for ruining so many lives and businesses' (Kremer, 2020). In her Parler post, Kremer also refers to her August Twitter ban, 'for tweeting that a pedophile that had just been arrested should be hung in the town square. I feel muzzled and I HATE it. The censorship is real …' (Kremer, 2020).

Calls for extreme forms of violence, such as 'hanging' presumed enemies of Trump or the alt-right, appear to increase after allegations of voter fraud occur on Parler (see Figure 5.16 and Figure 5.17). However, the increase in violent posts could also be the result of other factors such as the increased number of posts that are generally made after claims of fraud, or the growth of the Parler network over time as its membership was in a growth phase.

The line graph (see Figure 5.16) and word cloud (see Figure 5.17) are both compiled from parleys containing violent keywords. While some phrases are innocuous such as 'murder rate' many of the keywords relate to threats of violence targeted towards specific individuals or organizations. Examples of those targeted include the left-wing anti-fascist group 'Antifa' and 'George Soros' who is a billionaire philanthropist the far-right claim is responsible for voter fraud and moreover, who QAnon claim is a central figure in a pedophilia network. Also targeted are Democrats, including nearly every major Democratic figure including Bill Clinton and Hillary Clinton, Alexandria Ocasio-Cortez, President Joe Biden and members of Biden's family.

In the word cloud, it is important to note that while 'Trump Supporters' and 'Proud Boys' feature prominently, they are not the proposed targets of violence but rather the instigators.

FIGURE 5.17 Word Cloud of Parleys Calling for Death, including 'hanging,' 'firing squads,' 'lethal injection' and other calls for death

Source: Copyright David VanDyke.

Conclusion

Parler has a conservative or alt-right bias for many reasons, including its funding origins and the strong echo-chamber effect occurring on a platform that is much smaller and far less moderated than its rivals. Trump's campaign used the Parler network to raise funds while also attempting to increase distrust in the electoral system. Parler's most popular citizens (in terms of post views and upvotes), including Marjorie Taylor Greene and Rudy Giuliani, also worked to perpetuate the election fraud narrative and inspire Parler citizens to take action on January 6, 2021.

Within Parler's highly polarized ecosystem, many of its users were only exposed to far-right content, as Parler's voting system ensured that criticisms of the far-right and claims dispelling election fraud were down-voted and therefore less likely to be viewed by users. This was further exacerbated by an astroturfing campaign promoting a highly visible message about the importance of January 6th.

The growing political fervor of Parler's citizens and their use of increasingly violent rhetoric culminated with the January 6th Capitol insurrection, an event that was shocking to the outside world but much less of a surprise to the Parler citizens who had spent the previous weeks discussing and planning the event.

References

Acosta, RT (2021) 'Supreme Court of the State of New York Appellate Division, First Judicial Department,' [Online]. Available at: www.nycourts.gov/courts/ad1/calendar/List_Word/2021/06_Jun/24/PDF/Matter%20of%20Giuliani%20(2021–00506)%20PCpdf (Accessed: 31 August 2021).

adatascienti.st (2021) 'A Parler Archive,' [Online]. Available at: https://parler.adatascienti.st/ (Accessed: 31 August 2021).

Aliapoulios, M, Bevensee, E, Blackburn, J, Bradlyn, B, De Cristofaro, E, Stringhini, G and Zannettou, S (2021) 'An early look at the parler online social network,' *Proceedings of the International AAAI Conference on Web and Social Media*, 15(1): 943–951 [Preprint]. Available at: http://arxiv.org/abs/2101.03820 (Accessed: 12 July 2021).

Begg, IM, Anas, A and Farinacci, S (1992) 'Dissociation of processes in belief: Source recollection, statement familiarity, and the illusion of truth,' *Journal of Experimental Psychology: General*, 121(4): 446–458. https://doi.org/10.1037/0096-3445.121.4.446.

@Deantolley07 (2020) 'We will stop it. Forget the courts. Forget the electoral college. They are all compromised! We the people's Army will win back freedom. 1776 again!,' *Parler*, 23 December [Online]. Available at: https://parler.adatascienti.st/comment/02181a6d9af54c89ae88db3fadf17a83 (Accessed: 12 July 2021).

Dixit, S (2021) 'Who is Parler hacker @donk_enby? Deleted posts provide 'very incriminating' evidence against US Capitol riots,' *Media, Entertainment, Arts WorldWide*, 11 January [Online]. Available at: https://meaww.com/who-is-parler-hacker-donkenby-deleted-posts-very-incriminating-data-dump-us-capitol-riots-trump (Accessed: 31 August 2021).

Federal Election Commission (2021) 'Greene for congress disbursements,' *FECgov* [Online]. Available at: www.fec.gov/data/disbursements/ (Accessed: 30 September 2021).

Gardiner, B (2021) '@anonymousdata_ While you're waiting for the archive.... I was on Parler quite a bit in the weeks before Jan 6th. It seemed every 5th post was a promoted post from Green, excessive, annoying utter saturation, & always the same:,' @Bo_Gardiner, 16 January. Available at: https://twitter.com/Bo_Gardiner/status/1350309593365307393 (Accessed: 30 September 2021).

Giuliani, R (2020) 'After the last exam of Democrat Dominion machines in Michigan showed 86% of ballots subject to adjudication and 63% inaccuracies, crooked Democrats in Arizona are trying to coverup these vote stealing machines. Criminals coverup. Innocent people would help you review the records. Think they are guilty?,' *Parler*, 18 December [Online]. Available at: https://parler.adatascienti.st/post/344d7074a9484f0f9b8177d25a b30b63 (Accessed: 12 July 2021).

Goot, M (2021) 'Stefanik under fire for holding event with anti-Muslim conspiracy theorist,' *The Post-Star* [Online]. Available at: https://poststar.com/news/local/govt-and-poli tics/stefanik-under-fire-for-holding-event-with-anti-muslim-conspiracy-theorist/article_ e585e384-9b25-59cb-80a3-79fa7facf773.html (Accessed: 27 August 2021).

Greene, MT (2020) 'On January 6 on the House floor, I will OBJECT to fraudulent electoral votes from several states at the Capitol…,' *Parler*, 22 December [Online]. Available at: https://parler.adatascienti.st/post/90e725e001cf45a6b9523ab2f1f0c148 (Accessed: 12 July 2021).

Greene for Congress (2021) 'Fight for Trump—Stop the steal,' Greene for Congress [Online]. Available at: https://secure.anedot.com/greene-for congress-inc/fight-for-trump-par1222 (Accessed: 30 September 2021).

Halberstam, Y and Knight, B (2016) 'Homophily, group size, and the diffusion of political information in social networks: Evidence from Twitter,' *Journal of Public Economics*, 143: 73–88. https://doi.org/10.1016/j.jpubeco.2016.08.011.

Hasher, L, Goldstein, D and Toppino, T (1977) 'Frequency and the conference of referential validity,' *Journal of Verbal Learning and Verbal Behavior*, 16 (1): 107–112. https://doi.org/10.1016/S0022-5371(77)80012–80011.

Kremer, A (2020) 'I am in Twitter jail for 12 hours for tweeting that the Nashville Mayor should be 'tarred and feathered…,' *Parler*, 19 September [Online]. Available at: https://pa rler.adatascienti.st/post/da1be957969547c78f963003bc024641 (Accessed: 12 July 2021).

Nally, L (2021) 'The hacker who archived Parler explains how she did it (and what comes next)' *Vice*, 12 January [Online]. Available at: www.vice.com/en/article/n7vqew/the-ha cker-who-archived-parler-explains-how-she-did-it-and-what-comes-next (Accessed: 31 August 2021).

Presler, S (2020a) 'Calling All Pennsylvanians: Show up TODAY in Gettysburg & bring your stop the steal signs. Wyndham Gettysburg Hotel 95 Presidential Circle @ 12:30 p. m.,' *Parler*, 25 November [Online]. Available at: https://parler.adatascienti.st/post/ 09b8e9e980f04a77831654cfc3cd7361 (Accessed: 12 July 2021).

Presler, S (2020b) 'I feel this deeply & intensely within my bones. I promise you & I make a commitment that I will do everything within my power to re-elect President @real-DonaldTrump. We are fighting for the soul of our country,' *Parler*, 27 June [Online]. Available at: https://parler.adatascienti.st/post/4038ff2696904843ad1290090925934d (Accessed: 12 July 2021).

Presler, S (2020c) 'I'm in DC, preparing for the Stop The Steal rally tomorrow & there are Trumpers everywhere. The best way I can describe it is a "love fest",' *Parler*, 14 November [Online]. Available at: https://parler.adatascienti.st/post/13c4a9128743461da bfc2c0bd30d1924 (Accessed:12 July 2021).

Reuters (2021) '"Let's have trial by combat" over election – Giuliani' *Reuters*, 6 January [Online Video]. Available at: https://reut.rs/2KY4AAz (Accessed: 27 August 2021).

Team Trump (2020) 'Help stop voter suppression, irregularities and fraud! Tell us what you are seeing. Report a case: djt45.co/stopfraud Call: (888) 503–3526,' *Parler*, 7 November [Online].

Available at: https://parler.adatascienti.st/post/6bb1c1c7cbe14c2689c68f100416bf32 (Accessed: 12 July 2021).

@Tobias47kills (2021) 'Can we all just march on Washington DC fully armed …,' *Parler*, 28 December [Online]. Available at: https://parler.adatascienti.st/comment/027c3f298f754a08b654d2311327b141 (Accessed: 12 July 2021).

Trump, D (2020) [Twitter] 19 December. 'Peter Navarro releases 36-page report alleging election fraud.' Available at: https://media-cdn.factba.se/realdonaldtrump-twitter/1340185773220515840.jpg (Accessed: 10 July 2021).

Trump Team (2020) 'Welcome to Parler! Help us MAKE AMERICA GREAT AGAIN by clicking the link below. Be sure to text TRUMP to 88022!,' *Parler*, 17 June [Online]. Available at: https://parler.adatascienti.st/research (Accessed: 12 July 2021).

Tufte, E (2001) *The visual display of quantitative information*. Cheshire: Graphic Press.

Wood, L (2020a) 'Chinese Communists used computer fraud & mail ballot fraud to interfere with our national election. They thought we could be had & they could overthrow our duly elected President without firing a shot. They were wrong,' *Parler*, 13 November [Online]. Available at: https://parler.adatascienti.st/post/243c38dae05d4982afd4dc19db50e0ca (Accessed: 12 July 2021).

Wood, L (2020b) 'Dominion voting machines were rigged in Antrim County, MI They were rigged across the nation. Evidence is overwhelming & conclusive,' *Parler*, 24 December [Online]. Available at: https://parler.adatascienti.st/post/708683a18b8c4bf7bf2c3ca845660e8a (Accessed: 12 July 2021).

Wood, L (2020c) 'STOP THE SUNDAY ATTEMPT TO DESTROY EVIDENCE OF VOTING FRAUD IN GEORGIA,' *Parler*, 29 November [Online]. Available at: https://parler.adatascienti.st/post/0881f5a48008449ca26d5f8271df1458 (Accessed: 12 July 2021).

Wood, L (2021) 'A sobering but well-reasoned analysis of the current situation facing our President @realDonaldTrump, our country, & our future as a free people. The time has arrived for each American citizen to take a stand. Patriot or Traitor?,' *Parler*, 5 January [Online]. Available at: https://parler.adatascienti.st/post/fa62e72a3c0749b9ba2878d330ae2c95 (Accessed: 12 July 2021).

6

PHOTOGRAPHING THE SPECTACLE

Curating a Crisis

Miranda McKee

For those not in Washington, DC, on January 6th, 2021, first impressions were shaped by startling imagery, headlines, and looping video footage dominating the online mediascape. News coverage of the events led with visuals portraying a fevered delirium, a cosplayed chaos, with an emphasis on both playful costumes and concerted violence redolent with historically relevant symbolism. *ProPublica* (Groeger et al., 2021a) would later share an archive of images, texts, and videos shared on Parler by the rioters themselves (see Chapter 5), providing first-person accounts of the events that unfolded, ultimately revealing a disorganized mob with an array of intentions.

In this chapter, we look at two distinct groups who communicated those intentions through visual imagery at the Capitol: first, the self-representation of the rioters, and second, the mainstream media images from photojournalists on the ground that day. The still and moving images that emerged from the Capitol riots tell a deeper story than a mere description of the events (Jurgenson, 2019). These artifacts present a window into the sociocultural conditions at play for those in attendance on January 6th, with implications for the broader direction of democracy in the United States. The visual documents posted by the Capitol rioters themselves depict a series of performances that may betray an uncertainty within thinly constructed narratives grounded in exhortations to 'Make America Great Again.' In contrast, selected photos captured by photojournalists on the scene lay bare the extent of the existential crisis taking place within the American extreme right.

To read these images, we have various tools at our disposal. We begin by considering the technological developments that have led to the widespread use of photos and video by ordinary citizens, as well as the cultural context within which the 'social photo' has become a common method of communication. The historical relevance of the camera and snapshot, as well as the recent developments of both smartphones and social media, must all be considered as they each play a vital

DOI: 10.4324/9781003246862-8

role in the capacity of a subject to engage in visual-cultural self-representations. In addition to this, critical theory as a subject, from McLuhan (1977) to Berger (1997), paired with recent reflections on social photography from Jurgenson (2019), further assist in the deeper processes of decoding visual symbols. In this analysis, we illustrate how photographs may be understood to both embed and construct the culture within which they are created.

Thus, the rioters' own video footage, uploaded to Parler (Groeger et al., 2021a), depicts violence from an insider's perspective, fraught with uncertainty, confusion and an insistent need to be seen, powerfully paired with symbolism indicative of a significant loss of and attempts to reinstate an identity. In an ironic twist of fate, through the discoverability of social media and the Parler dataset rescued by @donk_enby, the rioters' footage also *exposes* their identities to scrutiny, simultaneously serving as self-incriminating evidence. Ultimately, a collective roused by Trump's spurious rhetoric led citizen videographers to express, curate, and craft nostalgic themes, as misinformed as they were dangerous.

In contrast to first-hand accounts, photojournalists delivered an outsider's point of view, locating the rioters within a legacy of political history, where riots reveal the contours of the particular contemporary ideologies driving them. While Republicans, including Senator Ron Johnson, attempted to downplay the seriousness of the event, claiming 'This didn't seem like an armed insurrection to me' (Johnson, 2021, cited in Elfrink, 2021), a more critical perspective—visible in the media itself—can delve into and attempt to understand the costumes, posturings, and performances, presenting a sobering reality wherein five people lost their lives.

Of great symbolic import is the fact that, on the day of the Capitol riots, the Confederate flag reached further inside the Capitol building than it ever did during the Civil War. Moreover, politically speaking, a crowd intoxicated by social-media-driven self-assurance was able to delay—but not prevent—the democratic process of certifying the results of the election, and more importantly for our purposes here, to document their efforts well. The visual documentation of the event itself also transformed over time from spectacle to evidentiary, as the photographs provided by rioters and journalists alike led to hundreds of arrests, combined with further evidentiary material from surveillance and body-worn cameras, however, these last are outside the scope of this chapter.

The Social Photo

To locate ourselves in contemporary visual culture, we must first consider the trajectory of photography that has delivered us to this moment. Following its inception, the development of the photographic medium and its use originally progressed at a significantly slower pace than that of the technologies and practices of digital photography today. After the first photograph was stabilized circa 1826, a full ten years passed before a human figure was portrayed (Rosenblum et al., 2020). More than seventy years passed again before the first affordable camera was produced—a Brownie by Kodak—democratizing photography with a mass-produced and easy-to-use apparatus (Pritchard, 2015). The invention of the Brownie meant that creating a photograph was no longer reserved for the elite, with the technology now made accessible to a much wider portion of the population. With a quicker shutter speed, the subject matter captured could be more impromptu. The power to document images was finally in the hands of the average family: the snapshot was born.

Approximately 70 years later, the era of digital photography emerged in the 1970s (Estrin, 2015) when cameras became increasingly smaller while simultaneously offering a choice of functions: to save, delete, and/or print the photos captured. These early digital cameras were not incredibly high resolution but began to improve as the cost of the electronic elements decreased (The Editors of Encyclopaedia Britannica, 2020). By the early 2000s, however, high-resolution cameras had become a standard feature in internet-connected smartphones (Hill, 2013), adding a new and important function—*to share*—initially by text or email and eventually via social media platforms as applications for smartphone integration developed (Haridy, 2019). Although Facebook was launched in 2004 at Harvard and always offered an opportunity to upload images, it was later in 2006 when the platform became accessible on mobile devices (Brügger, 2015). Facebook users were able to upload videos from 2007 onward (Brügger, 2015); however, it was Snapchat developers who introduced the concept of 'stories' in 2013 (Etherington, 2013). This short, ephemeral video content proved popular (McRoberts et al., 2017), and Instagram and Facebook eventually followed suit, providing their users with similar functionality in 2016 (McRoberts et al., 2017) and 2017, respectively (Dillet, 2017).

From 2010 onward, both the quality and quantity of digital photography increased exponentially (Haridy, 2019). The rapid development of digital photography technology and its integration with smartphone functionality provided a significant portion of the population with the ability to capture, manipulate, and publish images with a device that they could carry in their pockets. Never before had we been able to capture images, edit them to our liking, and disseminate them instantaneously across the globe to a ready and waiting audience of social media friends. With the rapid uptake of these technologies, everyday communications were no longer limited to text; people could express themselves through both still and moving images that were of increasingly higher quality.

Within current media ecosystems, digital citizens are able to visually communicate with others instantaneously, in large part thanks to the integration of smartphone camera technology with social media platforms. Our digital lives are immersed in what Nathan Jurgenson (2019), a sociologist at TikTok, defines as the 'Social Photo' which includes 'snapshot photography, personal photography, domestic photography, vernacular photography, networked images, [and] banal imaging' (p. 16). As such, the social photo becomes 'an image not a photograph' (Ritchin, 2009, cited in Jurgenson, 2019, p. 24). For Jurgenson (2019), what makes a photo a social photo is the intention of the author to use it as a form of communication. Jurgenson (2019, p. 41) claims that the social photo is not just a documentation of life, but that 'life itself becomes shaped by the logic of documentation' because social photos are captured with the intent to share on social media.

Through social photography, particularly on video-focused platforms like TikTok, YouTube, and Snapchat, as well as in Facebook and Instagram 'stories,' a significant portion of the population regularly documents themselves, thus playing a 'lead role,' performing for their audience of followers. Once a social photo is published, the audience is then tasked with evaluating the content within the socio-cultural context that it is received, namely 'the relations between power, identity and reality' that influence both the production and the audience's interpretation (Jurgenson, 2019, p. 26).

In 2020, the pandemic shifted a significant portion of social interactions online due to various states of lockdown, which placed even further emphasis on the documentation online of one's social existence. This factor plays a significant role in shaping the types of photographs and videos that emerged from the Capitol riots—as well as our interpretations of those social photos within the broader cultural context of our time.

Jurgenson (2019, p. 12) importantly points to a momentous shift in the way photography and imaging now function in society with their integration into social media and social uses: 'How we see, what we can see, what both social visibility and invisibility mean are changing.' The way we see and interpret images is shaped by both our history and our socio-technical, political, and cultural context. Social visibility achieved through social media shapes identities, a sense of self, and how we situate ourselves in the world.

Jurgenson's idea here is not new, however. Berger's (1972) powerful work, aptly titled 'Ways of Seeing,' brought to BBC television audiences the practice of decoding visual art by examining the cultural influences that have shaped *the way we see one another* from century to century. In order to 'read' visual imagery, we must therefore consider the cultural framework within which it has been created and circulated. Specific to the issue at hand, we must ask ourselves how the socio-technical, political, and cultural contexts all ultimately influenced the imagery that emerged from the Capitol rioters producing social photos.

The Social Media Riot

To culturally situate the imagery emerging from the Capitol riots, we must add to the technological trajectory of cameras described above, a consideration of the sociological trajectory of social media practices, including not just production but also consumption. It is therefore essential to discuss the landscape of audio-visual storytelling that shapes our contemporary digital lives.

While the average American may consume radio broadcasts and cable television from time to time, these are now considered to be waning residual media. Video streaming services like Netflix and video platforms like TikTok and YouTube are no longer emergent media but have become dominant media forms that have escalating daily consumption rates (Koetsier, 2020). Thanks in part to the pandemic, the average time spent consuming online content has doubled, according to a study of over 10,000 people in five countries, including France, Germany, Spain, the UK, and the US (DoubleVerify and Sapio Research, 2020).

Yet, it is not just the amount of media consumption but also the consequent formation of narratives that we must be attentive to. In a recent workshop for writers, Netflix shared a pitch deck that emphasized that the 'hero should be proactive in trying to obtain their goal. Overly reactive heroes are boring' (Mack, n.d.). Linking this to the rally prior to the riot, Donald Trump Jr. was quoted saying, 'You can be a hero, or you can be a zero. And the choice is yours. But we are all watching. The whole world is watching' (Mangan, 2021). The linguistic resonances between how Netflix constructs narratives and how political figures do so is remarkable.

Returning to the Netflix screenwriting pitch deck, under the description of 'key ingredients' for a good story pitch, Netflix stressed that the lead character must have a call to action, a quest to fulfill their destiny, and a need to stand up for themselves (Mack, n.d.). While it is reasonable to acknowledge that contemporary audiences have mastered the willful suspension of disbelief, one must also consider the influence of commercial narratives on the construction of our social realities, value systems, cultural norms, and identities. The individuals and groups who fought their way into the Capitol building similarly were heeding calls to action from Trump Sr. and Trump Jr. alike to stop the steal and become heroes, they considered 'storming the Capitol' to be their quest, and they felt the need to stand up for themselves against a perceived corrupt democracy, and thereby to engage in performances as the proactive heroes in their own narratives.

One compelling 'way of seeing' or interpreting self-produced visual evidence during the Capitol riots, therefore, is to consider this imagery through the lens of performance. The performances of the Capitol rioters began in the lead-up to January 6, 2021. We know that the riot was planned in advance, as Mike German, a former FBI agent specializing in counterterrorism explains,

> It wasn't as if this was a spontaneous gathering. This was an event that had been planned for weeks, and it was very clear in the social media activity and public statements of these militants what they intended to do.
> *(German, 2021, cited in Devereaux, 2021, para. 3)*

Even without knowing this, the costumes evident amongst the crowd bear evidence of forethought and preparation. In a visual symbol now synonymous with the Capitol riots, Jacob Anthony Chansley, aka Jake Angeli, aka the QAnon Shaman (see Figure 6.1), is depicted in multiple photographs roaming the Capitol grounds and Senate chamber in full red-white-and-blue face paint, wearing a fur headdress with horns, and carrying a spear-like staff from which he had hung the American flag. Aaron Mostofsky, an equally prominent figure in mainstream media coverage, as the son of a prominent Brooklyn Judge, was dressed in what appeared to be a full-body fur animal skin, shielded by a bulletproof Police vest.

FIGURE 6.1 QAnon Shaman aka Jake Angeli aka Jacob Anthony Chansley
Source: Photo by TheUnseen011101, October 25, 2020, Wikimedia Commons, Public Domain, https://commons.wikimedia.org/wiki/File:Jake_Angeli_(Qanon_Shamon), _seen_holding_a_Qanon_sign_(cropped).jpg, *edited by David VanDyke.*

Researcher in apparel and textile design, Thèrèsa Winge, spoke to *The Atlantic*, considering the potential motivations behind these costumes. She argues that they were 'most likely intended to visually harken [to] the spirit of the Indigenous warrior' (Winkie, 2021). The adoption of a quasi-nostalgia for misrepresented Indigenous 'warriors' portrayed in the 1950s and 60s Wild West Hollywood films needs to be problematized, particularly in light of the great replacement theory, which suggests that white European settlers are the so-called 'native sons' and rightful owners of America.

Chansley himself claimed in a 2020 interview that he made a habit of wearing fur, painting his face, and going shirtless with the objective of attracting attention, which he hoped would provide him with an audience with whom he could speak about QAnon and other conspiracy theories (Ruelas, 2021). He did indeed draw attention through his appearance, as did others such as Mostofsky in similar outfits. The initial 'fame' that the media provided through the wide distribution of the visual spectacle subsequently shifted focus and after time gave access to further visual evidence, leading to a more serious, evidential purpose as hundreds of rioters were later arrested. After the riot, when Chansley appeared in court, the US District Judge Lamberth dismissed his claim of innocence, stating that the 'Defendant's perception of his actions on January 6th as peaceful, benign and well-intentioned shows a detachment from reality' (Lamberth, 2021, cited in Shepherd, 2021, para. 12). Not only did many of the rioters perform for an audience, whether it was their own followers, fellow rioters, or the viewers of photojournalistic works, as indicated by Lamberth, the narrative driving their performances seems to have a limited connection with contemporary urban realities. And yet, despite this disconnect, their actions undertaken in these particular costumes produced very real consequences.

Furthermore, Chansley and Mostofsky were not the only participants donning elaborate costumes. One man crossed through the water of the Capitol reflecting pool dressed from head to toe as George Washington. Others were seen wearing costumes of the American symbol of the eagle, Lady Liberty, Uncle Sam, and more—key signifiers of American power brought to life in idolatrous pageantry, but, like Chansley and Mostofksy, with no clear connection between the costumes, performances, and actions undertaken.

More serious in tone, a significant number of Capitol rioters came dressed in army fatigues, varying from basic camouflage clothing to full tactical gear. Painted faces, flags, and symbols ranging from QAnon, the Proud Boys, and the Oath Keepers, to icons including the Confederate flag and the date, 1776, of the US Declaration of Independence—allowed in-groups to identify one another amongst the sea of protesters. It was clear the rioters wore these symbols with pride, waving matching flags and chanting related slogans. There is a strong sense of identity building that takes place through costume, the demonstration of which becomes visually evident in photographs and videos of the crowd, with strong correlative visual evidence signifying group belonging. This documentation does not come solely from photojournalists who were present on the day, many of whom were at best not welcomed and, in some cases, violently attacked by those within the crowd (Fargo, 2021). Rather, an overwhelming number of photographs and videos were created by the rioters themselves, a behavior and provenance important to consider when evaluating the images produced as indicative of performances of particular identities and actions. Moreover, for the Capitol rioters belonging to militias or gangs and dressed in military gear with insignia, the outfits and symbolic signifiers were not spurious but rather were strongly connected not just to their identities but also to the actions they would undertake linked to the specific political objectives they had in mind.

Visual Documents

Throughout the riot, thousands of videos were uploaded to the online platform Parler, which described itself as a 'Free Speech Social Network' (Parler, n.d.) predominantly used by those whose dissemination of disinformation or hate speech had them kicked off other social media platforms. Although content produced at the Capitol riots was quickly deleted by Amazon (Parler's cloud-hosting service) for inciting violence, ProPublica had already archived over 500 videos, later making this content accessible online (Groeger et al., 2021a). Upon review of this archive, the 'selfie soliloquy' stands out as a key recurring style. Rioters turned their cameras towards themselves, speaking in a self-assured, energized tone. Some described the experience of being tear-gassed or maced, while many others celebrated breaching the Capitol building as a personal and collective victory. In all of these videos, the orator would posture themselves in such a manner that made it clear they were speaking to a perceived audience. These documents were not intended for personal reflection; they addressed a spectator. Thus, the intention to perform—and to be seen performing—has the potential to tell us more about the Capitol rioters than they reveal in their script alone. It provides an interpretive lens for understanding their actions within the context of what one might call—building on Jurgenson—the 'social video,' used in the construction of the trope of a rioter as a form of identity performance.

To understand this drive to perform, McLuhan's reflections on the many uses of media for identity building provide useful insights. Long before social media existed, McLuhan (1994) referred to media and technologies as an 'extension of man.' He argued that 'any extension, whether of skin, hand, or foot, affects the whole psychic and social complex' (McLuhan, 1994, p. 4). Building from this premise, McLuhan (1994) argued that, just as the wheel extends our legs and thus our ability to move, the phone extends our voice and our ability to speak. By corollary, the computer extends our minds and our ability to think, and digital media as a whole may extend our central nervous system, which controls both the body and the mind (Bobbitt, 2011). In this way, social media and the social photo or video become an extension of identity, of ways of knowing oneself and of being known. Writing on the topic of the selfie and identity building, Jurgenson (2019, p. 71) argues:

Photos don't just depict the self but are a procedure for self-knowledge, a mode of thinking about the self. This identity work is deciding to remember something as quintessentially me, a choice, a performance, memorialized within the frame.

Observing the photos and videos that were self-produced by the Capitol rioters means that we are also observing 'the ongoing process of identity construction' (Jurgenson, 2019, p. 71), a performance of the self-under-construction.

If we are to understand the visual content from the Capitol riots as part of a process of identity building, it is also key to consider the specific behaviors portrayed in order to understand the specific identities or selves under construction, particularly within the context and against the backdrop of a violent insurrection. Yet, how may we comprehend the relationship between identity construction and violence? Here, McLuhan (1977, p. 2) provides additional context:

> Ordinary people find the need for violence as they lose their identities. It is only the threat to people's identity that makes them violent. Terrorists, hijackers—these are people minus identity. They are determined to make it somehow, to get coverage, to get noticed.

McLuhan (1977) further explains somewhat famously that while new technologies have created a 'global village,' the closer people get to one another, the more savage and impatient they may become with one another. McLuhan (1977, p. 3) provides Hitler as an example, who used radio to extend the reach of his voice, building an identity for the 'Aryan' race through unspeakable acts of violence. While there is a significant difference between the horror of Nazi activities and what unfolded at the Capitol riots, the reference provides context to violence when witnessed in its full spectrum, especially in its relationship to identity building. Bringing McLuhan's (1977) point of view into a contemporary setting, we can imagine that the global village he envisioned now functionally exists in online spaces where people interact as if shoulder to shoulder. The close proximity that global citizens have to one another influences the nature of online interactions, and as McLuhan (1977) warned, has the potential to promote a new source of violence. The contemporary violence of specific identity production has emerged from within social interactions occurring online.

A subset of white Americans, emboldened by Trump's accusatory rhetoric and anti-immigration policies, were motivated to carve out identities based on exclusion, elevating the role of the 'patriot' while simultaneously vilifying the racialized 'other.' Visual documents and the acts of violence created under the purview of this narrative apprehension appear to proclaim, 'This is me, this is who I am, I'm important.' One might ask, who else would feel the need to make such a proclamation, except an individual who feels their identity threatened?

As we know from Chapter 3, corroborated by a report by Pape (2021, p. 19), the rate of insurrectionists who lived in particular counties was 'four times higher in counties where the % of non-Hispanic whites had declined the most.' Those who felt their historically privileged white perspective or identity was being negated by the growing population of non-white others perceived this as a risk to their identity and social rights; thus, their relative status within an increasingly precarious social, cultural, and economic milieu was perceived to be at risk. This perception also drives the tendency not just to believe in the great replacement theory, but to be fearful rather than welcoming of increasing racial diversity.

The Parler videos further reveal individuals who wished to stake their identities in the Capitol building itself by placing their flags upon the Capitol grounds, including the floor inside the building itself, chanting 'Our House,' (anonymous, 2021, cited in Groeger et al., 2021b, 00:01) implying that the center of American democracy belongs to them, in other words, belongs specifically to some citizens to the exclusion of others. The responses of the rioters, as captured in the visual documentation that they themselves produced, was ultimately shaped by violent outbursts that reflected a larger crisis of identity happening within white, middle-class America.

Although we now know through visual symbols that racist and xenophobic groups like the Proud Boys and the Oath Keepers were involved in the riots, Pape and Ruby (2021, para. 7) found that 'a large majority of suspects in the Capitol riot have no connection to existing far-right militias, white-nationalist gangs, or other established violent organizations.' The study focused on the first 193 people to be charged with breaking and entering the Capitol building or breaking through the barricades surrounding the Capitol grounds. If these people did not identify with the militias, gangs, and violent organizations, who did they identify with?

From this study, we learn that 'the overwhelming reason for action, cited again and again in court documents, was that arrestees were following Trump's orders to keep Congress from certifying Joe Biden as the presidential-election winner' (Pape and Ruby, 2021, para. 6). Rioters interestingly did not emerge from the reddest or most Republican of states; the same study found that over half of those arrested came from counties that Biden had won, blue or Democratic states, thus it seems they were there to contest their state being governed by Democrats.

If the global village that McLuhan (1977) describes has threatened the identity of a segment of the American population, Trump has offered a narrative identity as well as a community within which to belong.

The Curated Riot

We can learn more about the identity that participants in the Capitol riots were attempting to construct for themselves by revisiting the Parler video content. A performance becomes interesting because it is *curated* for the viewer. The content may be inspired by a true story or entirely fabricated, but in either case, it is purposefully designed to be consumed by an audience. We can learn a great deal by paying attention to the narrative the rioters have chosen to share with their audience, as well as what they unintentionally reveal.

A video shot at 2:35pm ET and uploaded to Parler begins with a man who yells, 'You paid for this' (anonymous, 2021, cited in Groeger et al., 2021c, 00:00), as the group he is a part of enters the Capitol building. As the group ascends a set of stairs that open onto the Rotunda, there is an audible sense of awe and wonder. 'Oh my God,' (anonymous, 2021, cited in Groeger et al., 2021c, 00:29), someone says in reaction to the grandiose architecture. In many videos, we hear the crowd chant, 'Our house,' (anonymous, 2021, cited in Groeger et al., 2021b, 00:01), and yet, even though the building is, under normal circumstances, open to the public for tours, it seems clear many had never visited before. One man appears visibly emotional in a Parler video shot at 2:42pm ET, almost brought to tears as 'Glory, glory alleluia' (anonymous, 2021, cited in Groeger et al., 2021d, 00:11) is sung by rioters in the Rotunda. Their voices dramatically ricochet and echo through the dome. Inspired to pray, he and others bow their heads together and film themselves from below, their heads appearing as dark silhouettes against the golden dome above (see Figure 6.2). It is visually striking, appearing to be a profound experience for these men. As they prayed, it became clear that by facing down, with their phone camera facing upwards, they were likely gazing upon their own orchestrated silhouettes on the floor, visually echoing what was captured in the video. Toward the end of their prayer, one man flashes what looks to be a hang-ten sign with his hand, confirming they are indeed aware of the curated visual being recorded.

Prayer as an activity was common throughout the day, as were both groups and individuals breaking out in song. Religious rites, the collective singing of the American National Anthem, and the chanting of various ideological slogans taken together reinforced a homogenous identity that served to unite the crowd in a feeling of common purpose. The curated experience thus took on an ethereal, existential tone, as though the rioters were living through a transformative religious experience. Having breached the perimeter, some rioters appeared euphoric. It may be that the act of breaching the Capitol building was able to provide a temporary sense of validation to those seeking identity, their act of confrontation and transgression a quest that they had embarked upon and somehow miraculously achieved.

At the same time, 2:42pm ET, in another part of the building, a Parler video was shot, following a group of rioters as they aimlessly wandered the halls, clearly unsure of their location or where they should go next. We hear them shout, 'Defend the constitution, defend your liberty,' and, 'Seventeen-seventy-six!' (anonymous, 2021, cited in Groeger et al., 2021e, 00:05 and 00:22) as one man further ahead of them violently kicks each door that he passes. In terms of constructing an identity, their words may have been purposeful, but their actions betrayed an underlying confusion and lack of direction. In an ironic twist, the same video ends with a man forcefully yelling, 'You're afraid of Antifa? Well guess what? America showed up!' while another woman overlaps his voice with her own concern, 'Where's the rest of everybody? There's not enough of us. They're gonna bring the Feds in,' (anonymous, 2021, cited in Groeger et al., 2021e, 00:23).

FIGURE 6.2 Rioters lean forward and pray below the Capitol Rotunda ceiling
Source: Miranda McKee's impression of video still from Parler footage taken January 6, 2021, and Rotunda ceiling photographed by Yael Clusman, Unsplash License, https://unsplash.com/photos/K3YhnnjC5D0, *compiled by Miranda McKee.*

Passionate exclamations echoed throughout the crowd—adopted from social interactions both online and in-person—yet no particular rhetoric was backed up by a cohesive and coherent plan that would have given sense or direction to this particular group who had entered into the building, similar to those in the Rotunda who sang, prayed, and chanted in place.

In yet another video uploaded to Parler shot at 3:38pm ET, one man is interviewed by another participant outside the Capitol building, as the latter performs the role of citizen journalist (anonymous, 2021, cited in Groeger et al., 2021f). Dressed in camouflage, wearing a Three-Percenter patch, the interviewee explains in great detail how he and 30 others had managed to enter the Capitol building, describing how they were roaming the halls and admitting, 'We had no idea where we were going,' (anonymous, 2021, cited in Groeger et al., 2021f, 01:13) even though he says that he previously had a tour of the building. The citizen journalist behind the camera laughs and sincerely exclaims, 'Wow, incredible' (anonymous, 2021, cited in Groeger et al., 2021f, 01:16). Further into his description, the interviewee says, 'We took the uh, main chamber in there, uh … uh … whatever room is under the dome' (anonymous, 2021, cited in Groeger et al., 2021f, 03:37) and the citizen journalist replies, 'So we overtook the Capitol.… What do we do now?' (anonymous, 2021, cited in Groeger et al., 2021f, 03:44). In this moment they take the role of a direct-action journalist, an interviewer who is also participating in the action (Jeppesen, 2016). The interviewee seems unsure, responding, 'We need another shift to take over,' (anonymous, 2021, cited in Groeger et al., 2021f, 03:56) and begins to describe how his group exited the building. He ends by saying that he hopes they 'are able to maintain the momentum' and 'actually get what we came here for' (anonymous, 2021, cited in Groeger et al., 2021f, 04:13), an objective that he fails to unpack.

Through this footage, we may recognize the passion that accompanies the pursuit of a shared cause, paired with a lack of clarity in the stated purpose of their actions. There is a sense that, rather than a failure to achieve more advanced or coherent political goals, the performance itself was the goal; an identity-building exercise to contest the election's outcome without any other defined objective. By entering the Capitol, rioters answered the call from Trump's speech earlier that day, demanding that they march down to the Capitol and 'fight like hell' (Trump, 2021, para. 4). Mirroring Trump's vague yet defiant utterances, the rioters' actions too became defiant yet disorganized. In the end, the identity they fought so hard to perform remained unformed.

In addition to identity-building performances that seem to lack coherent over-arching actionable objectives, it is essential to highlight the broader theme of nostalgia that permeated the visual and discursive symbolism captured in the video and photographic documentation of the Capitol riots. References to 1776, the Confederate flag, the Betsy Ross flag, and the Gadsden flag all point to a past that the rioters clearly glorify. Trump celebrates this nostalgia with his well-known slogan, 'Make America Great Again' (MAGA), an expression visually evident on hats, T-shirts, and flags throughout the January 6th rally, march, and riot; a slogan that serves to declare belief in a collective past that was in some way greater than the present. The MAGA slogan clearly alludes to a nostalgic American imaginary, undeniably a period where people of color and women figured much less prominently in the halls of power, underlining the inferred racist and misogynist undertones.

McLuhan (1977) spoke of the dangers of nostalgia, describing it as an indication of having lost one's identity. Speaking of the financial crisis of 2008, Oliete-Aldea

(2012) describes an environment that may easily correlate to the collective conditions under the COVID-19 pandemic: 'With no faith in the future, what remains is to hark back to past times where socio-economic relations, if not perfect, were, at least, better defined' (p. 349). Oliete-Aldea (2012) also attends to the idea of nostalgia in times of crisis, emphasizing how the rise of 'this anxiety has provoked a nostalgic search for the shelter of a community' (p. 347). The unpredictable nature of the pandemic has rendered our collective visions of the future inaccessible, making it easy to fall prey to the appeal of living in an imaginary past. In the case of MAGA proponents, it is a past in which America is imagined to have been a 'pure white' country, despite the historical truths of colonization and slavery, which are erased in this nostalgic imaginary.

We must, therefore, following McLuhan, attend to the dangers of nostalgia. To provide an example that connects with our current circumstances, consider the story of a collective that was developed in 1915 by an ex-minister who prioritized Christian virtue and patriotic pride. The group intended to be the savior of a nation in peril. Their goals included restricting immigration, bettering government, reverting to the Constitution, improving law enforcement, and increasing allegiance to the flag. This group was the Ku Klux Klan under the direction of its founder, William J. Simmons (Baker, 2016). Baker (2016, para. 9) explains that 'The Klan's message of 100 percent Americanism and restrictive immigration resonated in the 1920s, and their message gains traction, again and again, every time white Americans encounter social change and shifting demographics.' The current instability created by the pandemic has triggered an identity crisis within white America, and the knee-jerk white nostalgia that Trump has both capitalized upon and intensified manifests itself in the autobiographical visual and discursive content created by the Capitol rioters.

To complete our analysis of the visual documentation that has memorialized the events that took place on January 6, 2021, we must also consider the work of professional photographers on the ground, as these images provide a compelling contrast to the content shared via Parler. While rioters engaged in the social construction and performance of their collective identity through social photos and videos used to communicate their experiences and construct their identities to an audience, photojournalists captured an array of juxtapositions that unexpectedly transpired before them, while, unlike the riot participants, leaving themselves out of the picture.

Take as an example the photo of millennial 36-year-old Adam Johnson (see Figure 6.3) carrying Nancy Pelosi's lectern through the Capitol Rotunda, smiling and waving to the photographer, Win McNamee, who is Chief Photographer at Getty Images.

The joy that Adam Johnson expresses as he poses for the photo must certainly have dissipated when he was arrested on federal charges (anonymous, 2021, cited in Groeger et al., 2021b, 00:01) in large part due to the pictorial evidence presented (Munoz, 2021). Behind Johnson in the Rotunda is a depiction of the *Surrender of General Burgoyne*, painted by John Trumbull. The painting portrays the surrender of

FIGURE 6.3 Adam Johnson carries the lectern of Speaker of the House Nancy Pelosi through the Rotunda of the Capitol building, January 6, 2021
Source: Photo by Win McNamee/Getty Images News.

the British General in 1777 during the American Revolutionary War, a significant turning point for the Americans which contributed to their overall victory. As described by the *Architect of the Capitol* website (n.d., para. 2), 'The scene suggests peace rather than combat or hostility,' a sentiment which stands in opposition to the events unfolding as the Capitol building was being stormed. McNamee's photograph of Johnson thus provides a disturbing juxtaposition: a rioter gleefully thieving the lectern, itself a symbol of the American democratic process, after storming the building and interrupting that very democratic process, and then posing in front of a visual depiction which represents a key moment in the nation's formation during an event which sees the nation on the precipice of chaos and fragmentation.

The performative behavior of the rioters—and specifically of Johnson in this instance—is particularly incongruent with the visual reality captured in the photo, from both past and present. Despite his gleeful expression, Johnson does not embody peace, victory, or nation-building in this photo, but rather the conflict, chaos, and disintegration of American politics. Further, Johnson willfully and perhaps unwittingly poses for a photo that documents his performance of a fairly serious crime (see Chapter 8) that, one would imagine, in any other circumstances he would never dream of committing.

Another instance in which the images of the historic portraits in the Capitol seem to conflict with the iconography of the rioters is a photograph taken by New York Times photographer Erin Schaff depicting a middle-aged rioter inside the Capitol building resting a huge Confederate flag on his shoulder (see Figure 6.4).

FIGURE 6.4 Kevin Seefried holds Confederate flag inside the Capitol building, with Aaron Mostofsky in foreground, January 6, 2021
Source: Copyright Erin Schaff/The New York Times/Redux.

Directly behind him hangs a portrait of Justin Smith Morrill, an abolitionist and advocate for higher education who initiated legislation that provided greater access to college for America's working class (Michigan State University, n.d.).

According to Blair, a professor emeritus of history at Penn State, as described to the *New York Times*, the presence of the Confederate flag inside the Capitol is remarkable, particularly because 'the man carrying the flag faced less stringent security than that encountered by the Confederate soldiers who failed to penetrate Union forts guarding the Capitol' (Blair, 2021, cited in Cramer, 2021, para. 12). In other words, Confederate flags had moved deeper into Washington, DC, on the day of the Capitol riots than they ever did during the Civil War. The man in the photo is now known to the FBI as Kevin Seefried. He and his son Hunter were both arrested on charges of unlawful entry after Hunter bragged at work about being inside the Capitol building with his father (del Rio, Goldman, Benner, and Ives, 2021). In a form of foreshadowing, Seefried's hand is raised to his face as if to shield his shame. He looks in the opposite direction of Morrill's gaze as captured in the portrait, which aptly summarizes two entirely different, perhaps opposing, points of view. Closer to the lens and taking up a portion of the right-hand side of the frame, we catch a glimpse of Aaron Mostofsky. Fur-clad and carrying a stolen shield from the Capitol Police, his costume emphasizes the absurdity of the moment and strikes a strange contrast against the all-American-Dad attire embodied by Seefried and also against the seriousness of the portrait and politics of Morrill.

Perhaps it is not surprising that Johnson, Mostofsky, and Seefried are acting in opposition to those portrayed in the hallowed halls of power, as indeed power is what they were there to contest. What is interesting here is how the rioters posed and narrated themselves in relation to the iconography of the Capitol in contradictory ways, both claiming the house as their own and purporting to share the political positions of those represented on the walls, posing for selfies with their arms around the statues while also calling into question and physically interrupting the democratic process; whereas the professional photographers captured the juxtaposition and contrast of the rioters' behaviors over and against the historical images and iconography in a subtle way that reveals just exactly what is at stake in the contradictions.

Conclusion of Visual Analysis

The truth about what happened on the Capitol grounds is multilayered. A visual analysis of self-generated imagery from the rioters points to a desperate need to be seen, to proclaim one's identity—at times violently—and to document and disseminate this imagery as part of a performance of self to an expected online audience. Through the Parler footage, we may begin to understand the existential crisis being experienced by a significant portion of the population, those seduced by Trump's nostalgic rhetoric. The performative acts of the rioters reveal a collective anxiety further heightened by their participation in social media, which threatens their sense of self and elicits a violent reaction, reflecting McLuhan's (1977) observations regarding the global village.

The documentation captured by photojournalists on the day helps to both reveal and construct the multilayered narrative of political history currently being mobilized in the United States. What we extrapolate through a critical visual analysis is the contemporary socio-technical context and constructions of the rioters and their relationship to media, both social and otherwise, which played a central role in the events that unfolded before, during, and after the riot.

Visual documentation from all sources began circulating with a focus on the attention-grabbing nature of the spectacle before transitioning into a focus on the evidentiary aspect of the images, admissible in a court of law. At a time when visual storytelling has reached a new peak, the story of an American identity crisis continues to unfold before our collective eyes.

References

Architect of the Capitol (n.d.) 'Architect of the Capitol, Surrender of General Burgoyne' [Online]. Available at: www.aoc.gov/explore-capitol-campus/art/surrender-general-burgoyne (Accessed: 30 September 2021).

Baker, K J (2016) 'Donald Trump's language is similar to the 1920s Ku Klux Klan: Nationalism and anti-immigration,' *The Atlantic*, 12 March [Online]. Available at: www.theatlantic.com/politics/archive/2016/03/donald-trump-kkk/473190/ (Accessed: 25 April 2021).

Berger, J (1972) 'Ways of Seeing,' *BBC* [Online]. Available at: www.bbc.co.uk/programm es/p00hmb29 (Accessed: 28 September 2021).

Berger, J (1997) *Ways of seeing*. London, UK: Penguin Books.

Bobbitt, D (2011) 'Teaching McLuhan: Understanding *Understanding media*,' *Enculturation* [Online]. Available at: http://enculturation.net/teaching-mcluhan (Accessed: 25 April 2021).

Brügger, N (2015) 'A brief history of Facebook as a media text: The development of an empty structure,' *First Monday* 20(5) [Online]. https://doi.org/10.5210/fm.v20i5.5423.

Cramer, M (2021) 'Confederate flag an unnerving sight in Capitol,' *The New York Times*, 9 January [Online]. Available at: www.nytimes.com/2021/01/09/us/politics/confedera te-flag-capitol.html (Accessed: 26 August 2021).

Del Rio, GMN, Goldman, A, Benner, K and Ives, M (2021) 'Several more Capitol rioters have been arrested including man who carried a Confederate flag inside building,' *The New York Times*, 14 January [Online]. Available at: www.nytimes.com/2021/01/14/us/ Kevin-Seefried-arrested.html (Accessed: 26 April 2021).

Devereaux, R (2021) 'Storming of the Capitol was openly planned but ignored by law enforcement,' *The Intercept*, 7 January [Online]. Available at: https://theintercept.com/ 2021/01/07/capitol-trump-violence-law-enforcement/ (Accessed: 26 April 2021).

Dillet, R (2017) 'Facebook launches stories in the main Facebook app,' *TechCrunch*, 28 March [Online]. Available at: https://social.techcrunch.com/2017/03/28/facebook-la unches-stories-in-the-main-facebook-app/ (Accessed: 27 September 2021).

DoubleVerify and Sapio Research (2020) 'Four fundamental shifts in media & advertising during 2020,' 23 September [Online]. Available at: https://doubleverify.com/four- fundamental-shifts-in-media-and-advertising-during-2020/ (Accessed: 28 September 2021).

Dowling, S (2015) 'The most important cardboard box ever?,' *BBC News*, 5 January [Online]. Available at: www.bbc.com/news/magazine-30530268 (Accessed: 26 August 2021).

Elfrink, T (2021) 'Sen. Ron Johnson plays down Capitol riots: "This didn't seem like an armed insurrection to me",' *Washington Post*, 16 February [Online]. Available at: www.w ashingtonpost.com/nation/2021/02/16/ron-johnson-capitol-riots-downplays/ (Accessed: 30 September 2021).

Estrin, J (2015) 'Kodak's first digital moment,' *The New York Times Lens Blog*, 12 August [Online]. Available at: https://lens.blogs.nytimes.com/2015/08/12/kodaks-first-digita l-moment/ (Accessed: 26 April 2021).

Etherington, D (2013) 'Snapchat gets its own timeline with Snapchat stories, 24-hour photo & video tales,' *TechCrunch*, 3 October [Online]. Available at: https://social.techcrunch. com/2013/10/03/snapchat-gets-its-own-timeline-with-snapchat-stories-24-hour-photo- video-tales/ (Accessed: 27 September 2021).

Fargo, A (2021) 'Why the news media may not want to share Capitol Riot images with the police,' *The Conversation*, 15 January [Online]. Available at: http://theconversation.com/ why-the-news-media-may-not-want-to-share-capitol-riot-images-with-the-police-153076 (Accessed: 26 April 2021).

Groeger, LV, Kao, J, Shaw, A, Syed, M and Eliahou, M (2021a) 'What Parler saw during the attack on the Capitol,' *ProPublica*, 17 January [Online]. Available at: https://projects. propublica.org/parler-capitol-videos/ (Accessed: 25 April 2021).

Haridy, R (2019) 'Smartphones, streaming & social media: Tech that shaped us in the 2010s,' *New Atlas*, 5 December [Online]. Available at: https://newatlas.com/computers/ smartphones-streaming-social-media-technology-decade-transformed-2010s/ (Accessed: 26 April 2021).

Hill, S (2013) 'A complete history of the camera phone,' *digitaltrends*, 11 August [Online]. Available at: www.digitaltrends.com/mobile/camera-phone-history/ (Accessed: 26 August 2021).

Jeppesen, S (2016) 'Direct-action Journalism: Resilience in Grassroots Autonomous Media,' *Journal of Applied Journalism and Media Studies*, 5 (3): 383–403.

Jurgenson, N (2019) *The social photo: On photography and social media*. New York, NY: Verso Books.

Koetsier, J (2020) 'Global online content consumption doubled in 2020,' *Forbes*, 26 September [Online]. Available at: www.forbes.com/sites/johnkoetsier/2020/09/26/global-online-content-consumption-doubled-in-2020/ (Accessed: 24 April 2021).

McRoberts, S, Ma, H, Hall, A and Yarosh, S (2017) 'Share first, save later: Performance of self through Snapchat stories,' in *Proceedings of the 2017 CHI Conference Extended Abstracts on Human Factors in Computing Systems* 17: 6902–6911. New York, NY: Association for Computing Machinery.Available at: https://doi.org/10.1145/3025453.3025771.

Mack, C (n.d.) 'Stage 32 next level education: Television pitch workshop,' *Stage 32* [Online]. Available at: www.stage32.com/webinars/Stage-32-%20-Netflix-Present-Television-Pitch-Workshop (Accessed: 24 April 2021).

Mangan, D (2021) 'Donald Trump Jr. video shows happy family, friends backstage at rally prior to Capitol Riot that killed 5,' *CNBC*, 9 January [Online]. Available at: www.cnbc.com/2021/01/08/capitol-riots-video-shows-trump-family-before-rally.html (Accessed: 6 September 2021).

McLuhan, M (1977) 'Violence as a quest for identity,' TV Ontario: The Mike McManus Show [Online]. Available at: www.marshallmcluhanspeaks.com/sayings/1977-violence-as-a-quest-for-identity/index.html (Accessed: 28 September 2021).

McLuhan, M (1994) *Understanding media: The extensions of man*. Cambridge, MA: MIT Press.

Michigan State University (n.d.) 'Justin Smith Morrill,' Michigan State University [Online]. Available at: https://curriculum.chm.msu.edu/about/the-academy-and-learning-societies/justin-smith-morrill (Accessed: 26 April 2021).

Mike, TS (2015) 'The evolution of the camera phone,' *CMSIT Australia*, 14 May [Online]. Available at: https://cmsit.com.au/the-history-of-camera-phones/ (Accessed: 22 April 2021).

Munoz, CR (2021) 'Adam Johnson, Manatee County man accused of taking lectern during US Capitol Riot, appears in Federal Court,' *Sarasota Herald-Tribune*, 11 January [Online]. Available at: www.heraldtribune.com/story/news/crime/2021/01/11/florida-man-accused-grabbing-nancy-pelosis-lectern-during-washington-riot-charged-federal-crimes/6628390002/ (Accessed: 25 April 2021).

Oliete-Aldea, E (2012) 'Fear and nostalgia in times of crisis: The paradoxes of globalization in Oliver Stone's *Money Never Sleeps* (2010),' *Culture Unbound* 4(2): 347–366. doi:10.3384/cu.2000.1525.124347.

Pape, RA (2021) 'Understanding American domestic terrorism: Mobilization potential and risk factors of a new threat trajectory,' The University of Chicago, 6 April [Online] Available at: https://d3qi0qp55mx5f5.cloudfront.net/cpost/i/docs/americas_insurrectionists_online_2021_04_06.pdf?mtime=1617807009 (Accessed: 21 September 2021).

Pape, RA and Ruby, K (2021) 'The Capitol Rioters aren't like other extremists,' *The Atlantic*, 2 February [Online]. Available at: www.theatlantic.com/ideas/archive/2021/02/the-capitol-rioters-arent-like-other-extremists/617895/ (Accessed: 25 April 2021).

Parler (n.d.) 'Parler free speech social network' [Online]. Available at: https://parler.com/ (Accessed: 25 April 2021).

Pritchard, M (2015) *A history of photography in 50 cameras*. Richmond Hill, Canada: Firefly Books.

Robinson, A (2021) 'House Speaker Nancy Pelosi's lectern, stolen in Capitol Riot, returned,' *ABC News*, 13 January [Online]. Available at: https://abcnews.go.com/Politic s/house-speaker-nancy-pelosis-lectern-stolen-capitol-riot/story?id=75231676 (Accessed: 7 September 2021).

Rosenblum, N (2020) 'History of photography,' *Encyclopedia Britannica*, 3 December [Online]. Available at: www.britannica.com/technology/photography (Accessed: 22 April 2021).

Ruelas, R (2021) 'Longtime Arizona QAnon supporter in horned helmet joins storming of US Capitol,' *The Arizona Republic*, 6 January [Online]. Available at: www.azcentra l.com/story/news/politics/arizona/2021/01/06/arizona-qanon-supporter-jake-angeli-join s-storming-u-s-capitol/6568513002/ (Accessed: 6 September 2021).

Shepherd, K (2021) '"QAnon Shaman" stays in jail as judge slams his arguments: "So frivolous as to insult the court's intelligence",' *Washington Post*, 9 March [Online]. Available at: www.washingtonpost.com/nation/2021/03/09/qanon-shaman-jacob-chansley-jail/ (Accessed: 6 September 2021).

The Editors of Encyclopaedia Britannica (2020) 'Digital camera,' *Encyclopedia Britannica* [Online]. Available at: www.britannica.com/technology/digital-camera (Accessed: 28 September 2021).

Trump, D (2021) 'Read Trump's Jan. 6 speech, a key part of impeachment trial,' *NPR*, 10 February [Online]. Available at: www.npr.org/2021/02/10/966396848/read-trumps-ja n-6-speech-a-key-part-of-impeachment-trial (Accessed: 7 September 2021).

Winkie, L (2021) 'What those animal pelts tell us about the future of the far right,' *The Atlantic*, 12 January [Online]. Available at: www.theatlantic.com/culture/archive/2021/ 01/why-capitol-rioters-wore-animal-pelts/617639/ (Accessed: 25 April 2021).

PART 3

Race, Class, Gender, Crime, and Affect at the Riots and Beyond

7

AWAKENING THE BEAST AT THE CAPITOL RIOTS

Affect, Cruelty, and QAnon

iowyth hezel ulthiin

Situated in a world already on fire, the events of the Capitol riots are a spark of outrage against state power on the part of a pacified public within an immersive media experience under COVID-19 lockdowns. Hyper-saturated with robust information flows, subjects in this milieu became further immersed in overwhelming sensual stimulation, revealing a reality lurking under the façade of civility, a raw animalistic substrate (see Figure 7.1). The result of this mediatized provocation can be seen as culminating in the storming of the US Capitol building, a gathering of subjects within an increasingly uncertain world, having been aggravated by a 24/7 rage and fear machine, and suffering the predictable side-effects of contemporary media ecosystems that cross paths with emerging global realities like pandemics and climate change catastrophes.

In this chapter, we begin to unpack and contemplate the intersections of emotional affect—which can be understood to bind and move individuals into patterns of action or experience (Ahmed, 2004)—and the body within the culture of media and information hyper-saturation, the shared roots of fear, anger, and anxiety that laid the foundations for not just the Capitol riots, but also the embrace of conspiracy theories and the decision to engage in direct action, both seen as forms of symbolic pushback against the violence of a punishing state.

The Theatre of Cruelty

In situating this argument, we turn to Artaud's (1978/1964) Theatre of Cruelty, harkening back to the early 1930s in an era preceding television, where Artaud proposed a system to awaken the petite-bourgeois from their polite torpor. Artaud wanted to provoke the audience into action by submerging them within a sensually overwhelming environment, exposing the banal horror lurking within the passive theatre goer and prodding them into action—positive or negative. He

DOI: 10.4324/9781003246862-10

FIGURE 7.1 A Capitol rioter screams 'Freedom' in the Senate chamber, January 6, 2021
Source: Copyright iowyth hezel ulthiin, ulthiin's impression of photograph by Win McNamee.

believed such provocations would expose the façade of civility, that which mediates a version of polite reality, revealing a deeper reality, an animalistic ground. We argue that the immersive, saturated media environment under the unique circumstances of COVID-19 mimics the set and setting of Artaud's Theatre of Cruelty, submerging the subject in overwhelming sensual stimulation, priming them to engage in reactive and perhaps even violent actions. In the United States, this resulted in the storming of the US Capitol, where agitators expressed a deep affective dissonance, emerging from within the animalistic bowels of an increasingly uncertain world.

Setting Artaud's vision against Agamben's 'state of exception' and Precario's 'immunized and *de-munized*,' we may understand the Capitol riots as a predictable side-effect of contemporary media ecosystems as they intersect with emerging global realities. In *The Theatre and Its Double*, Artaud (1978/1964, p. 88) argues that 'whether they admit it or not, whether a conscious or unconscious act, at heart audiences are searching for a poetic state of mind, a transcendent condition by means of life, crime, drugs, war or insurrection.' The audience's entertainment creates the ground for their collective understanding of reality-as-story. Artaud believed that theatre wasn't separate from real life, that distinctions between the two were illusory, and that by assaulting the audience with stimulation, divisions between audience and stage actor would become transformed, as the boundary between audience and the role of social actor blurred, and spectators were agitated out of their stupor into states of poetry in which reality became the stage where they could ultimately act within and upon the world.

Unleashing forces within a passive subject may upend suppression put in place by the forces of civilization. Unaddressed feelings of alienation and helplessness serve as cultural shadows, creating conditions for acting out fantasy scenarios that provide direction, meaning, purpose, and identity to otherwise disenfranchised modern subjects, abject precisely due to the ultimate emptiness of their privilege. When the American dream is realized, it contains nothing more than an intensifying state of despair; what else might one cling to but a sinking ship and the hopes it signifies? The agitated affect of subjects under social restriction, facing the threat of annihilation from without (COVID) and within (despair), requires an exorcism which, lacking any sensible outlet, might emerge through acts of fantasy. For, as we know, 'All the world's a stage, / And all the men and women merely players' (Shakespeare, 2021 2.7.6). In the world that is given, citizens must play their parts in ways that satisfy and ground their desires, hopes, and dreams.

Previously articulated narrativization lies in wait for the evocation of the 'dog-whistle,' or as Artaud (1978/1964, p. 92) put it, a 'chaotic development of dream images in the brain' which are then carried out by 'a genuine enslavement of the attention.' Leading up to the spectacle of January 6th, Trump claimed that China would soon own the US if he failed to be re-elected (Solender, 2020), taking other actions to undermine the electoral process, including targeted attacks on mail-in voting (overwhelmingly used by Democrats), increasing voter restrictions (overwhelmingly affecting Black voters), and questioning the security of voting machines. Embedded in these narratives are subtle cues toward social and racial tensions which may be set into motion through skillfully wielded probes embedded as meta-narratives within the reportage of events, conveyed through an embedded lens or perspective.

Despite its name, Artaud's vision was not advanced for the cause of authoritarian politics and yet there is a kind of violence imbued in his vision, reflected in the assault on the observer, a provocation into action based on so-called subconscious cruelty. Yet, we must ask, is this cruelty the innate ground out of which humanity emerges, or is it a response to cruel and inhuman conditions to which humanity has become subject? Serwer's (2018) article entitled, 'The Cruelty Is the Point,' suggests that messaging surrounding the Trump movement has had cruelty as its core, indeed that cruelty had become the social adhesive, offering a channel to an affective dissonance bursting at the seams. Serwer (2018 para. 11) suggests that 'only the President and his allies … are entitled to the rights and protections of the law, and if necessary, immunity from it. The rest of us are entitled only to cruelty, by their whim.'

Not only do we have a neoliberal political theatre with the ever-present threat of a disintegrating social safety net, but we also have a 360-degree media environment that promotes and aggravates the concerns of a vulnerable populace looking to direct and relieve their angst. It is in the continual assault on our emotions that this particular theatre of cruelty is manifest. In fanning the flames of paranoia against the 'other,' this form of political spectacle may awaken the animal drive within its audience, becoming manifest in armed demonstrations (Censky, 2020) as well as in an unholy alliance among vegans, QAnon believers, and Neo-Nazis (Schaer, 2020), to which we might add new-agers, alt-right hippies, health food adherents, anti-vaxxers, anti-authoritarians, and militia groups, where commonly assumed divides between left and right become dissolute under the onslaught of an endless chorus of shouting, paranoid voices.

The absolute deluge of both actual facts and 'alternative facts' in an environment of fear, anxiety, and tension may easily result in the impairment of both cognitive function and reasoning (Falshlunger, Lehner, and Treiblmaier, 2016). The perception of a social threat can activate bodily systems meant to deal with stressors (i.e., fight or flight responses) (Kemeny, 2003) and at the same time, stress related cortisol spikes may 'exacerbate vigilance for threat cues' (Akinola, 2012). The science echoes more poetic descriptions in Artaud's (1978/1964) manifesto. He describes the theatre as both 'dissociatory, vibratory action on our sensibility' (p. 63). The art is meant to break through to the hidden, animalistic impulses at the heart of humanity, to reveal a deeper truth under a polite middle-class civility, all of which is to be experienced as liberatory.

One might see the use of provocative semiotic communication through gesture and tone as a kind of metaphysical symbolism expressed through figures such as Donald Trump, Alex Jones, or Fox News. Their affective tones carry a vibratory and sensual relationship to the subject matter which they are communicating, a dance of anger and terror. From the beginning of the Trump Presidency, and perhaps even earlier, this vibratory push towards an impulsive expression of violent urges is evident. As early as 2016, right-wing media pundit Ann Coulter (2016) tweeted, 'we would like to see a little more violence from the innocent Trump supporters set upon by violent leftist hoodlums.' In an interview in August 2020, Kellyanne Conway, Senior Counselor to the President in the Trump administration from 2017 to 2020 said, 'The more chaos and anarchy and vandalism and violence reigns, the better it is for the very clear choice of who's best on public safety and law and order' (Conway, cited in Vigdor, 2020, para. 2). Perhaps most potently, Rudy Giuliani (2021) calls for 'trial by combat' while standing on a dais in front of the White House at the 'Save America' rally before the riots. To bring the state into order, one must rise to violence. But whose order and whose violence?

There is a sensual logic in the incessant, intense, and unrelenting narrativizing of violence and cruelty coming from the 24-hour news cycle provoking an immobilized public into reaction. We see a culmination in the surreal storming of the US Capitol building on January 6, 2021, which some have compared to a Live-Action-Role-Play (LARP) event (Walther, 2021) a place where identities and desires might be embodied. We see people in costume, including military style uniforms, play-acting as revolutionaries (see Chapter 9) and the incident was recorded and photographed with many in the mob brandishing their faces as weapons of expression, seemingly oblivious of the political attempt to disrupt the democratic process in a chaotic action that left five dead (see Chapter 8). In this context, we may begin to unpack and contemplate the intersections of the human body within the culture of sensual bombardment through media and information saturation as it melds media and social media narratives with the so-called 'real-life' spaces of embodied action—perhaps even to the extent where they are no longer distinguishable.

Rhizomatic Media Flows—Flat, Organic, and Timeless

In the Big Flat Now, Self (2018, para. 2) argues that 'flatness has neither a limit nor a horizon. It has permanently changed our relationship with time and place.' This flatness comes from communication systems making up the contemporary, from the free distribution of cultural forms and the levelling of information flows within communication ecosystems. The coming of COVID-19 serves to further flatten a landscape, both incoherent and endless, suspending the lively world within a container of ambiguity. Self (2018, para. 1) further argues that many current media forms lack 'hierarchy or centrality,' a once editorialized version of truth has become democratized and that democratization has brought forth a frothing narrative, one lacking coherence, meaning, or collective vision. Pettitt's (2013) notion of the 'Gutenberg Parenthesis' further suggests that in secondary orality, literate information flows turn from grand narratives, becoming complex, local, disorderly, and individual. This chaotic restructuring of social life has given rise to new forms of cultural production, given the freedom to construct, construe, and recontextualize the facts of the world into a newly flexible matrix of the real, making connections between self and other in new alliances, alignments, and agreements.

Yet, despite prevailing anxieties, a hopeful imaginary remains. There is the promise of a collective worldwide awakening, with roots running the political gamut from consciousness-raising feminist spirituality, to progressive political activism, from environmentalism and new age sentiments, to, now we argue, the far-right conspiracy theory, QAnon. QAnon's version of this liberatory philosophy ascribes heroic qualities to the unlikely patron of Donald Trump, a purportedly messianic figure sent to shake up a stagnant world politics run by elite insiders upholding the evils of an incestuous political and business class. The promise of a global awakening seems all the more relevant in a world already filled with anxiety over social rifts and global environmental collapse.

Conversely, in considering the rise in conspiratorial thinking, one might wonder why a public—or fragments of a public—might choose *not* to express their concern, seemingly dulled or numbed to the multiplying ills of the world. Webber Nicholsen (2002) speaks of the tendency to stay silent about environmental destruction, speaking of the pressure to stay silent to our dependency and vulnerability. In speaking our love for the world out loud, there is a danger of destroying the tender filaments that link us to those things we cherish most, also drawing notice and perhaps harm to ourselves in the process through the exposure of our deepest human vulnerabilities. Imagine for a moment a singular savior emerging, one who has the power to elevate humanity above abject corrupt powers and environmental catastrophes. The eponymous Q writes,

Stay TOGETHER.
  Be STRONG.
  Get ORGANIZED.
  Be HEARD.
  FIGHT the censorship.
  You, the PEOPLE, have ALL the POWER.
  You simply forgot how to PLAY.
  TOGETHER you are INVINCIBLE.
  They want you divided.
  They want you silenced.
  MAKE NOISE.
  We are WITH you.
  MAKE IT RAIN.
  Q

(WWG1WGA, 2019, p. 51)

In facing a world where global environmental catastrophe piles upon a health crisis that in turn portends an impending social collapse, pointing to the true ills of this world connects one with their own utter vulnerability within a matrix of relations of power seemingly beyond their control. The Q narratives further take advantage of the unmooring of a central logic which undermines trust in consensus reality, taking advantage of information flows that present no collective order. The opening of reality to democratic participation also subjects reality to the complication, attrition, and potential destruction of common truths that may have, at one time, brought unity while also being seen as a common oppressive factor. Complicating the issue, Duffield (2020, para. 22), a disinformation analyst at Blackbird. AI, says that progressive political ideologies have been:

> enfeebled by late capitalism's centrist normativism, divesting mainstream left-wing politics of meaningful social currency or practical efficacy.... This reduces political debate away from theory, ideology and causal reasoning to pitched identity-driven battles between Us and Them—a cosmic dramaturgy easily transposed onto QAnon's Manichean reading of world politics.

So-called vanguards of freedom and progress have been absorbed by market ideologies, moving toward strident individualism under a supposed free market.

The frenzied affective politics of this new world disorder touches upon individuals beyond the social media sphere. Regardless of how it is understood, it has produced gunmen with semi-automatic rifles showing up at pizza places looking for child-sex-dungeons and Viking Shamans entering the Capitol seeking to either upend democracy or to save it—or both, in the same action.

With the arrival of the enigmatic COVID-19, a match has been introduced to the tinder of our post-rational condition. Pillars that once grounded any substantial determination of truth are now eroded by emerging rhizomatic terrains giving birth to fragmented organic communication networks. The spaces most free from limits become, perhaps puzzlingly, the most toxic. Communications ecosystems become a tangled network of corporate media, citizen participation, and inter-state disinformation campaigns involving both real world trolling and algorithm-driven artificial intelligence (AI) bots. Our collective-fever-dream becomes a 360-degree alternative reality simulation, one that may entice, enrapture, and ensnare global citizens in a rush of stimulus that cuts to the quick of human consciousness, stimulating the nervous system into modes of action that precede rational thought. This effect precisely is Artaud's theatre of cruelty in action.

Biopolitics: A Siege on the Body

During the early stages of the pandemic, before a crystalized discourse had emerged, French philosopher Giorgio Agamben (2020) mobilized his well-known concept of a 'state of exception' on the Italian website *Il Manifesto*. He critiqued responses to the crisis by governments—many of which had imposed lockdown measures to prevent the spread of the virus—arguing that governments had created a problematic 'state of exception.' This, he predicted, would further increase normalization of forms of 'war' (e.g., the war on terror, the war on drugs, the war on COVID, etc.) triggering further extraordinary state measures which would in turn further curtail freedoms.

Patton (2011, p. 105) relates Agamben's 'state of exception' to a previous viral pandemic, namely H1N1, in which she posits that diseased bodies, once declared so, are forever rendered 'suspect,' and moreover, measures put into place during these extraordinary times are not easily undone. During the H1N1 pandemic, public scrutiny of the World Health Organization (WHO) ran rampant, with unsubstantiated claims made that the WHO was price fixing with drug companies (Patton, 2011). While the WHO had limited powers to enforce public health recommendations, nonetheless they were an authoritative voice that wielded power through the proposal of state actions. For those suspicious of and perhaps previously traumatized by the state, well-meaning recommendations by the WHO were seen as suspect. PEW Research Center's (2019, para. 1) work on public trust in the US government found that it currently 'remains near historic lows' with only 17% of Americans saying that they would trust their government 'to do what is right' in a crisis. One may wish to dismiss the concerns of the anti-mask, lockdown, or anti-vaccine crowd as the result of stupidity or a lack of education, but there is a cynicism toward state actors that runs deeper than ignorance, presenting perhaps a kind of cultural logic to which the vulnerable may attach themselves in search of comfort and protection.

During the pandemic, an exceptionally vocal US movement has been protesting against government imposition of lockdowns and quarantine measures. A second study by PEW Research Center has shown that a surprising number of Americans (three in ten) believed that the Coronavirus was intentionally constructed in a lab (Schaeffer, 2020). Such latent distrust of authority creates a vulnerability to ideological manipulation. This has led those skeptical of neo-liberal governmental forces, media, and mainstream Western medicine to become fodder for astroturfing campaigns—top-down corporate or state campaigns manipulated to appear as if they are grassroots movements. The largely white protests against the COVID lockdowns might be yet another demonstration of the fracturing of the middle class (Reid, 2016). We can see a convergence of New Age Practitioners (Meltzer, 2021) with the 'Boogaloo Bois' movement, a group calling for a second civil war in the United States, recognizable in their Hawaiian shirts (and often carrying automatic weapons) (Evans and Wilson, 2020), whose critiques of police and the state find easy receptivity among those who want the government to fall. There is therefore a coalescing of anti-state sentiment, uniting a once-diverse crowd within disparate social milieus, collectively railing against the pandemic body-politic.

Preciado (2020) suggests that in a time of illness, issues of the 'immunized and *de-munized*' become exacerbated, where the immunized are drawn close and the *de-munized* have their communal identities undermined in fundamental ways. In this moment, when those in quarantine also become the 'de-munized' of society, like inmates or prisoners, captured migrants or the poor, there is an increased pressure to implicate oneself as existing among the immunized. Thus, perhaps vocally opposing the wearing of masks might mark one out as inviolate just as the wearing of masks might, to place oneself above defamation brought on by the disease. Further, once lockdown—feared to be a permanent state-of-exemption—becomes fully imposed, even when one may finally go outside, the skin of our bodies becomes the quarantine; our bodies become 'suspect.'

Preciado (2020, para. 16) warns that the body 'has become the new territory where the violent border politics that we have been designing and testing for years on "others" are now expressed.' The body is also where we experience the tug-of-war over socioeconomic control. The chaotic boundary between anti-mask, anti-lockdown protests and Black Lives Matter anti-police brutality protests, attempts to draw out the notion of *homo sacer*, one who exists outside of state protection and thus becomes disposable. This is exemplified by the murder of Black individuals at the hands of the state—experienced viscerally—and set against the martyrdom experienced at the hands of the state by anti-government protesters, experienced largely in the alt-right public imaginary. In both the anti-vaxxer and the anti-racist protests, it is in the boundaries of the skin, of the body itself, that the war for control is waged. Moreover, perhaps even more fundamentally so, it is within the boundaries of the mind—these protest imaginaries—that the tug-of-war for 'the real' is being waged and staged.

The Awakening of QAnon

As a whole, conspiracy theories may be considered mythologies, laying claim to centrality and authority in the lives of those so engaged. Such is the fervor of QAnon adherents that they believe themselves to be witnessing an unravelling mystery, one that upends collectively held social meaning, proving it to be a malicious lie. The closing down of society under the COVID-19 pandemic serves as an ideal setting for an alternative-reality-game wherein we can make-believe that a global cabal is installing a New World Order. The Trump presidency becomes a force for hope, perhaps precisely due to the surrealism of unfolding events, where the reality-TV-star turned President was predicted in an episode of the Simpsons in the year 2000 as a joke (Greaney and Marcantel, 2000). When this is what we know to be true, how much more surreal is the coming of the 'storm' (as Q would put it) to uproot the corruption of the world?

A simple or dismissive view of conspiracy theories is insufficient to understand the complex dynamics at play in our current geopolitical climate. Domestically in the United States, there are determined efforts by corporate-funded lobbyists and think-tanks to destabilize the social underpinnings of the welfare state, including attempts at capitalist enclosure of socially held institutions such as schools and hospitals. Internationally, foreign actors are attempting to destabilize liberal democracies and the global hegemony of the US–Europe axis of power. Whether this amounts to good or ill, evidence of these interlocking sites of democratic erosion are in plain sight and do not need a labyrinthine conspiracy narrative to explain them. Yet, the energy of displeasure awakened by a fragmented and disturbed public has been given an easy flow through the creation of infrastructure by those interested in mobilizing these forces for economic and political purposes.

In an FBI memo (Phoenix Field Office of the FBI, 2019, p. 5), they note that a 'factor driving the intensity of conspiracy theorizing in the United States … is the uncovering of real conspiracies or cover-ups involving illegal, harmful, or unconstitutional activities by government officials or leading political figures.' Controversies surrounding the whistleblowing of Edward Snowdon, Chelsea Manning and Wikileaks—whose ethos in disclosing heretofore classified documents, they believed would 'lead to a more knowledgeable public and ultimately to a more accountable, responsive, and effective state' (Fenster, 2012, p. 770)—have added to a growing list of disturbing and unresolved issues involving state-level crimes against humanity. In not-too-distant memory, we see the Bush administration's handling of the intelligence regarding alleged weapons of mass destruction that never existed, the Iraq War, and the torture of prisoners in the Abu Ghraib detention center. Both President Bush and former UK Prime Minister Tony Blair were tried in absentia and convicted of 'crimes against peace, crimes against humanity, and genocide as a result of their roles in the Iraq War' by the Kuala Lumpur War Crime Tribunal (Falk, 2011, para. 1).

Add to this the explosive revelations in the case of Jeffrey Epstein, who was jailed in 2008 for 13 months and subsequently arrested again in 2019 on charges of child sex trafficking and prostitution, embodying the most ghoulish claims of QAnon, that of a child sex trafficking ring taking place at highest levels of the power strata. Epstein would later die in prison due to a purported suicide (Boboltz, 2019), the incident becoming an internet meme with the phrase 'Epstein didn't kill himself' appearing in surprising contexts (Grey Ellis ,2019), similar to the phenomenon of 'Rick Rolling' (Dubs, 2009). The phrase was even mentioned in a speech by Ricky Gervais during the 2020 Golden Globes, signaling a sentiment of suspicion around the death of someone who had ties to an actual cabal of powerful elite individuals. The most notable figure implicated in the scandal was Prince Andrew, the Queen of England's second son, whose victim gave testimony in a popular Netflix documentary, *Filthy Rich* (Dickson, 2020), with further coverage in *The Guardian* (Osborne, 2019). In a recent Reddit comment, user hereforthefeast (2021) posted a list of Republican party insiders who have been indicted on charges of human trafficking, child-sex-trafficking, and child pornography. We cannot say that it is easy for the American public to process the knowledge of these state and elite atrocities, knowing full well that the perpetrators have not been (and may never be) brought to justice.

It becomes difficult to put forward an argument that the public should trust what have long been considered reputable sources (the state, the media, etc.), given that these same sources are known to willfully mislead the public, to the detriment of the public itself. When one considers this, in concert with media monopolies, partisan media outlets, and the Trump administration's notorious reputation for uttering falsehoods (Kessler et al., 2021), a sophisticated and critical mindset seems requisite for life within contemporary democracies. Chomsky and Herman's (1988) *Manufacturing Consent*, popularized in a 1992 documentary now on YouTube, details the insidious manner in which power systems may coerce speech. This very title—*Manufacturing Consent*—is cited in *QAnon: An Invitation to the Great Awakening* (2019), a compilation assembled by a collective of anonymous internet persons who go under the moniker WWG1WGA (which stands for: where we go one, we go all). But it is not a QAnon conspiracy to say that the media play a knowledge gatekeeping role: there is a widespread folk understanding in Western societies of the manipulation of media representations, making it nearly impossible to point to mainstream media sources as a means to debunk conspiratorial thinking. Indeed, there is a built-in response to any attempted debunking: 'that's just what they want you to believe.'

In *QAnon: An Invitation to the Great Awakening* (2019) there are detailed instructions for disseminating information via visual memes in order to avoid algorithmic censorship, which is a known operational mechanism within other groups such as the 'Bujahadeen,' neo-civil war hopefuls (Goldenberg, 2020). Interestingly Goldenberg (2020), as part of the Network Contagion Research Institute, points to the use of memes as faster and more efficient at mobilizing potentially inflammatory or dangerous content than has been previously thought. In addition to this, QAnon mobilizes a rather complex analysis of media literacy narratives referencing the likes of media and communications scholars Chomsky,

Lippmann, and Popper for the purposes of attempting to understand how Trump as a mythical figure will contend with media control in order to accomplish Q's aims. It may be said that the QAnon narrative has correctly identified some of the causes and mechanisms of oppression, yet their identification of the means by which one may transcend this oppression is rightly contested. This references back to Webber Nicholsen's (2002) reflections on silence. Why might QAnon followers be afraid to voice the obvious critiques of the ills that they seem most fixated on? Could it be a symptom of the fear that birthed QAnon, that in voicing the collective course of action to rise above the corruption and misery of the world, one might destroy that most fragile and delicate hope of salvation? LaFrance (2020), in interviews with Q believers, notes that the suspicion of 'fake news' drives some believers even deeper into the movement, the thought being that any critique of the movement's aims is motivated by bad actors. The hope that holds the Q narrative together is fragile, built on shifting sands.

Further, 'The FBI assesses these conspiracy theories very likely will emerge, spread, and evolve in the modern information marketplace, occasionally driving both groups and individual extremists to carry out criminal or violent acts' (Phoenix Field Office of the FBI, 2019, p. 1). This isn't relegated to a group of fringe weirdos, either. At the time of writing, Kaplan (2020) on the website *Media Matters for America*, had compiled a list of 43 current or former congressional candidates who have documented associations with the Q narrative. Belief in Q is gaining hold within the institutions of power in the United States and elsewhere, including being explicitly championed by Marjorie Taylor Greene (see Chapter 5). This seems to reflect a feedback mechanism, exemplified in Donald Trump's famous obsession with Fox News (Gertz, 2018) where state actors begin to consume, believe, and then produce less truthful propaganda. Beyond this, and due to the fact that the QAnon narrative is assembled from a series of disparate and often vague anonymous posts, LaFrance (2020) points out that this narrative has the unique quality of having flexible boundaries that can change and pivot when needed.

How do we approach the explosion of conspiracy theories, alternative facts, and echo chambers in an environment where major issues are brought to the fore by both journalists and whistleblowers and then are left with little closure, progress, or remediation? A tweet by the account for *Existential Comics*, references the 2016 publishing of the Panama Papers in the newspaper *Süddeutsche Zeitung*, expressing a commonly held sentiment in saying 'Remember when the Panama Paper revealed that the ultra rich all had a secret tax-evasion island where they hid their assets, and nothing happened?' (Existential Comics, 2019). Beyond nothing happening, a lead investigative journalist into the Panama Papers scandal, Daphne Caruana Galizia, died under mysterious circumstances in Malta in 2017, the victim of a car bombing (Garside, 2017).

Those seeking a sense of justice for any of these events may ultimately be disappointed. A public that is craving security and a sense of direction may find more appeal in the QAnon narrative than in facing an unknown, faceless, powerful, and wealthy elite who seem immune to consequence for illegal actions taken in the open. In the face of this, the realms of media and information literacy cannot remain apolitical but must attend to a field of communications that is bringing public attention to the injustices of the world to a public who lack any directive as to what to then do about any of it. It may seem (and be) off the wall to take an AR-15 rifle into a pizza restaurant (Kennedy, 2017) but considering the seriousness of the global realities we are all facing, is it any more sane to do nothing?

Limitations of a Revolution

As we have thus far established, affect, decision making in the halls of power, and fundamental concepts such as goodness, freedom, and justice may be manipulated by those once deemed credible. Valid and real feelings of injustice, fear, or insecurity may be funneled into tangible action, especially when carried out within the frenzied pace of an over-mediatized 24/7 communications environment. In Mercer's (2010) article 'Emotional Beliefs' he points to the neurological foundations of decision making, contending that it is not possible to make rational decisions *without* emotion. Studies of those who have lost their ability to feel emotions due to brain surgery, have been found to have lost their ability to engage in rational decision making. Mercer notes that those who have developed a foundation of belief do so by navigating complex emotional fields, constantly attempting to define the credibility of sources based on one's feelings, founded on a network of rather abstract concepts around trustworthiness. To distinguish the good from the bad brings us to create an emotional framework that serves as the basis for fundamental notions of justice. A Trump tweet calling for the left-wing anti-fascist ethos, Antifa, to be designated a domestic terrorist organization (Smith, 2020) predictably led to hysteria in Klamath Falls, Oregon where individuals believed buses full of Antifa terrorists were travelling to their town to attend a protest (Elliott, 2020). If you believe the President of the United States to be credible, or see online messages shared by trusted people in your life, like friends, or family members, you might be led to experience a sense of fear, outrage, and paranoia that may lead to violence.

In a media vacuum where access to a reader's attention is available for whoever can get there first, we see a struggle for control over what is real with those engaged in online social media, news, and other sources being exposed to what could be characterized as an aggressively manipulative environment where one's emotions may be preyed upon to direct one's action towards a wanted goal (such as profits for social media companies, but also political and social objectives). This comes up with the astroturfing efforts by the Dorr brothers, who are guns rights activists mining right-wing political outrage for the purpose of 'data harvesting' (Graves, 2020; Zadronzny and Collins, 2020a). It also comes up with QAnon piggybacking on emotional currents of insecurity, the desire for justice around issues of child sexual exploitation, the growing disparity between the rich and poor, and calls for racial justice which, in some cases, become reduced to a means to sell merchandise (Zadronzny and Collins, 2020b).

There is power and money in the ability to hold attention and to inspire an emotional reaction. Returning to Artaud's theatre of cruelty, the glut of information accessible to the public becomes an onslaught, when there is no model for *how* to process this information. It becomes, instead, a barrage of sensory information that speaks to the animalistic and instinctual impulses within the audience, prodding them to flow into convenient channels to exorcise the feelings that build up as a response to the deluge, whether it be political or capitalist in nature. The key factor in the theatre of cruelty was not the *why* of the reaction but, rather, the reaction itself; unmoored from motivation it becomes an expression of the purely libidinal sense of the subconscious, the animal, and in Artaud's vision, the potential for latent cruelty within humanity. Yet, does it not make sense for cruelty to be the result of an onslaught to the senses? Perhaps it is not the *truth* of humanity that we are seeing, but instead, a tendril in the rhizome of human expression.

We see here the way that human beings react when the ground of truth is found to move, when the speed of communication means that the gatekeepers of sense are undermined by both good and bad actors alike. It is a time of great social upheaval but also of great political and epistemological manipulation, where the populace is chained within a 360-degree media environment from which it is nearly impossible to delink. Here, a struggle for the real is waged within our very minds. Yet, the same human needs remain as in Maslow's (1943) theory. It is often stated dismissively that people who believe in conspiracy theories are seeking security, craving an explanation to make sense of their lives. Yet, is the need for security not a fundamental mechanism of human psycho-emotional makeup?

Perhaps what is needed is for people to be brave enough to put voice to the hidden desperation that so many are feeling. In a recent TikTok made by a mother who was sucked into the Capitol riots narrative, she says that she believed the rapture to be possible and even immanent. She later posted a video of her feet and legs in slippers and pyjamas in a doctor's office. A title overlaying the video reads, 'I really hope I get help because I feel like I'm screaming and no one hears me' (Vanderbilt, 2021). It was recently revealed that 68% of QAnon followers arrested after the Capitol riots reported that they had received mental health diagnoses (Moskalenko, 2021), often being reported in the media with a sense of superiority and condescension, as though the vulnerability of their mental health had exposed a moral lack in the individuals, rather than a deeply concerning trend in North American society at large.

It doesn't appear as though QAnon can be simply dismissed as the product of stupidity or ignorance. Instead, it might be understood to have emerged within the interstices of love, hope, fear, anger, and violence played out within information flows that exist as hotly contested territories of influence, manipulation, and control. Pointing fingers at individuals who take up conspiracy narratives lets the real architects of these flows escape culpability.

A cultural, political, and economic elite are currently engaged in a turf war over the 'real,' in which the emotional pain of individuals becomes fodder to be channeled into action that ultimately serves the flow of both capital and power. It is not that individuals are innocent of wrongdoing, but in limiting the scope of one's analysis to the individual alone, one could easily miss the machinations of a propaganda machine bent on awakening the masses to express their libidinal impulses for directed aims. It is this machine that needs to be encountered and dismantled, this battleground which must be acknowledged, understood, and deconstructed.

References

Agamben, G (2020) 'Lo stato d'eccezione provocato da un'emergenza immotivata,' *il manifesto*, 25 February [Online]. Available at: https://ilmanifesto.it/lo-stato-deccezione-provocato-da-unemergenza-immotivata/ (Accessed: 15 September 2021).

Ahmed, S (2004) *The cultural politics of emotion*. Edinburgh: Edinburgh University Press.

Akinola, M (2012) 'Stress-induced cortisol facilitates threat-related decision making among police officers,' *Behavioral Neuroscience*, 126(1): 167–174. https://doi.org/10.1037/a0026657.

Anderson, C (2020) 'Reopen domains: Shut the front door,' *DomainTools*, 24 April [Online]. Available at: www.domaintools.com/resources/blog/reopen-domains-shut-the-front-dorr (Accessed: 11 May 2020).

Artaud, A (1978) *The theatre and its double* (V Corti, Trans.). Alma Classics (original published in 1964).

Phoenix Field Office of the FBI (2019) 'Anti-government, identity based, and fringe political conspiracy theories very likely motivate some domestic extremists to commit criminal, sometimes violent activity' [Online]. Available at: www.scribd.com/document/420379775/FBI-Conspiracy-Theory-Redacted#download&from_embed (Accessed: 15 September 2021).

Baum, D (2016) 'Legalize it all,' *Harper's Magazine*, April [Online]. Available at: https://harpers.org/archive/2016/04/legalize-it-all/ (Accessed: 7 June 2020).

Beckett, L (2020) 'Older people would rather die than let Covid-19 harm US economy – Texas official,' *The Guardian*, 24 March [Online] Available at: www.theguardian.com/world/2020/mar/24/older-people-would-rather-die-than-let-covid-19-lockdown-harm-us-economy-texas-official-dan-patrick (Accessed: 7 June 2020).

Binder, M (2020) 'The right-wing family pushing anti-quarantine events on Facebook,' *Mashable*, 20 April [Online]. Available at: https://mashable.com/article/facebook-groups-right-wing-anti-quarantine-protests/ (Accessed: 30 April 2020).

Boboltz, S (2019) 'A timeline of sex offender Jeffrey Epstein's convictions and new allegations,' *HuffPost Canada*, 11 July [Online]. Available at: www.huffpost.com/entry/jeffrey-epstein-timeline_n_5d2763c8e4b02a5a5d57857f (Accessed: 7 June 2020).

Brown, L (2020) 'Idaho representative compares Coronavirus lockdown to Nazi Germany,' *New York Post*, 20 April [Online]. Available at: https://nypost.com/2020/04/20/idaho-representative-compares-lockdown-to-nazi-treatment-of-jews/ (Accessed: 7 June 2020).

Censky, A (2020) 'Heavily armed protesters gather again at Michigan Capitol to decry stay-at-home order,' *NPR*, 14 May [Online]. Available at: www.npr.org/2020/05/14/855918852/heavily-armed-protesters-gather-again-at-michigans-Capitol-denouncing-home-order (Accessed: 7 June 2020).

Chomsky, N, Achbar, M and Wintonick, P (2002) *Manufacturing consent: Noam Chomsky and the media: A film*. New York: Zeitgeist Video.

Chotiner, I (2020) 'How pandemics change history,' *The New Yorker*, 4 March [Online]. Available at: www.newyorker.com/news/q-and-a/how-pandemics-change-history (Accessed: 7 June 2020).

Coulter, A [@AnnCoulter] (2016) 'We would like to see a little more violence from the innocent Trump supporters set upon by violent leftist hoodlums,' *Twitter*, 13 March [Tweet]. Available at: https://twitter.com/AnnCoulter/status/709151593913061378?ref_src=twsrc%5Etfw%7Ctwcamp%5Etweetembed%7Ctwterm%5E709151593913061378%7Ctwgr%5E%7Ctwcon%5Es1_&ref_url=https%3A%2F%2Fthehill.com%2Fblogs%2Fblog-briefing-room%2Fnews%2F272864-coulter-id-like-to-see-a-little-more-violence-from-trump (Accessed: 7 June 2020).

Dickson, EJ (2020) '7 Shocking revelations from Netflix's new Jeffrey Epstein documentary,' *Rolling Stone*, 28 May [Online]. Available at: www.rollingstone.com/culture/culture-features/jeffrey-epstein-filthy-rich-netflix-documentary-1006535/ (Accessed: 7 June 2020).

Dubs, J (2009) 'Rickroll,' *Know Your Meme* [Online]. Available at: https://knowyourmeme.com/memes/rickroll (Accessed: 7 June 2020).

Duffield, R (2020) 'The global QAnon phenomenon: The "great awakening" worldwide,' *Blackbird.AI*, 20 October [Online]. Available at: https://blackbirdai.medium.com/qanon-goes-global-c96ddc6e930b (Accessed: 3 February 2021).

Elliott, JK (2020) 'Small-town vigilantes duped into standing guard for Antifa "bus invasion" hoax,' *Global News*, 8 June [Online]. Available at: https://globalnews.ca/news/7038764/antifa-bus-george-floyd-protests/ (Accessed: 10 June 2020).

Evans, R and Wilson, J (2020) 'The boogaloo movement is not what you think,' *Bellingcat*, 27 May [Online]. Available at:www.bellingcat.com/news/2020/05/27/the-boogaloo-movement-is-not-what-you-think/ (Accessed: 7 June 2020).

Existential Comics [@existentialcoms]. (2019) 'Remember when the Panama Papers revealed that the ultra rich all had a secret tax-evasion island where they hid their assets, and nothing happened? Well, you'd think the ultra rich having a secret rape island would be taken a little more seriously, but it's not looking good,' *Twitter*, 11 August [Tweet]. Available at: https://twitter.com/existentialcoms/status/1160625727433166848?lang=en (Accessed: 15 September 2021).

Falk, R (2011) 'Kuala Lumpur tribunal: Bush and Blair guilty,' *Al Jazeera*, 28 November [Online]. Available at: www.aljazeera.com/indepth/opinion/2011/11/20111128105712109215.html (Accessed: 7 June 2020).

Falschlunger, L, Lehner, O and Treiblmaier, H (2016) 'InfoVis: The impact of information overload on decision making outcome in high complexity settings,' *SIGHCwe 2016 Proceedings*, 3 [Online]. Available at: https://aisel.aisnet.org/sighci2016/3 (Accessed: 28 September 2021).

Fenster, M (2012) 'Disclosure's effects: WikiLeaks and transparency,' *Iowa Law Review*, 97(3), 753.

Gabbatt, A (2021) '"Incited by the president": Politicians blame Trump for insurrection of Capitol Hill,' *The Guardian*, 7 January [Online]. Available at: www.theguardian.com/us-news/2021/jan/06/donald-trump-politicians-insurrection-Capitol-hill (Accessed: 15 September 2021).

Garside, J (2017) 'Malta car bomb kills Panama Papers journalist,' *The Guardian*, 16 October [Online]. Available at: www.theguardian.com/world/2017/oct/16/malta-car-bomb-kills-panama-papers-journalist (Accessed: 10 June 2020).

Gertz, M (2018) 'I've studied the Trump-Fox feedback loop for months. It's crazier than you think,' *Politico*, 1 May [Online]. Available at: www.politico.com/magazine/story/2018/01/05/trump-media-feedback-loop-216248 (Accessed: 7 June 2020).

Giroux, HA (2010) 'Neoliberalism, pedagogy, and cultural politics: Beyond the theatre of cruelty.' In Z Leonardo (ed.), *Handbook of cultural politics and education* (Vol. 4). Sense Publishers, 49–70.

Giuliani, R (2021) 'Rudy Giuliani speech transcript at Trump's Washington, DC rally: Wants "trial by combat",' *Rev*, 6 January [Online]. Available at: www.rev.com/blog/tra nscripts/rudy-giuliani-speech-transcript-at-trumps-washington-d-c-rally-wants-trial-by-c ombat (Accessed: 10 June 2021).

Goldenberg, A (2020) 'Cyber swarming, memetic warfare and viral insurgency: How domestic militants organize on memes to incite violent insurrection and terror against government and law enforcement,' *Network Contagion Research Institute* [Online]. Available at: https://ncri.io/reports/cyber-swarming-memetic-warfare-and-viral-insur gency-how-domestic-militants-organize-on-memes-to-incite-violent-insurrection-and-te rror-against-government-and-law-enforcement/ (Accessed: 9 June 2020).

Graves, L (2020) 'Who's behind the "Reopen" protests?' *The New York Times*, 22 April [Online]. Available at: www.nytimes.com/2020/04/22/opinion/coronavirus-protests-a stroturf.html (Accessed: 7 June 2020).

Greaney, D (Writer) and Marcantel, M (Director) (2000) 'Bart to the Future' (11, 17), 19 March [TV series episode]. In *The Simpsons*. 20th Century Fox.

Grey Ellis, E (2019) '"Epstein didn't kill himself" and the meme-ing of conspiracy,' *Wired*, 15 November [Online]. Available at: www.wired.com/story/epstein-didnt-kill-himself-conspiracy/ (Accessed: 10 June 2020).

Han, B-C (2015) *The burnout society* (E Butler, Trans.). Stanford Briefs.

hereforthefeast (2021) 'Maybe the satanic sex cult were the friends we voted for along the way … this is just amazing,' *Reddit*, 3 April [Online]. Available at: www.reddit.com/ r/LeopardsAteMyFace/comments/misr9j/maybe_the_satanic_sex_cult_were_the_friends _we/ (Accessed: 6 April 2021).

Kaplan, A (2020) 'Here are the QAnon supporters running for Congress in 2020,' *Media Matters for America*, 1 July [Online]. Available at: www.mediamatters.org/qanon-conspiracy-theory/ here-are-qanon-supporters-running-congress-2020 (Accessed: 15 September 2021).

Kemeny, ME (2003) 'The psychobiology of stress,' *Current Directions in Psychological Science*, 12(4): 124–129. https://doi.org/10.1111/1467-8721.01246.

Kennedy, M (2017) '"Pizzagate" gunman sentenced to 4 years in prison,' *NPR*, 22 June [Online]. Available at: www.npr.org/sections/thetwo-way/2017/06/22/533941689/p izzagate-gunman-sentenced-to-4-years-in-prison (Accessed: 7 June 2020).

Kessler, G, Rizzo, S and Kelly, M (2021) 'Trump's false or misleading claims total 30,573 over 4 years,' *Washington Post*, 24 January [Online]. Available at:www.washingtonpost. com/politics/2021/01/24/trumps-false-or-misleading-claims-total-30573-over-four-yea rs/. (Accessed: 25 January 2021).

LaFrance, A (2020) 'The prophecies of Q,' *The Atlantic*, June [Online]. Available at: www.theatlantic.com/magazine/archive/2020/06/qanon-nothing-can-stop-what-is-com ing/610567/ (Accessed: 20 May 2020).

Maslow, AH (1943) 'A theory of human motivation,' *Psychological Review*, 50(4): 370–396. doi:10.1037/h0054346.

Meltzer, M (2021) 'How new age spirituality and sensitive masculinity led to QAnon,' *Washington Post*, 19 April [Online]. Available at: www.washingtonpost.com/magazine/ 2021/03/29/qanon-new-age-spirituality/ (Accessed: 10 June 2021).

Mercer, J (2010) 'Emotional beliefs.' *International Organization*, 64(1): 1–31.

Moskalenko, S (2021) 'Many QAnon followers report having mental health diagnoses,' *The Conversation*, 25 March [Online]. http://theconversation.com/many-qanon-followers-rep ort-having-mental-health-diagnoses-157299 (Accessed: 15 September 2021).

Osborne, L (2019) 'Prince Andrew and Jeffrey Epstein: What you need to know,' *The Guardian*, 7 December [Online]. Available at: www.theguardian.com/uk-news/2019/dec/07/prince-andrew-jeffrey-epstein-what-you-need-to-know (Accessed: 7 June 2020).

Patton, C (2011) 'Pandemic, empire and the permanent state of exception,' *Economic and Political Weekly*, 46(13): 103–110.

Pettitt, T (2013) 'Bracketing the Gutenberg Parenthesis', *Explorations in Media Ecology*, 11(2): 95–114.

PEW Research Center (2019) 'Public trust in government: 1958–2019,' Pew Research Center, 11 April [Online]. Available at: www.people-press.org/2019/04/11/public-trust-in-government-1958-2019/ (Accessed: 7 June 2020).

Preciado, PB (2020) 'Learning from the virus,' *Artforum* [Online]. Available at: www.artforum.com/print/202005/paul-b-preciado-82823 (Accessed: 10 June 2021).

Reid, M (2016) 'Inequality, neoliberalism, and the unmaking of the middle class,' *The Indy*, 27 February [Online]. Available at: https://theindependent.ca/2016/02/27/inequality-neoliberalism-and-the-unmaking-of-the-middle-class/ (Accessed: 10 May 2020).

Schaer, C (2020) 'Neo-Nazis, QAnon nuts, and hardcore vegans unite to protest Germany's lockdown,' *The Daily Beast*, 13 May [Online]. Available at: www.thedailybeast.com/neo-nazis-qanon-nuts-and-hardcore-vegans-unite-to-protest-germanys-lockdown (Accessed: 7 June 2020).

Schaeffer, K (2020, April 8) 'Nearly three-in-ten Americans believe COVID-19 was made in a lab,' *Pew Research Center* [Online]. Available at: www.pewresearch.org/fact-tank/2020/04/08/nearly-three-in-ten-americans-believe-covid-19-was-made-in-a-lab/ (Accessed: 30 December 2021).

Self, J (2018) 'The big flat now: Power, flatness, and nowness in the third millennium,' *032c*, 16 December [Online]. Available at: https://032c.com/the-big-flat-now-power-flatness-and-nowness-in-the-third-millennium (Accessed: 10 June 2020).

Serwer, A (2018) 'The cruelty is the point,' *The Atlantic*, 3 October [Online]. Available at: www.theatlantic.com/ideas/archive/2018/10/the-cruelty-is-the-point/572104/ (Accessed: 15 September 2021).

Shakespeare, W (2021) *As You Like It*. Retrieved from: www.sparknotes.com/nofear/shakespeare/asyoulikeit/page_96/#:~:text=All%20the%20world's%20a%20stage%2C&text=The%20whole%20world%20is%20a,life%20separated%20into%20seven%20acts (Original publication 1623).

Smith, A (2020) 'Trump says he will designate Antifa a terrorist organization as GOP points fingers at extremists,' *NBC News*, 31 May [Online]. Available at: www.nbcnews.com/politics/politics-news/trump-says-he-will-designate-antifa-terrorist-organization-gop-points-n1220321 (Accessed: 7 June 2020).

Solender, A (2020) '"You're Gonna Have to Speak Chinese": Trump Warns of Hostile Foreign Takeovers if Biden Wins,' *Forbes*, 11 August [Online]. Available at: www.forbes.com/sites/andrewsolender/2020/08/11/youre-gonna-have-to-learn-to-speak-chinese-trump-warns-of-hostile-foreign-takeovers-if-biden-wins/?sh=678da3a154a6 (Accessed: 24 September 2021).

Vanderbilt, A [@ashleyvanderbilt] (2021) '#mentalhealthmatters #ptsdawareness #leavingcult45 #mentalhealth #mentalhealthcrisis,' *TikTok* [Online Video]. Available at: www.tiktok.com/@notsurewhattoputhere/video/6935477471139630341?is_copy_url=1&is_from_webapp=v1&referer_url=https%3A%2F%2Fwww.businessinsider.com%2F&referer_video_id=6919975959353429253 (Accessed: 15 September 2021).

Vigdor, N (2020) 'Conway says the more violence erupts, "the better it is" for Trump's re-election prospects,' *The New York Times*, 27 August [Online]. Available at: www.nytimes.com/2020/08/27/us/elections/conway-says-the-more-violence-erupts-the-better-it-is-for-trumps-re-election-prospects.html (Accessed: 10 June 2021).

Walther, M (2021) 'The limits of LARPing,' *The Week*, 6 January [Online]. Available at: https://theweek.com/articles/959235/limits-larping (Accessed: 15 September 2021).

Webber Nicholsen, S (2002) *The love of nature and the end of the world: The unspoken dimensions of environmental concern*. Boston: MIT Press.

WWG1WGA [Where we go one we go all] (eds.) (2019) *QAnon: An invitation to the great awakening*. Dallas: Relentlessly Creative Books.

Zadronzny, B and Collins, B (2020a) 'Conservative activist family behind "grassroots" anti-quarantine Facebook events,' *NBC News*, 20 April [Online]. Available at: www.nbcnews.com/tech/social-media/conservative-activist-family-behind-grassroots-anti-quar antine-facebook-events-n1188021 (Accessed: 7 June 2020).

Zadronzny, B and Collins, B (2020b) 'Like the fringe conspiracy theory Qanon? There's plenty of merch for sale on Amazon,' *NBC News*, 18 June [Online]. Available at: www.nbcnews.com/business/business-news/fringe-conspiracy-theory-qanon-there-s-plenty-m erch-sale-amazon-n892561 (Accessed: 7 June 2020).

8

PERFORMANCE CRIME AND SELF-SURVEILLANT SUBJECTS IN THE CAPITOL RIOTS

Sandra Jeppesen

They have the appearance of reality. True crimes. As a form of true crime, performance crime takes this appearance of reality one step further—the real-life performers of crime intentionally document and share the moment of committing the crime, willfully or unwittingly providing evidence to be used against them through self-surveillance. They film, photograph, record, snap, tweet, share, post, parley, and otherwise provide traces of self-surveillant digital evidence of their own commission of crimes. The crime is performed only to be documented, shared, have an audience, receive applause, and thus yield the perpetrator notoriety and fame as the subject of the performance. The achievement of fame exceeds the enactment of the crime. The performance may not even be understood as a crime by the performer. In the extreme, the performer sees only the mediatization and not the crime, as in a recent case where two TikTok influencers filmed themselves robbing a bank for the fame and were surprised when charges were laid (BBC Tech, 2020). This form of self-surveillance was rampant at the Capitol riots which, I argue, is a quintessential example of performance crime. A self-surveillant subject loves performance crime, and performance crime loves a self-surveillant subject.

In performance crime, 'crimes are committed as part of a new media content production agenda aimed at recording and disseminating acts as a means of self-representation and promotion' (Surette, 2015, p. 196). The riots consisted of multiple concomitant but incohesive performances, many of which were criminalized, that played out on three types of stages. First, they took place on the *political stage* in a politics of contestation called for by outgoing President Donald Trump and supporters to stop an allegedly stolen election, with an undergirding politics of white supremacy, misogyny, xenophobia, and transphobia. Second, as observed in the previous chapter, following Goffman's theories, the riots played out on the *front stage of identity*, with identity performances of whiteness, white

DOI: 10.4324/9781003246862-11

supremacy, masculinity, femininity, military, historical and fictional figures, and so on. Third, they took place on what José Marichal (2013) calls the *digital front stage* of self-surveillant subjects on social media, which facilitates the performance, depiction, and dissemination of possible political selves. These are 'private performances that are socially mediated in ways that allow for large scale public consumption' (Surette, 2015, p. 199). While presenting images shot or live-streamed in real-time, the digital front stage is also a dramaturgical stage in which non-fiction events, disinformation, fake news, and other misrepresentations of the truth are constructed to appear real. Many of the rioters' performances may have been true performances, but many were also grounded in untruths.

In this chapter, we first consider riots as performance, followed by an analysis of three key mediatized performance types that played out that day—discursive, material, and political.

Performance Riot

Riots are arguably always performative. A protest march becomes a riot when the barricades protecting a state structure or other property or person(s) have been breached. As discussed in Chapter 1, 'The moment when the partisans of riot exceed the police capacity for management, when the cops make their first retreat, is the moment when the riot becomes fully itself' (Clover, 2016, p. 16). Thus, the riot is initiated with this performance of transgression.

In the mainstream media on January 6, we saw images of tug-of-wars between protesters and police, the former attempting to pull down the barricades and the latter tasked with preventing them. As inciting performance—or group of performances in several locations surrounding the Capitol—it was after the barricades fell that the intensity of the *performance riot* escalated.

Social movement scholars note that protests often produce a range of actions known as a repertoire of contention (Tarrow, 1993). Within this repertoire, participants choose actions and perform them in ways they think will best accomplish their objectives. These can be understood through a typology consisting of three types with increasing levels of action:

a   Low-action type: vigils, press releases, petitions (online and offline), festival-like marches, and speeches;
b   Medium-action type: civil disobedience, sit-ins, occupations, lockdowns, tree-sits, blockades, and protest camps—physical refusals that protect or claim symbolic spaces; and
c   High-action type: direct action, black bloc tactics, property destruction, barricade removal, and engagement with police.

Global justice activists labeled these three levels of action a 'diversity of tactics' within the repertoire of contention (Conway, 2003; Frazer, 2019; Hurl, 2005). Riots clearly fit into the high-action type as participants transgress some form of barricades in high-action inciting incidents. Riots may also include low- and medium-action types, but these do not define the riot. While not all direct actions are riotous (e.g., community gardens are a form of direct action), all riots are direct actions, with high levels of physical, performative, and communicative participation.

Communications scholars note the repertoire of contention is accompanied and accomplished by a repertoire of communication, a toolbox of communications strategies used to organize, coordinate, and communicate actions before, during, and after the protest (Mattoni, 2013). Paolo Gerbaudo (2012) refers to a choreography of assembly, what I call a *choreography of contention*, as activists use social media texts, photos, and videos to choreograph actions to achieve stated objectives. This choreography is undertaken by key action initiators who coordinate decision-making, develop and implement communication strategies, respond to police actions, and so on, according to a predictable script of contention (by participants) and criminalization (by police). Engaged in the choreography of contention, performance rioters become self-surveillant subjects, mediatizing key riotous moments.

Riot performance would be nothing without police violence. Police have a repertoire of riot policing mapped out in playbooks known as 'soft hat' or command and control, and 'hard hat' or the Miami model (Vitale, 2008). These models define performative police practices, including discrediting activists, preemptively arresting leaders (through social media surveillance), sowing conflict, infiltrating general assemblies, denying protest permits, and kettling, detaining, and arresting large numbers of participants. Weapons used include rubber bullets, tear gas, sonic booms, flashbangs, pepper spray, batons, tasers, and live ammunition. Police also use interpersonal engagements that include pain compliance holds, physical assault, and escalating violence. These actions can have injurious effects, up to and including death. The mediatized performances of police are considered further in Chapter 11.

The mediatized performance riots of January 6 played out in some predictable and some innovative ways. Rioters produced *discursive* disgruntlement, which led to *material* interventions with varying levels of *political* strategy—three types of performance riot mapped below.

Performance Riot Types

Three performance riot types played out at the Capitol. This analysis excludes the low-action participants, marchers who turned back at the barricades.

a   Discursive type: visual, textual, or auditory performances such as placards, signs, slogans, graffiti, costumes, hats, tattoos, and T-shirts, focusing predominantly on communicative action;

b   Material type: non-strategic performances of bravery that consist of material or physical interventions, uncoordinated and non-confrontational, such as occupiers, climbers, and thieves; and c Political type: strategic performances enact political objectives of insurrection, overthrowing the state, capturing politicians, and pre-empting democratic process.

Below we provide an analysis of specific cases of the three performance riot types (see Table 8.1), however, a comprehensive mapping of all performance riots at the Capitol that day is beyond our scope.

Discursive performance riot type

Once inside the Capitol building, discursive performance rioters made predominantly symbolic interventions. They did not engage in aggressive physical actions, nor did they seem to have a cohesive political objective beyond being there. Messages expressing specific ideologies were visible on flags, patches, hats, T-shirts, and tattoos representing QAnon, 1776, Oath Keepers, Three Percenters, Proud Boys, and so on, often linked to white supremacy. Many echoed Trump's disinformation campaign #stopthesteal, already amplified by the right-wing media apparatus to emerge as the regime of truth about the election—for some Americans. *New York Times* journalists suggest the insurrection was 'the culmination of a sustained assault by the president and his enablers on fact-based reality' (Barry et al., 2021). In the discursive performance riot type, non-fact-based discourses, conspiracies, and ideologies abound.

Discursive performance riot types fall into four sub-categories: shaman, truth-teller, historical re-enactor, and the Republican leadership.

The Shaman

Likely the most widely publicized image of the Capitol riots was the image of Jake Angeli, aka Jacob Chansley, aka the QAnon Shaman, discussed at length in Chapter 7. Key characteristics of this performance riot included:

TABLE 8.1 Discursive, Material, and Political Performance Riot Types

Performance riot types	Sub-types	Actions	Self-production of media
Discursive	The shaman Truth tellers and sloganeers Historical re-enactors Republican leadership	Communicative action through clothing, flags, placards, hats, expressing coded white supremacy	High
Material	Climbers Occupiers Thieves	Non-strategic performances of bravery to gain social capital	Medium
Political	Street fighters Insurrectionists	Breaking barricades, windows, fighting police, attempting to stop certification of election	Low

Source: Copyright Sandra Jeppesen.

a   sartorial signifiers of white supremacy and paganism such as the Norse tattoos prominently displayed on the chest;

b   visual signifiers of power conveyed through sharp objects such as the horns of the hat worn, and the sharpened 6-foot staff or spear;

c   ideological signifiers of patriotism and American mythologizing such as the John Bunyan-like fur hat, the American flag tied to the staff, the American flag iconography painted on the face, and the discursive signifier of screaming the word 'freedom'; and

d   the co-optation of Indigenous spiritual signifiers indicated by the use of 'shaman' and shamanistic claims.

While Chansley's was not the only shaman performance riot that day, the mainstream media has framed the Q Shaman as the Capitol riots' leading actor on the digital and identity front stage, despite the fact he played little to no role in organizing the riots and did not engage in aggressive action while in the Capitol. This media framing is arguably due to the vivid visual discursive signifiers, potentially qualifying him for the award of best-dressed rioter. At the same time, we must bear in mind his proximity and adherence—despite being now denounced—to the QAnon conspiracy, #stopthesteal disinformation, and patriot or white supremacy ideologies. There is a key photo of Proud Boy Dominic Pezzola (who broke the first window) with his arm around the Q Shaman inside the Capitol (NBC Chicago, 2021, photo 11).

Truth Tellers and Sloganeers

The overwhelming 'truth' conveyed by truther performance rioters was #stopthesteal, a discursive regime of truth demonstrating how false ideas can yield material consequences. For Michel Foucault (1978), a regime of truth consists of the powerful insistent circulation of a set of ideological notions that, although mostly false, are widely held to be true. The circulation of a constellation of false ideas as the truth serves an ideological function invisible to those who believe it, with material influence on their lives. It also typically supports a regime of political power. The #stopthesteal discourse, patently untrue, circulated prior to and during the Capitol riots in social media, conservative mainstream media, and alt-right media as a regime of truth. The denunciation of this regime of truth as a lie in democratic or liberal mainstream media served only to reinforce the truthiness of the claim for those believing it.

The #stopthesteal performance riots were accompanied by overt white supremacist discourses that, among others (see Figure 8.1), included:

a   the white power OK hand gesture used by the Proud Boys and other white supremacist groups (Washington Post Staff, 2021);

b   the Confederate flag used by white supremacists, including the KKK, and the Betsy Ross Flag, an 'early design of the US flag [that] has been co-opted by some white supremacist groups to idolize a time when women and people of color had no power' (Washington Post Staff, 2021);

c   the Three (or III) Percenters, an anti-government 'far-right militia group' (Barry et al., 2021) of self-designated patriots, that references the percentage of people it is believed to have fought in the revolutionary war against the British (Washington Post Staff, 2021);

d   1776 memorabilia such as the message propagated by Republican Marjorie Taylor Greene that January 6 would be the 'Republicans' "1776 moment"' (Washington Post Staff, 2021), with some participants wearing T-shirts reading 'MAGA Civil War January 6, 2021' or "Keep America Great" (George-Parkin, 2021);

e   'Don't Tread on Me' images and the Gadsden Flag, featuring a threatening rattlesnake, now considered symbols of white supremacy, often used by gun-rights and limited-government libertarians (Walker, 2016); and

f   rioters shouting 'the N word' at Black police officers while physically assaulting them (Wagner et al., 2021).

White supremacy is thus a predominant discourse among truther performance rioters that bears further analysis. Robert Pape (2021, para. 4) has found, in a

FIGURE 8.1 Discourses, flags, banners, T-shirts, and hats with historical and contemporary white supremacist iconography

Source: Wikimedia Commons, CC BY-SA 4.0, by TapTheForwardAssist https://commons. wikimedia.org/wiki/File:DC_Capitol_Storming_IMG_7958.jpg.

preliminary analysis of the first 377 arrestees (now over 700), that they are 95% white. The rate of insurrectionary participation or rioting among arrestees is higher in American counties where the percentage white population is in decline. As Pape (2021, para. 6) has found, 'Counties with the most significant declines in the non-Hispanic White population are the most likely to produce insurrectionists who now face charges.' Statistically speaking, Pape's (2021, para. 9):

> Analysis of the 250 counties where those charged or arrested live reveals that the counties that had the greatest decline in white population had an 18 percent chance of sending an insurrectionist to D.C., while the counties that saw the least decline in the white population had only a 3 percent chance.

The rioters arguably experienced the demographic shift as evidence of the Great Replacement Theory (GRT). Like #stopthesteal, the key issue with GRT is not just its truthiness but also its xenophobic, white supremacist scaffolding.

While the truther sartorial discourses expressed historical mythologizing and white supremacy, slogans and chants in selfie videos included levels of aggression from cursing to death threats. Performance rioters chanted 'Take the Capitol' or declared 'DC is a motherfuckin' war zone!' Oath Keepers filmed themselves yelling, 'We're in the fucking Capitol!' and 'In the Capitol, overran the Capitol!' Other selfie videos pronounced, 'Here we come Nancy … you fucking bitch,' a gendered physical threat. Yet others demanded 'Hang Mike Pence!' a death threat backed up by the material object of a hangman's scaffold erected on the Capitol grounds. Rioters photographed themselves beside graffiti that said 'Murder the Media' (Khavin et al., 2021), purportedly the name of a citizen journalism outlet, whose members include the leader of the Hawaii Proud Boys (Jankowicz, 2021).

The dominant white supremacist visual, textual, and sartorial discourses conveyed through aggressive selfie audio and video messaging constructed an overarching discursive field of a violent hypermasculine white supremacy intent on interrupting the peaceful transition of power, propelled to action through false discursive regimes of truth, and promoting insurrectionary (white) patriotism against the alleged Great Replacement.

Historical Re-enactors

Much of the white supremacist discursive regime hearkens back to a nostalgia for the wild west—and extremely racist and colonial—roots of America. The historical aspects of the 1776 memorabilia, the Confederate and Gadsden flags, and the imagining of January 6, 2021 as a Republican revolution were supported by many other costumes and outfits beyond participants' self-representations. Truther performance rioters participated in the riots while wearing full-fledged costumes of ideologically connected, mythologized American patriotic figures. These included several George Washingtons, a Lady Liberty, an Uncle Sam, and even a Captain America filmed literally climbing the Capitol building. The historical re-enactors, linked to the MAGA Civil War discourse, underlined the visual and textual discursive slogans. They romanticized historical moments through American national symbols and characters alluding to the past, attempting to rewrite (or prewrite) the contemporary historical moment of the riots, framing it as a revolutionary action that might remake 1776 and rebirth America.

Interestingly, only one of the costumes worn by the performance rioters was that of a real historical figure—George Washington. The historicity of the historical re-enactments can thus be called into question, as the sartorial signifiers reference a perceived symbolic power rather than real historical events.

Republican Leadership

Perhaps the most powerful—and most alarming—discursive interventions came not from the performance rioters themselves but from the Republican social and political leadership. While not having physically transgressed the barricades, some have been shown to have contributed to the discursive incitement to riot (Wagner et al., 2021).

Donald Trump's lawyer Rudy Giuliani at a speech given at Donald Trump's 'Save America' rally on January 6, 2021, said that since they had lost legal challenges to the election results, 'let's have trial by combat' (Giuliani, 2021). Steve Bannon, Trump's former political strategist, declared on his January 5th podcast that on January 6th, 'all hell is going to break loose,' a phrase he repeated twice for emphasis (Evon, 2021). In his own 'Save America' speech, Trump constantly reiterated the regime of truth of #stopthesteal, urging supporters to show strength, march to the Capitol, and 'fight like hell' (Trump as cited in Naylor, 2021). During the riots, he refused to denounce the rioters, instead delaying his response and eventually sharing messages of approval and even 'love.' Similarly, in the first Presidential debate on September 29, 2020, Trump refused to denounce white supremacists when asked directly, instead saying, 'Proud Boys stand back and stand by' (Frenkel and Karni, 2020). These statements arguably emboldened not just the Proud Boys but many rioters who repeatedly claimed in their altercations with police on January 6th, 'I was invited here by the President' or 'Trump sent me' (Khavin et al., 2021).

The multiple, consistent incitements to violence by many powerful Republicans are currently being downplayed by Trump backers, along with the egregiousness of the violence itself. Representative Andrew Clyde, photographed barricading a door during the riots, now claims the rioters' actions were like 'a normal tourist visit' (Shammas, 2021). And Giuliani claims he was alluding to *Game of Thrones* (Durkee, 2021), therefore his 'comment was not a call to violence' and 'incited no violent response' (Crump, 2021). Middlebury College in Vermont has revoked Giuliani's honorary degree for 'fomenting the violent uprising against our nation's Capitol' (Crump, 2021). These denials of incitement to violence, however, erase neither the incitements nor the violence: the fact remains that five people died violently that day.

Thus, while historical re-enactors were basing their performance riots on myths and legends rather than actual history, politicians are attempting to rewrite history and elude accountability by creating their own myths and legends. The digital media recorded that day is being used evidentiarily to hold rioters accountable, but it remains to be seen whether the same accountability will befall the powerful.

Material Performance Riot Type

Material performance rioters, we argue, made non-instrumental interventions at the Capitol. In her participatory study of the squatter movement in Amsterdam, Nazima Kadir (2016, p. 65) noted the importance of 'non-instrumental acts of bravery' in which participants took incredible material actions that had however no strategic objective, demonstrating 'the skill of acting courageously during direct actions [which] is mainly symbolic and has almost no functional practicality' (Kadir, 2016, p. 65). These actions involved great risk to the participant,

FIGURE 8.2 Tweet by Ava DuVernay, capturing climbers, occupiers, and thieves
Source: Copyright iowyth hezel ulthiin, ulthiin's impression of the original tweet (DuVernay, 2021).

including arrest or police violence, and generated great credibility for participants, despite not making a strategic contribution. Indeed, 'the very lack of strategic practicality of an act of bravery constructs it as more honest, and ergo reflects the deeply held convictions of the activist who performs' it (Kadir, 2016, p. 66). In the Capitol riots, we see highly mediatized predominantly non-instrumental acts of bravery manifest as three key material performance types: climbers, occupiers, and thieves, captured nicely in a composite tweet by *Selma* film director, Ava DuVernay, drawing attention to Trump's controversial tweet (see Figure 8.2).

Climbers

A surprising number of riot participants took it upon themselves to attempt to scale the wall constituting the West (Senate) side of the building. Participants on the ground are depicted in mainstream media taking selfies with climbing performance rioters in the background, transforming the Capitol building into a gym climbing wall with its evenly spaced hand and footholds (Jason Andrew in Paybarah and Lewis, 2021). Some climbers repurposed barricades (referred to incorrectly as 'bike stands' in mainstream media) as ladders, placing them sideways against the wall.

FIGURE 8.3 A climber inside the Capitol building carrying a backpack and wearing a helmet, climbing over and repelling down the wall from the balcony above the Senate floor

Source: Copyright iowyth hezel ulthiin, ulthiin's impression of original photo by Win McNamee, 'A man hanging from the balcony in the Senate chamber'.

The climbers, some, we recall, with police and military training, seemed adept at moving vertically across architectural environments, similar to parkour. Parkour, also known as freerunning, was originally used by the French military and is now an urban sport in which participants move quickly through built environments, using obstacles in their path to propel them through the landscape (Atkinson, 2009). The climber performance rioters mimicked parkour moves, both inside and outside the Capitol building (see Figure 8.3). On the outside, for example, there is a photo of a climber in a Captain America costume accompanied by someone in a leopard print fleece jacket, integrating discursive into material performances. Inside, there is a photo of a parkour climber hanging above the Senate floor, having climbed up and thrown himself over the balcony wall (McNamee, 2021).

These climbing actions are non-instrumental acts of bravery undertaken by unorganized participants with no political objectives. They are climbing from an outdoor location to a secondary outdoor location exterior to the Capitol building, thus their vertical ingress does not readily provide admission to the building. They seem to be climbing—and filming it—as part of the spectacle of the riot, achieving a non-strategic expression of physical prowess and domination over the Capitol building itself. These are therefore non-instrumental acts of bravery that make good photos, generating social capital for the participants despite being politically incoherent and providing no direct ingress into the Capitol. Most people took the stairs.

Occupiers

Occupiers are the third group of material performance rioters depicted committing non-instrumental acts of bravery. Attempting to locate lawmakers, finding offices abandoned, occupiers sat in chairs, ate food, read papers, put their feet up on desks, and wrote threatening messages, documenting this on social media. The occupation of offices had no strategic advantage, but nonetheless, these performances, like those of the climbers, were widely mediatized, creating social capital for participants.

Perhaps the most mediatized of these was the occupation of Nancy Pelosi's aide's office by 60-year-old Arkansas man Richard Barnett, now charged with a federal crime (Barry et al., 2021). Barnett had draped his American flag over the filing cabinet, taken a seat in what he thought was Pelosi's chair (actually that of an aide), had his phone out, and one booted foot up on the desk (see Figure 8.4). Photos of him holding an envelope removed from her office appeared in social and mainstream media alike, linking occupiers to thieves and demonstrating the permeability of these groups and types.

Another image of occupier performance rioters features several of them occupying the Senate dais, including the QAnon Shaman (performing both discursive and material acts), cell phones at the ready, used to document their acts, becoming self-surveillant subjects through instantaneous mediatization.

FIGURE 8.4 Richard Barnett occupies Nancy Pelosi's aide's desk
Source: Photo by Saul Loeb/AFP via Getty Images.

Thieves

Another popular photo of the riots was taken by photographer Win McNamee of a gleeful Adam Johnson making off with Nancy Pelosi's lectern (Acevedo, 2021). Wearing a Trump toque and scarf, with shoulder-length reddish hair and a short beard, Johnson pauses to wave at McNamee with a mischievous smile (see Figure 6.3). While this may be the most famous theft that occurred that day, material performance rioters engaged in theft ran rampant, producing a stream of self-surveillant photos of office ransackings (Khavin et al., 2021). A female rioter carrying an American flag over her shoulder is shown in the January 6th rundown in the *New York Times* carrying a broken sign that clearly reads, 'Speaker of the House Nancy Pelosi,' which was 'taken as a trophy' (Levenson, 2021). Another female rioter, 22-year-old Riley June Williams, has been arrested for allegedly removing or assisting in the removal of Pelosi's laptop (Moghe, 2021). Apparently, 'anything taken from Speaker Nancy Pelosi's office was especially popular with the crowd' (Rosenberg, 2021), illustrating how thieves gained social capital, with one rioter boasting about how popular he had become on his dating app, which 'blew up' after participating in the riots.

The theft of these items, stolen from not just Pelosi's office but throughout the Capitol building, was widely documented and shared on social media. Theft of politically symbolic materials was a non-instrumental act of bravery that did not lead to the accomplishment of strategic political objectives, but did result in the increase in social capital for the rioters, whether the attention was positive (more dates) or negative (arrest).

The symbolic action of taking trophies signifies the political commitment of the rioters. Kadir argues that 'acts of bravery visually perform a genuine and non-instrumental conviction quickly and dramatically' (Kadir, 2016, p. 65), creating an appearance of authentic political commitment with neither the long-term demonstration of political skills nor the short-term accomplishment of political objectives. If indeed the political objective was to apprehend Pelosi, the performance rioter-thieves instead apprehended signifiers of her power.

In sum, rather than engaging in political riots, the riotous performances of climbers, occupiers, and thieves are based on roles derived from social media discourse that then took place in a real-world space, performances which were then filmed and re-inserted into the social media space. The front stage identitarian and digital performances of social media materialized in the material world, as participants engaged in Bakhtinian carnivalesque performances transgressing even their own normative social behaviors of everyday life—a fact many have articulated in their legal defense. While highly mediatized for 'riot points' or riot-based social capital, these performances did not achieve any political objectives.

Political Performance Type

The political performance rioters, on the other hand, performed instrumental acts with strategic objectives allegedly coordinated by militia groups and white nationalist gangs, who constituted ten percent of the initial 377 arrested (Pape and Ruby, 2021). They planned and engaged in riot performances with political objectives, predominantly communicating on Parler, Zello, and walkie-talkies, as street fighters and insurrectionists.

Street Fighters

The Proud Boys, a group of white ethnonationalists and neofascists (Barry et al., 2021) whose everyday group tactics typically include street fighting, marched together to the Capitol building in a small but growing crowd of (mostly) men, numbering in the hundreds.

In the mainstream media and selfie videos of the day, they can be seen leading the onslaught on the barricades, fighting police in hand-to-hand combat. At many geographical points and chronological times, they can be seen attacking various police lines with mace, pepper spray, bear spray, tasers, a metal whip, hockey sticks, and large wooden sticks brought with them, as well as objects of opportunity found on-site such as fire extinguishers, the barricades themselves, and so on (FBI, 2021; The New York Times, 2021). Many wore gas masks to protect against police deployment of tear gas and pepper spray, as well as their own use of aerosol irritants against the police. Street fighters engaged in 2–6 hours of fighting with police at various barricades and building entry points (FBI, 2021; The New York Times, 2021), injuring at least 140 officers (Jackman, 2021), one of whom died that day. Brian Sicknik was sprayed with bear spray that brought on a fatal stroke. It was allegedly also Proud Boys who confronted mainstream journalists and destroyed their equipment, forcing them to retreat and report at a distance from the Capitol (Nicholson, 2021). While the Proud Boys led the street fighting performance rioters, they were joined by militia groups such as the Oath Keepers and Three Percenters, as well as many unaffiliated participants who showed up alone or with a friend or two. These unorganized people comprised approximately 90% of the mob of 800 who breached the Capitol (Pape and Ruby, 2021).

According to the New York Times video investigations (2021), the Proud Boys contingent, including unaffiliated followers, fought several hours to remove barricades on the West side of the Capitol. In the video, a group then departs the West side and moves to the East side, taking down a largely unpoliced section of barricade there. Massive groups then surged toward the building on all sides. The street fighter performance rioters had the strategic objective to break through the barricades and approach and eventually breach the building, which they accomplished by performances that created opportunities for protesters—not yet rioters—to join them.

Insurrectionists

The moment at which the crowd breaches the building through a broken window was shown repeatedly on mainstream media and distributed widely on social media. In the video, you can see a group of men dressed in militia fatigues

FIGURE 8.5 Smashing a window, Dominic Pezzola of the Proud Boys is the first to breach the Capitol building

Source: Court documents, Public domain, via https://www.democratandchronicle.com/story/news/2021/02/10/dominic-pezzola-rochester-ny-charged-in-capitol-riot-said-he-was-duped-by-trump/4361809001/.

and helmets, carrying backpacks and gear. One participant with shoulder-length salt and pepper hair repeatedly hits the window with a police shield, soon breaking it out. This person is Proud Boy Dominic Pezzola (Khavin et al., 2021). Adjacent reinforced windows are broken with a limited shattering of glass, and the remaining segments removed (see Figure 8.5). Very quickly, several people climb through the windows—the first breach of the day. Police inside run toward the window, but stop short, not taking any action to block the window or prevent further ingress. The first few rioters in the building smash open locked doors from the inside, letting in hundreds of people amassed outside the doors.

A group soon attempts to breach into the House Chamber, slower to evacuate than the Senate. This also happens through breaking a window which is smashed out by a rioter repeatedly pounding it with his fist, wearing a helmet like a glove. As the window is repeatedly hit, a rioter says, 'He's got a gun,' pointing out that an officer inside the House Chamber has a gun trained on them. The first person through the broken window is Ashli Babbit, helped up by two of her male co-participants. Babbit is immediately shot in the shoulder and falls backward into the hallway. Many lawmakers still in the House are quickly escorted out a side door. The smashing of windows to achieve ingress has the express insurrectionist objective of intervening against the democratic process of certifying President Joe Biden's election win. Many organizers used the term 'insurrection' on Parler, discussing ways in which they would violently overthrow the government.

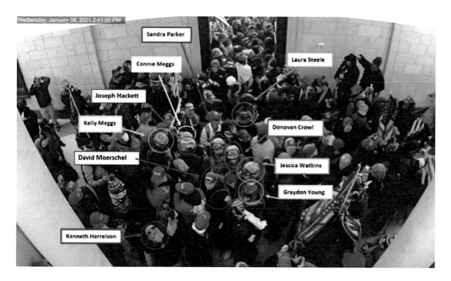

FIGURE 8.6 Ten Oath Keepers inside Capitol building identified in surveillance footage
Source: United States Department of Justice, U.S. v David Moerschel complaint via https://www.wa shingtonpost.com/context/u-s-v-david-moerschel-complaint/0b66dc72-2f54-49e3-931f-c b41e0cfdf03/.

Insurrectionist performance rioters also included members of the Oath Keepers seen in video footage moving to the front of the crowd in a military formation called a 'stack,' a line of people one behind the other, one hand on the shoulder of the person in front. They are outfitted as militia, wearing flak jackets, military pants, camo hats and helmets, and carrying gear in backpacks (see Figure 8.6). They used walkie-talkie radios on an open channel, plus the communications push-to-talk walkie-talkie app Zello. Many attempted not to be photographed and took fewer selfies or selfie-videos than the discursive and material performance rioters, avoiding widespread discoverability through self-surveillance, and maintaining communications among a select group on their channel. The Department of Justice has charged at least sixteen defendants from the Oath Keepers in a seditious conspiracy case (Department of Justice, 2021), including Oath Keepers leader Stewart Rhodes.

The various political performance rioters engaged in insurrection seem to have coordinated in advance with a clear political objective of using physical means to enter the building to prevent certification or #stopthesteal through fighting (Trump's word) or combat (Giuliani's word), an act characterized by Pape and Ruby (2021) as 'political violence.'

Finally, the discursive, material, and political types of performance rioters did not act separately, nor were their actions mutually exclusive. The question remains regarding whether their actions were criminal.

Riot as Crime

Riots are political activities that have been criminalized, with conspiring, organizing, and leading riots seen as more egregious in the eyes of the law than following or participating in a riot. Riots often occur through planning and coordination by a small number of people who mobilize a much larger number of people to follow their lead, getting caught up in the action. Most people who participate in riots do not set out to do so but later discover that participating in a protest that shifts from low-action to high-action is considered rioting by the criminal justice system.

There are some key distinctions we must first make in our negotiation of the concept of riots as a crime. We do not necessarily take the side of the state in criminalizing riots, nor do we condemn riots as political events, as these have long had their place on the political stage in times of political upheaval, including insurrections, uprisings, revolutions, and so on. These political actions are all part and parcel of the ongoing historical process of state formation, reformation, and revolution. To condemn riots would be to stand on the side of the powerful who have outlawed them in order to safeguard that very power. Riots are often the last energetic outpouring of the disenfranchised who cannot stand the oppression one minute longer, as we know from historical analyses of riots and revolutions (Badiou, 2012; Clover, 2016; Fanon, 2007).

We also challenge and deconstruct the binary violent/non-violent protesters, which characterizes marches, vigils, and speeches as peaceful and appropriate political actions, while denouncing civil disobedience, direct action, and riots as violent and thus inappropriate. First, the state typically uses the violent/non-violent protester binary to condemn the most vociferous protesters who are labeled violent to delegitimize their political claims and to privilege non-violent or passive actions. However, on the one hand, non-violent movements tend to protect the state, which is why they are condoned by the state (Gelderloos, 2007). And on the other hand, violent, direct action or civil disobedience actions often are more successful at achieving their political objectives. Thus, some activists might privilege high-action events, reversing the binary to counter state power. But if we are to fully deconstruct the binary, we can see that non-violent actions may contain violence, and violent actions may contain non-violent elements. Repertoires of contention do not fall easily into this binary structure but may fall into many different types of action along a spectrum. Moreover, the spectrum of citizen actions is cooperative rather than competitive; rather than claiming one type as superior (competitive), all action types can support each other (cooperative). Therefore, in deconstructing this binary, which serves the state, we can understand the important complexities of civic actions in staking claims against the state.

A theory of protest must delineate without judgment the spectrum of political citizen action. Political tactics for social transformation up to and including revolution should not be judged by the groups that engage in them. Protesters emerge from all political spectrums, but it is the politics of the protesters—not their tactics—that should be judged on their own grounds. We must therefore separate the white supremacist politics of the Capitol rioters from their chosen political tactics. We condemn white supremacy but neither condemn nor condone riots. Rather we support the right to protest in a free democracy, as well as the right to push the limits of protest, contesting not just corrupt governments but also government control over citizen tactics to contest corrupt governments. If the state is an authoritarian institution, that authority must be called into question, especially regarding the criminalization of dissent. Therefore, rather than take a side regarding riots, in this book we are analyzing the mediatization of the riots and the role digital media have played in constructing multiple complex meanings.

What is clear is that the rioters have been criminalized, with nearly 600 arrestees and further investigations underway. Many participants face common charges such as 'parading, demonstrating or picketing in a Capitol building,' 'obstruction of an official proceeding,' assaulting or obstructing a police officer, disorderly conduct, and so on. Others face serious charges such as conspiracy, reserved for key members of the Oath Keepers and the Proud Boys (Department of Justice, 2021; Hall et al., 2021). All of these charges are backed up by extensive video and photographic evidence, such that *Insider* journalist Madison Hall and colleagues (2021) call the riots 'one of the most documented crimes in US history.'

The Capitol Riots as Performance Crime

Having established the Capitol rioters as engaged in both performances and crimes, we turn to an analysis of *performance crime*. Performance crime is defined as the commission of a crime that includes, as part of its foundational invention, the filming and online sharing of the crime's commission. Contemporary performance crime is generative of its own social media audience, availing itself of the affordances of discoverability and virality. Performance crime is situated in cultural criminology at the crossroads of criminology and media studies. Cultural criminology considers not just the legal repercussions or social causes of crime but also the ways in which crime is constructed by and constructs particular cultural and media formations. For Majid Yar (2012, p. 248), an integral element of cultural criminology is the exploration of 'the mass media's role in constructing the reality of crime and deviance, and in generating new forms of social and legal control.'

Performance crimes are performed specifically with audiences in mind, with terrorist acts as one of the predominant categories throughout history (Surette, 2015). With social media, however, the crime performer has direct access to an audience, no longer constrained by mainstream media gatekeeping. '"Performances" are no longer rare events that are place and time bound to physical stages and scheduled broadcasts; they are now ephemeral renditions constantly created and repeatedly distributed in millions of social media interactions' (Surette, 2015, p. 197). Performers may be unwillingly captured on film and their images disseminated widely; they may also be unwittingly performing a crime, perhaps without realizing the seriousness or consequences of their actions (Surette, 2015, p. 196). Clearly, a key dimension of the performance of the Capitol riots was their mediatization, therefore, we argue it constitutes a mass performance crime.

Within social media performance crime, live streaming video is the genre of choice. Beall, Chen, and Terlip (2020, p. 146) argue that 'live streaming crimes represent the most controversial activities among all antisocial activities live streamed.' Live-streamed performance crimes tend to be based in oppression and hatred—misogyny, Islamophobia, and so on. An example of misogyny was Involuntary Celibate (InCel) Elliott Rodger, who live-streamed misogynist attacks on women. An example of racist Islamophobia was the New Zealand mosque shooter who live-streamed the killing of over 50 people on Twitch as if it were a video game (Mazer, 2020).

In the Capitol riots, the axis of oppression is white supremacy. Many participants live-streamed videos on social media platforms. 'However, unlike radio and television broadcasting, which are regulated … live streaming is not. Without any legal binding, live streaming is open to free-wheeling uses and misuses by social media users' (Beall et al., 2020, p. 145). Therefore, Capitol riot live streamers, in an unregulated context of media production and dissemination, gained access to an immediate synchronized audience. They could see how many people were logged onto their stream, and audience members could instantly respond with emojis, providing an interactive dimension. These interactions tend to resemble or have the look and feel, Beall et al. (2020) argue, of face-to-face interactions and communications due to their immediacy. While many scholars have considered the importance of live streaming protest in order to curb or document police brutality and to provide authentic reportage from within protests (Kumanyika,

2016; Thorburn, 2014), few have considered the complex prospect of live-streaming riots in which mass performance crimes are arguably committed.

It appears that, in the Capitol riots, increasing levels of intensity of action were most often paired with decreasing levels of self-mediatization. The more political their objectives and actions, the less likely participants were to live-stream those actions. This was at least partially because they had their hands too full to pull out a phone/camera, as they were moving in stack formations, tug-of-warring over barricades, banging down doors, smashing windows, and so on. In other words, the more self-surveillant mediatization of performances, the less participation in instrumental political acts of insurrection including the transgression of the barricades. Video was captured by those participating in low-action protest, using Go-Pros or equivalent technologies that captured video from the participants' points of view (POV). Video was also shot using reverse camera streaming, capturing the face and often words of the camera's user and the background events behind them. Much of the performance crime video live stream did not tend to show the most physical or high-action crimes, such as hand-to-hand combat with police.

Rather, mainstream and social media audiences on January 6th predominantly consumed performances of a) the discursive and b) the material types of rioters but not c) the political performance types who were attempting, by many accounts, to stage a coup, fighting cops with weapons and smashing their way into the Capitol. This means that the mainstream audience received a false impression of the riots as being predominantly low-action protests and people milling about in the rotunda.

The mainstream media also conveyed a false impression that not much policing was happening. This resulted in social media feeds and memes comparing the Capitol riots policing to the policing of Black Lives Matter. In images the audience had access to early on, the police were in retreat, let rioters pass by without much struggle, seemed in a state of disarray, did not have on riot gear, and were generally depicted as underprepared and non-confrontational.

However, the truth of the policing situation on January 6th is more complex than the limited image system available to us that day. The Capitol Police efforts were focused on keeping the rioters out of the Senate and the House, and later, out of the secret location, accessed through tunnels, where the lawmakers were sequestered for their safety. The police interactions with rioters at many places of ingress into the Capitol buildings were intense, on-going and long-lasting— upwards of six hours of pitched battles in some places—where officers engaged in hand-to-hand combat, some were dragged from the crowd and beaten violently, and over 140 officers suffered injuries and were hospitalized. One officer, Brian Sicknick, was sprayed with bear spray, which resulted in a stroke and subsequent death. Moreover, there were several police forces deployed that day, from the Capitol Police and Secret Police to the Washington DC municipal police, the FBI, and eventually when Mike Pence called them in, the National Guard, although there was an apparent breakdown in communications among the various police forces (Khavin et al., 2021). The policing of the riots is discussed in further detail in by Chenjerai Kumanyika in Chapter 11.

The performance crimes of the Capitol rioters are fairly complex, tending to fall into two categories: those committing crimes knowingly while live-streaming or posing for photos and those committing crimes unwittingly while live-streaming or posing for photos. A third group of those engaged in performance riots are those who were committing crimes knowingly while attempting to remain out of the camera's eye but who were unwittingly captured on film. This last group, however, is not considered performance crime as the mediatization of their actions was not part of their plan.

Conclusions

Despite the outpouring of performance crime images from January 6, 2021, many events were not filmed by the rioters. Self-surveillant images on social media have been supplemented in investigations by photos and video from professional journalists, police body-worn cameras, and surveillance cameras used to fill evidentiary gaps (FBI, 2021). These different sources of images remind us that the camera does not depict reality but frames and constructs a narrative. Something important is always outside the frame, omitted from the narrative of history.

Two paradoxes in the constructed relationship between mediatization and power arise. First, the most self-mediatized performances tended to be the least political, and vice versa, calling into question the cultural politics of the intentional invisibility of anti-surveillant subjects in an era of compulsive visibility. Second, Donald Trump, as a high-profile self-surveillant subject, promoted widely mediatized incitements to violence, with the question remaining whether his words and actions constitute a performance crime at the highest level, hidden in plain sight.

The many parallel, paradoxical and contradictory mediatized narratives of the Capitol riots are a new type of collective performance crime. While the pitched battle of January 6 is long over, the battle for the truth continues to play out in the digital mediascape. It is this battle that will shape the future of American democracy.

References

Acevedo, N (2021) 'Man Pictured Carrying Away Pelosi's Lectern, Two Others Charged in Capitol Riot,' *NBC News*, 9 January [Online]. Available at: www.nbcnews.com/news/us-news/man-pictured-carrying-pelosi-s-lectern-during-capitol-riot-arrested-n1253628 (Accessed: 23 September 2021).

Atkinson, M (2009) 'Parkour, anarcho-environmentalism, and poiesis,' *Journal of Sport and Social Issues*, 33(2). https://doi.org/10.1177/0193723509332582.

Badiou, A (2012) *The rebirth of history: Times of riots and uprisings.* London UK: Verso.

Barry, D, McIntire, M and Rosenberg, M (2021) '"Our President Wants Us Here": The Mob That Stormed the Capitol,' *The New York Times*, 9 January [Online]. Available at: www.nytimes.com/2021/01/09/us/capitol-rioters.html (Accessed: 23 September 2021).

BBC Tech (2020) 'TikTok Twins Charged Over Bank Robbery "Prank,"' *BBC News*, 6 August [Online]. Available at: www.bbc.com/news/technology-53681018 (Accessed: 23 September 2021).

Beall, ML, Chen, S-LS and Terlip, L (2020) 'You can doesn't mean you should: The rationale and ethics of live streaming crimes,' in Chen, S-LS, Chen, ZJ and Allaire N (eds.) *Legal and ethical issues of live streaming*. Lanham, MD: Rowman & Littlefield, pp. 145–156.

Broadwater, L and Fandos, N (2021) '"A Hit Man Sent Them." Police at the Capitol Recount the Horrors of Jan. 6 As the Inquiry Begins,' *The New York Times*, 27 July [Online]. Available at: www.nytimes.com/2021/07/27/us/jan-6-inquiry.html (Accessed: 23 September 2021).

Clover, J (2016) *Riot. Strike. Riot: The new era of uprisings*. London, UK: Verso.

CoEqual (n.d.) 'An oral history of the January 6th insurrection' [Online]. Available at: www.co-equal.org/jan-6 (Accessed: 13 August 2021).

Conway, J (2003) 'Civil resistance and the diversity of tactics in the anti-globalization movement: Problems of violence, silence, and solidarity in activist politics,' *Osgoode Hall Law Journal*, 41(2), 505–530.

Crump, J (2021) 'Giuliani Bizarrely Claims "Trial by Combat" Comments at MAGA Capitol Rally Were a Reference to Game of Thrones,' *The Independent*, 13 January [Online]. Available at: www.independent.co.uk/news/world/americas/us-politics/rudy-giuliani-rally-game-of-thrones-b1786613.html (Accessed: 23 September 2021).

Department of Justice (2021) 'Four Arrested in Sixteen-Defendant Oath Keeper Conspiracy Case for Activities Leading to US Capitol Breach,' June 3. [Online]. Available at: www.justice.gov/usao-dc/pr/four-arrested-sixteen-defendant-oath-keeper-conspiracy-case-activities-leading-us-capitol (Accessed: 24 August 2021).

Durkee, A (2021) 'Giuliani Claims His Call For "Trial By Combat" On Jan. 6 Shouldn't Have Been Taken Literally As Legal Woes Mount,' *Forbes*, 18 May [Online]. Available at: www.forbes.com/sites/alisondurkee/2021/05/18/giuliani-claims-his-call-for-trial-by-combat-on-jan-6-shouldnt-have-been-taken-literally-as-legal-woes-mount/ (Accessed: 23 September 2021).

DuVernay, A (2021) 'I know your pain,' 6 January [Twitter]. Available at: https://twitter.com/ava/status/1346938170156445699?lang=en (Accessed: 24 September 2021).

Evon, D (2021) 'Did Bannon Say "All Hell Is Going To Break Loose" Before Capitol Attack?' *Snopes*, 29 July [Online]. Available at: www.snopes.com/fact-check/bannon-hell-capitol-attack/ (Accessed: 24 September 2021).

Fanon, F (2007) *The wretched of the Earth*. New York: Grove Atlantic.

FBI (2021) 'Capitol violence' [Online]. Available at: www.fbi.gov/wanted/capitol-violence (Accessed: 24 September 2021).

Foucault, M (1978) *The history of sexuality*. New York: Pantheon.

Frazer, E J (2019) 'The diversity of tactics: Anarchism and political power,' *European Journal of Political Theory*, 18(4). https://doi.org/10.1177/1474885115627558.

Frenkel, S and Karni, A (2020) 'Proud Boys Celebrate Trump's "Stand By" Remark About Them at the Debate,' *The New York Times*, 29 September [Online]. Available at: www.nytimes.com/2020/09/29/us/trump-proud-boys-biden.html (Accessed: 24 September 2021).

Gelderloos, P (2007) *How nonviolence protects the State*. Cambridge, MA: South End Press.

George-Parkin, H (2021) 'Insurrection Merch Shows Just How Mainstream Extremism Has Become,' *Vox*, 12 January [Online]. Available at: www.vox.com/the-goods/22225538/capitol-insurrection-riot-sweatshirts-hats (Accessed: 24 September 2021).

Gerbaudo, P (2012) *Tweets and the streets: Social media and contemporary activism*. London UK: Pluto Press.

Giuliani, R (2021) 'Rudy Giuliani Speech Transcript at Trump's Washington, DC Rally: Wants "Trial by Combat",' *Rev*, 1 June [Online]. Available at: www.rev.com/blog/transcripts/rudy-giuliani-speech-transcript-at-trumps-washington-d-c-rally-wants-trial-by-combat (Accessed: 3 June 2021).

Hall, M, Gould, S, Harrington, R, Shamsian, J, Haroun, A, Ardrey, T and Snodgrass, E (2021) '591 People Have Been Charged in the Capitol Insurrection So Far. This Searchable Table Shows Them All,' *Insider*, 27 July [Online]. Available at: www.insider.com/all-the-us-cap itol-pro-trump-riot-arrests-charges-names-2021-1 (Accessed: 24 September 2021).

Hurl, C (2005) *Diversity of tactics: Coalescing new combinations*. Vancouver: UBC Press.

Jackman, T (2021) 'Police Union Says 140 Officers Injured in Capitol Riot,' *Washington Post*, 27 January [Online]. Available at: www.washingtonpost.com/local/public-safety/p olice-union-says-140-officers-injured-in-capitol-riot/2021/01/27/60743642-60e2-11eb-9430-e7c77b5b0297_story.html (Accessed: 24 September 2021).

Jankowicz, M (2021) '2 Men Who Posed with "Murder the Media" Scrawled on a Capitol Door Say They Were Just There to Report for Their Outlet, Murder the Media,' *Business Insider*, 14 January [Online]. Available at: www.businessinsider.com/capitol-riot-men-p osing-with-murder-the-media-claim-reporters-2021-1 (Accessed: 24 September 2021).

Kadir, N (2016) *The autonomous life? Paradoxes of hierarchy and authority in the squatters movement in Amsterdam*. Manchester: Manchester University Press.

Khavin, D, Willis, H, Hill, E, Reneau, N, Jordan, D, Engelbrecht, C, Triebert, C, Cooper, S, Browne, M and Botti, D (2021) 'Video: Day of Rage: An In-Depth Look at How a Mob Stormed the Capitol,' *The New York Times*, 30 June [Online]. Available at: www. nytimes.com/video/us/politics/100000007606996/capitol-riot-trump-supporters.html (Accessed: 24 September 2021).

Kumanyika, C (2016) 'Livestreaming in the Black Lives Matter network,' in Day, A (ed.) *DIY utopia: Cultural imagination and the remaking of the possible*. Lanham, MD: Lexington Books, pp. 169–188.

Levenson, M (2021) 'Today's Rampage at the Capitol, as It Happened,' *The New York Times*, 6 January [Online]. Available at: www.nytimes.com/live/2021/01/06/us/wa shington-dc-protests (Accessed: 24 September 2021).

Marichal, J (2013) 'Political Facebook groups: Micro-activism and the digital front stage,' *First Monday*, 18(12). https://doi.org/10.5210/fm.v18i12.4653.

Mattoni, A (2013) 'Repertoires of communication in social movement processes,' in Cammaerts, B, Mattoni, A and McCurdy, P (eds.) *Mediation and protest movements*. Bristol, UK: Intellect, pp. 39–56.

Mazer, S (2020) 'From performance to performativity: The Christchurch Mosque murders and what came after,' *Te Kaharoa*, 15(1). https://doi.org/10.24135/tekaharoa.v15i1.285.

McNamee, W (2021) 'Photos Show Chaos At The Capitol As Rioters Turn Violent,' *The San Francisco Chronicle*, 6 January, image 26 [Online]. Available at: www.sfchronicle. com/projects/2021/visuals/capitol-protests-photos/ (Accessed: 7 January 2021).

Moghe, S (2021) 'Woman Accused of Involvement in Pelosi Laptop Theft During Capitol Riot Released to Home Confinement,' *CNN*, 21 January [Online]. Available at: www.cnn. com/2021/01/21/politics/riley-williams-capitol-riot-pelosi-laptop/index.html (Accessed: 24 September 2021).

Naylor, B (2021) 'Read Trump's Jan. 6 Speech, A Key Part of Impeachment Trial,' *NPR*, 10 February [Online]. Available at: www.npr.org/2021/02/10/966396848/read-trump s-jan-6-speech-a-key-part-of-impeachment-trial (Accessed: 22 September 2021).

NBC Chicago (2021) 'Former Suburban CEO Pleads Guilty to Charges in US Capitol Riot,' *NBC Chicago*, 31 August [Online]. Available at: www.nbcchicago.com/news/loca l/former-suburban-ceo-pleads-guilty-to-charges-in-us-capitol-riot/2602432/ (Accessed: 24 September 2021).

Nicholson, K (2021) 'CBC Reporter Mobbed by Angry Trump Supporters in Washington,' *CBC News*, 6 January [Online]. Available at: www.cbc.ca/player/play/ 1841020995564 (Accessed: 24 September 2021).

Pape, R (2021) 'What an Analysis of 377 Americans Arrested or Charged in the Capitol Insurrection Tells Us,' *The Washington Post*, 6 April [Online]. Available at: https://perma. cc/B5L9-2KVV (Accessed: 24 September 2021).

Pape, R and Ruby, K (2021) 'The Capitol Rioters Aren't Like Other Extremists,' *The Atlantic*, 2 February [Online]. Available at: www.theatlantic.com/ideas/archive/2021/02/the-capitol-rioters-arent-like-other-extremists/617895/ (Accessed: 24 September 2021).

Paybarah, A and Lewis, B (2021) 'Stunning Images as a Mob Storms the US Capitol,' *The New York Times*, 7 January [Online]. Available at: www.nytimes.com/2021/01/06/us/politics/trump-riot-dc-capitol-photos.html (Accessed: 24 September 2021).

Rosenberg, M (2021) 'He Looted Speaker Pelosi's Office, and Then Bragged About It,' *The New York Times*, 7 January [Online]. Available at: www.nytimes.com/2021/01/06/us/politics/richard-barnett-pelosi.html (Accessed: 24 September 2021).

Shammas, B (2021) 'A GOP Congressman Compared Capitol Rioters to Tourists. Photos Show Him Barricading a Door,' *The Washington Post*, 18 May [Online]. Available at: www.washingtonpost.com/politics/2021/05/18/clyde-tourist-capitol-riot-photos/ (Accessed: 24 September 2021).

Surette, R (2015) 'Performance crime and justice,' *Current Issues in Criminal Justice*, 27(2). https://doi.org/10.1080/10345329.2015.12036041.

Tarrow, S (1993) 'Cycles of collective action: Between moments of madness and the repertoire of contention,' *Social Science History*, 17(2). https://doi.org/10.1017/S0145553200016850.

The New York Times (2021) 'Inside the Capitol Riot: An Exclusive Video Investigation,' *The New York Times*, 30 June [Online video]. Available at: www.nytimes.com/2021/06/30/us/jan-6-capitol-attack-takeaways.html (Accessed: 24 September 2021).

Thorburn, E D (2014) 'Social media, subjectivity, and surveillance: Moving on from Occupy, the rise of live streaming video,' *Communication and Critical/Cultural Studies*, 11(1). https://doi.org/10.1080/14791420.2013.827356.

Tumulty, K (2021) 'The Shameless Revisionism of the Capitol Attack Cannot Be Allowed to Take Root,' *The Washington Post*, 3 April [Online]. Available at: www.washingtonpost.com/opinions/2021/04/03/shameless-revisionism-capitol-attack-cannot-be-allowed-take-root/ (Accessed: 22 September 2021).

Vitale, A (2008) 'The command and control and Miami models at the 2004 Republican National Convention: New forms of policing protests,' *Mobilization: An International Quarterly*, 12(4). https://doi.org/10.17813/maiq.12.4.97541013681695q5.

Wagner, J, Bellware, K, Demirjian, K, Sotomayer, M, Alemany, J and Alfaro, M (2021) 'Police Officers Deliver Emotional Testimony About Violent Day at Capitol,' *The Washington Post*, 27 July [Online]. Available at: www.washingtonpost.com/politics/2021/07/27/jan-6-commission-hearing-live-updates/ (Accessed: 24 September 2021).

Walker, R (2016) 'The Shifting Symbolism of the Gadsden Flag,' *The New Yorker*, 2 October [Online]. Available at: www.newyorker.com/news/news-desk/the-shifting-symbolism-of-the-gadsden-flag (Accessed: 24 September 2021).

Washington Post Staff (2021) 'Identifying Far-Right Symbols That Appeared at the US Capitol Riot,' *Washington Post*, 15 January [Online]. Available at: www.washingtonpost.com/nation/interactive/2021/far-right-symbols-capitol-riot/ (Accessed: 24 September 2021).

Yar, M (2012) 'Crime, media and the will-to-representation: Reconsidering relationships in the new media age,' *Crime, Media, Culture*, 8(3). https://doi.org/10.1177/1741659012443227.

9

TAILGATERS AND MILITANTS

Unpacking Masculinities at the Capitol Riots

Michael Hoechsmann and David VanDyke

There is no question that the crowd that descended upon the Capitol was made up largely of angry, white men; the visual evidence demonstrates this, as do the arrest records after the fact. Of the many iconic moments of the Capitol riots, men scaling the side of the Capitol wall like Parkour athletes or video game characters, captured a general state of masculine jouissance at once both uplifting and troubling. Climbing that wall took courage, risk, strength, and agility, signifying a playful gamification of protest—as they are quite literally and physically getting to the next level. At the same time, the desire to traverse the wall at any physical cost demonstrates a desire for conquest and a desperation to overcome that are both endemic within a culture of masculine domination. Domination and aggression are present throughout the activities of the Capitol riots: fighting physically over barricades, hand-to-hand combat with police, smashing windows, transgressing and occupying the building itself, threatening security and staff, swearing and shouting, seeking trophies—all combine to create a hypermasculine narrative of victory and vanquishment over the Capitol building and its inhabitants. Describing how men staged their gender identities during the Capitol riots is the purview of this chapter.

Manly America

As elsewhere, there are a diverse range of masculinities in the US, but cowboys, vigilantes, and soldiers rank high in the popular (and populist) imaginary. From John Wayne to Rambo, Captain America, Batman, and The Terminator, representations of masculinity in popular culture have tended toward brooding, focused, and aggressive white men with increasingly buff, hypermasculinized bodies, infusing American film with tropes of hard masculinity and everyday violence (Jhally and Katz, 2000; Kellner, 2008). In society, acts of random gun violence in public

DOI: 10.4324/9781003246862-12

spaces, perpetrated almost exclusively by angry white men, are becoming alarmingly frequent in an increasingly militarized society. The US is rarely *not* at war, having conducted over one hundred known invasions of foreign countries within the last century, in addition to countless covert operations, some even to overthrow democratically elected governments. Used military equipment is now repurposed for domestic use within increasingly militarized police forces (see Chapter 11).

Though military veterans are celebrated upon returning home, many carry deep psychological wounds whose path toward healing seems little more than incidental to the very institutions that have created them, making them easy targets for stigmatization. The ideological and material reach of the American military-industrial complex is obvious to those outside the US, but less so within its borders, particularly those who are persuaded from a young age to see participation in warfare as an act of dignified 'service' performed for the benefit of the nation. What is perceived instead is an elaborate performance of sanitized violence, soldiers marching in parades or celebrated at National Football League (NFL) games—sport matches known for a mix of violence, daring, and bravado—and ultimately, the honoring of the flag and everything it claims to represent. The pageantry and rivalry of NFL games aptly mimic the theatre of war. When San Francisco 49ers' quarterback Colin Kaepernick saluted the US flag on bended knee to protest police treatment of Black Americans, his purported failure to uphold the dreamlike pageantry of the war-machine set off a maelstrom of indignation within the US political establishment, becoming a recurring theme of the Trump presidency, and resulting in Kaepernick's eventual removal from the team. Before each NFL game, the coach gives a motivational speech. January 6th participants heard such speeches from Rep. Mo Brooks (R-Ala.), Donald Trump Jr., Rudy Giuliani, and then-President Donald Trump, priming the crowd for action.

The men who gathered at the Capitol were a mix of characters who were predominantly white, male, and aged 30–60 years (Pape, 2021). The aesthetic of the gathering was reminiscent of a tailgate party, with participants donning team colors and logos—Make America Great Again (MAGA), Trump, and, to a lesser extent, Proud Boys, Three Percenters, Oath Keepers, and QAnon insignia, slogans, T-shirts, flags, and other paraphernalia (see Figure 9.1).

Though the participants might be loath to admit they had collectively converged on a particular 'look' for the gathering, there is viscerally and visibly apparent a rugged masculine chic that DMarge (2021), an Australian fashion site for men, succinctly describes via an archetypal character sketch:

He is an alpha male. He is physically masculine. He knows how to get things done. He takes no shit and no prisoners. He takes cues from the hard-as-nails men who came before him–the warriors, the adventurers, the blue-collar workers, the mountain men–and adapts them to 21st century life.

(Romano, 2021)

FIGURE 9.1 Tailgaters and Militants
Source: 'Balcony' by Tyler Merbler, used under CC 2.0 Generic / Cropped and Desaturated from original via https://flickr.com/photos/37527185@N05/50811893713/in/photostream/.

This alpha male is a bricoleur who cobbles together an aesthetic that combines allusions to blue-collar workplaces, military fields of engagement, and outdoor rugged recreation spaces:

> Start with traditional workwear, like flannel shirts, leather boots, wool coats, tweed trousers and denim. Then look to the military for field jackets, trench coats, and other earth-toned pieces that are tough and functional.… Remember that it never needs to be perfect.… These are work clothes. They have character.
> *(Romano, 2021)*

These are the archetypal outfits of the rugged alpha males that appeared at the Trump rally preceding the riots: amidst a sea of dark work clothes and tan military gear, an explosion of red MAGA baseball caps served as an iconic motif, alongside a panoply of stars and stripes paraphernalia that included not just the American flag but also the Confederate and Gadsden flags, symbols of both 'patriotism' and white supremacy.

If the Capitol riots were an NFL game, the fans would be the ones wearing MAGA hats and carrying American flags, while the players would be wearing Kevlar vests and other military wear, ready for action. Kevlar vests are not ordinary street clothing, the way military or camo fatigues, pants, and jackets now are, but rather they are specialized gear made for a specific task—only legal to wear in Washington, D.C. if you have not committed a felony (RCW 9.41.045, n.d.). Wearing Kevlar signifies readiness for a gunfight, the semiotic display of battle readiness. This is juxtaposed against the milieu of a tailgate party, with Kevlar-armored militia members using grenade pouches to hold cans of Pabst Blue Ribbon, White Claw, and water bottles, as seen in multiple videos of the day. Leader of the Proud Boys, Enrique Tarrio asked members to 'wear black' in DC so that 'small teams' of Proud Boys could 'blend in' (Parler post, Dec 29, 2020). Wearing black may have also served to blur the lines between Proud Boys and Antifa, known for their all-black attire, in attempts to divert blame onto Antifa, who in fact did not participate in the events that day (Zitser, 2021). Typically, Proud Boys can be seen wearing black Fred Perry polo shirts emblazoned with a gold laurel wreath and gold piping, or other official Proud Boy merchandise from 1776.store (co-owned by Tarrio). Bestsellers include a Proud Boy-themed set of Chuck Taylor shoes, and a variety of T-shirts with phrases such as: '1776 gang,' 'American supremacist,' 'Hunter [Biden] smokes crack,' and 'Kyle Rittenhouse did nothing wrong.'[1] The outfits donned by the Capitol rioters are semiotic signifiers of white supremacy, populism, racism, and so on, taken through an intersectional lens, also signifying a particular kind of rugged, aggressive white masculinity.

Toxic Trump

In terms of style, Donald Trump is cut from a different cloth, known for ill-fitting suits that hide his girth, a uniform he prefers everywhere except the golf course. When the occasion demands, Trump also dresses as an aristocrat, wearing tuxedos and bow ties to attend high society events. He is known to have an affection for Italian-made Brioni suits, a predilection he developed while filming his reality TV show, 'The Apprentice,' in which he always sported his trademark oversized red necktie. Power suits project financial wealth, but Trump carefully impresses upon his followers that he is one of the common people, not a member of the nation's political or economic elite. Despite straddling a fine line between being 'one of the guys' and the exclusive club of corporate magnates, it was reported that Trump was disappointed by the quality of apparel that signified and broadcast the social class of his followers at the Capitol riots:

> he was 'bemused' by the spectacle because he thought his supporters were literally fighting for him, according to a close adviser. But, this person said, he was turned off by what he considered the 'low-class' spectacle of people in ragtag costumes rummaging through the Capitol.
>
> *(Rucker, Parker, and Dawsey, 2021)*

Juxtaposed with this rummaging, ragtag spectacle, Trump's taste for ostentatious luxury is well known. His gilded three-story apartment in New York and his palatial enclave at Mar-A-Lago have both been widely exposed to the public eye. To cultivate his base, however, Trump disassembles his wealth and power, demonstrating his talent for making a connection with his audiences at political rallies through directness, intimacy and common language, as though he were speaking with every individual assembled, combined with a politics of brash spectacle that seem to resonate for many.

Trump's rise to political power relied on stoking the fires of discontent, tapping into and amplifying a wellspring of frustration, anger, and resentment among white American men toward three social groups—the educated elite, racialized immigrants, and women—yet his base depends on attracting voters from those same categories and distorting the concept of 'the elite' such that the financial elite be excluded while the political elite are derided. Collapsing and reaffirming differences and hierarchies as the moment requires, more than any pro-social policies, demonstrates what Bauman calls 'liquid modernity,' the slippage of identity and class markers in late capitalism (Bauman, 2013).

The rallying cry of Trump supporters is outrage. Their leader's outrageousness is not enough to turn them away, rather, many are drawn to his open willingness to insult and belittle racialized groups, women, people with disabilities, opposing politicians, other countries, and more. As discussed in Chapters 1–3, changes to the social and economic fabric of the US have left many white Americans upset and perplexed, and the emergence of the earlier Tea Party and the newer alt-right have both capitalized on this discontent. Trump may be seen simply as the politician who succeeded in tapping into this feeling, fanning the fires of discontent and outrage strategically and in equal proportions during the 2016 election campaign that swept him into power.

The noxious cocktail of regressive social and cultural values exemplified by the figure of Trump includes a strong dose of toxic masculinity, a term that has evolved 'as shorthand for characterizing homophobic and misogynist speech and violence by men' (Harrington, 2021, p. 349). Toxic masculinity captures a process of retrenchment of a narrow series of masculine traits that include power, sexual and social domination, aggression, and violence. Trump, a long-time narcissist, womanizer, and bully, deals with conflict by belittling his opponents and simultaneously proclaiming his own greatness—as in the MAGA slogan. Trump does not spare his female opponents from demeaning nicknames, which include terms such as 'Crooked'—Hillary Clinton, 'Pocohantas'—Elizabeth Warren, 'wacky' and 'lowlife'—Omarosa Manigault-Newman, 'Crazy Megyn'—Megyn Kelly (Schallhorn, 2018) and 'Evita' (Alexandria Ocasio-Cortez), the youngest on this list of defiled women, whom, Trump also adds, has an 'it factor' (Alberta, 2019).

Trump's predilection for younger women is well-documented, especially in his role as the former owner of the Miss Universe beauty pageant. His close personal friendship with notorious child-sex-trafficker Jeffery Epstein may have made under-age women available to him. Trump infamously quipped on a 2006 TV episode of 'The View' that 'if Ivanka weren't my daughter, perhaps I'd be dating her.' Trump embodies toxic masculinity in its most overt forms, proclaiming with a shameless braggadocio, that when he meets women he likes to 'grab 'em by the pussy,' (*New York Times*, 2016), without ever suffering any negative consequences. In fact, his base appears to reward him for this kind of outrageous misogynist expression that is seen to push back against 'political correctness' and 'cancel culture,' reinscribing the no-longer-acceptable entitlement of men to access women's bodies.

Masculinity Studies

Among the many culture wars of the time is the contemporary performance of white cis-male masculinity which can be encapsulated on a continuum from SNAG (sensitive new age guys of the 1990s) or metrosexual (the well-dressed urban professional male of the early 2000s) to the rugged he-man throwback to the 1950s-70s or earlier. The partial reconstruction of this dinosaur hypermasculine identity, which picks up momentum by a strand of masculinity in the 1980s and onwards, is a backlash against generational movements toward women taking on professional roles in the workplace and, particularly in middle classes, enhanced parenting and domestic roles expected on the part of men. The political-economic impact of these changes is to make families work harder than in the era of the 'family wage' of Fordist industrial America, and for women to bear the brunt of that double shift, working full-time jobs and engaging typically also in full responsibilities for unpaid domestic labor including the mental labor of organizing the household activities. The evolution of the sensitive-new-age-guy in Generation X, the metrosexual millennial, and feminist masculinities of today also offered a reprieve from the burden of a hard, emotionless, inexpressively aggressive masculinity, allowing men to experience the joy and other positive feelings of living in connection and cooperation with others, but even this came with an 'off switch.'

The author of *Iron John* (1990), men's movement leader Robert Bly, laments the trade-off made by men in the 1970s, saying that they had become 'soft' and lacked vitality. Men in this period became more thoughtful, gentle, ecologically sensitive, sympathetic to the harmony of the universe, and, according to Bly, desperately unhappy. 'By this process,' says Bly (1990, p. 2), 'he has not become more free. He's a nice boy who pleases not only his mother but also the young woman he is living with.' In contrast, the man of the 1950s:

> got to work early, labored responsibly, supported his wife and children, and admired discipline.... This sort of man didn't see women's souls well, but he appreciated their bodies; and his view of culture and America's part in it was boyish and optimistic.
>
> *(Bly, 1990, p. 1)*

While Bly expresses doubt about the sensitivity of the 1970s man, he also has strong reservations about the 1950s male, implying an awareness of toxic masculinity:

> Many of his qualities were strong and positive, but underneath the charm and bluff there was, and there remains, much isolation, deprivation, and passivity. *Unless he has an enemy, he isn't sure that he is alive.*
>
> *(Bly, 1990, p. 1, emphasis added)*

Building on Bly's 1950s male, we can see how these same characteristics—deprivation, isolation, an inability to understand women as completely human—festered into a full-blown toxic masculinity that includes: gender-based violence; sexual abuse and assault; proclivity for gun violence; anger and aggression; limited ability to express full range of emotions; and a combination of psycho-social elements unfortunately conducive to depression, with young males experiencing a rise in mental health issues.

Bly's scholarship embraces archetypes and historical accounts to conjure up an essentialist vision of rugged masculinity, but his not-so-subtle swipe at the impact of feminism on men diminishes the ultimate value of his work. Critiques of masculinity have been provided with fertile terrain in the so-called post-feminist era of the past 50 years, facing an upswing in the late 1980s. Feminist authors such as Raewyn Connell (formerly Robert W. Connell) and Lynne Segal produced nuanced works on the contradictions embedded in hegemonic masculinities, helping us to see men's lives in greater complexity, tempered by a clearer view of gender power and domination (Connell, 2005; Segal, 2006; Wedgwood, 2009). Also in the 1980s, pro-feminist, male writers such as Michael Kimmel and Michael Kaufman took a micro-lens to masculinities that have served to keep men within frames required by industrial capitalism and the bellicose state (Kaufman, 1987; Kimmel, 1987). Other authors, working in the terrain of popular culture, identify the role of culture in representing, (occasionally) resisting, and ultimately reproducing hegemonic masculinities (Easthope, 1990; Pfeil, 1995). While the outlook of masculinities researchers in this period is upbeat, there is always some doubt about the project of the transformed man, which includes an acknowledgement of the contradictions in any mass recuperation of male subjects. In his contribution to *Men in Feminism* (1987), Andrew Ross recalls his colleague's disappointingly non-insightful advice 'that the best [men] can do is "try not to be anti-feminist"' (86).

Toxic Masculinity 2.0

If some space was opened up in masculinity studies for examining, contesting and reimagining masculinities in the 1980s, it is met immediately with strong backlashes in the 1990s and into the 21st century; these backlashes attacked both feminism and pro-feminist masculinities activism by men. While male domination and violence continue to spread in everyday spaces such as the streets, homes, universities, workplaces, recreation spaces, religious institutions, the arts, and so on, with some limits maintained around what can be expressed in public. The weaponization of the internet by rage-filled, predominantly white men is a turning point where toxic masculinity finds a fertile, public expression in the anonymous spaces of the participatory Web 2.0, further amplified in the filter bubbles and echo chambers of Web 3.0. The internet has become a toxic, unsafe space for girls and women, especially those with public personas who have become direct targets for misogynist, hateful, violent threats, trolling, and doxing, with violent attacks sometimes moving from online to offline, or causing suicidal ideation and actual suicides by the young women targeted.

Unleashed by the constraints of public identity, toxic masculinity picks up steam online, exemplified by incidents such as GamerGate, where female video game developers were subjected to relentless violent harassment and threats, up to and including rape and death. The growth of the Incel (involuntarily celibate) movement and its associated violence, including femicide, reveals a deep well of unprocessed misogynist rage. With the election of Donald Trump in 2016, this enraged toxic masculinity was given a public ambassador, bringing a once hidden hatred out from the shadows into the public sphere.

The election of Trump has legitimated alt-right, anti-government, and white supremacist militia groups, in particular through Trump's refusal to denounce them. After the Charlottesville 'Unite the Right' rally on August 12, 2017, which included a number of acts of violence culminating in a vehicular homicide by a white supremacist adherent, Trump commented that 'there were very fine people on both sides' (The White House, 2017), refusing to condemn the racist, social, and physical violence of the white supremacist participants that day. This pattern of treading lightly around a growing alt-right white supremacist militia movement continued throughout Trump's presidency, highlighted again in 2020 during a presidential debate, mentioned earlier, where Trump called on the Proud Boys to 'stand back and stand by' (Associated Press, 2020). Stoking the flames of right-wing militias, Trump also decried the alleged rise of Antifa, an anti-fascist, anti-racist protest tactic that Trump mistakenly connected to acts of violence at Black Lives Matters protests in the summer of 2020.

Indeed, Trump seems willfully ignorant of who has committed specific acts in various protests and riots. Watching the Capitol riots unfold on television, Trump carried on with this interpretation of events:

> 'He kept saying: "The vast majority of them are peaceful. What about the riots this summer? What about the other side? No one cared when they were rioting. My people are peaceful. My people aren't thugs",' an administration official said. 'He didn't want to condemn his people.'
>
> *(Rucker, Parker, and Dawsey, 2021)*

It is interesting that Trump refers to the rioters as 'my people,' seeming to take responsibility for their actions and acknowledging that they were there for him, and following his directives. Moreover, his claim that they are not 'thugs' is a coded racialized statement which equates 'thugs' with racialized men, whereas 'his people' are mainly white and therefore not thugs. Trump's refusal to see that violence took place that day, committed by his supporters whom he encouraged to attend, and his denial of the threat their violent actions posed to the U.S. democratic process, is emblematic of his performance of hegemonic white masculinity which always has to be right, even if it means petulantly rewriting history immediately as it unfolds.

More sinister hyper-masculine ambitions are revealed by Trump's association with the Proud Boys and other right-wing militias. The Proud Boys hold socially conservative views toward gun ownership, immigration, family structures, and the role of women. They have a hierarchical membership structure, consisting of four levels of achievement or 'degrees' that demonstrate increasing loyalty and hypermasculine violence. According to the Proud Boys' By-laws, as cited in Kutner (2020, p. 3):

> The first degree requires an initiate to state the Proud Boys' fraternity creed; the second degree requires the initiate to be punched until he can name five breakfast cereals. Once the initiate succeeds, he is an official member; the third degree involves the new member getting a tattoo with Proud Boys phrases or symbols; the fourth degree requires the member to engage in violence on the group's behalf.

McDonald, Navarrete, and Van Vugt (2012, p. 672) argue that men are more likely to be drawn to groups containing hierarchical structures and are also more likely to share ideologies that 'legitimize existing hierarchical systems, including social conservatism, racism, patriotism and the explicit endorsement and support for wars of aggression.' This underlines the male warrior hypothesis that 'humans, particularly men, may possess psychological mechanisms enabling them to form coalitions capable of planning, initiating and executing acts of aggression on members of outgroups' (McDonald et al., 2012, p. 671). The Proud Boys contain many elements of this archetype. Based on dialogues shared by Proud Boys members on social media (particularly on Parler), outgroups that they find threatening include Antifa, Muslims, and non-Trump-supporters. Thus, at the Capitol riots we see the Proud Boys engaged in acts of aggression and violence that are expressions of intersectional racist, misogynist, white supremacist, hyper-masculinist logics and identities.

Men at the Riots

People—in particular the men—present at the Capitol on January 6th might be divided into two groups. First, there were Trump supporters casually dressed and accessorized with MAGA hats, American flags, alt-right T-shirts, and other discursive signifiers. Most of these citizens were not affiliated with a political group and were present based on disinformation regarding the alleged stolen election, a desire to see history in the making, and to have their voices heard. Participating in the march and the rally, only some of them transgressed the barricades.

Second, there were organized members of militias, white supremacists, and alt-right groups such as the Three Percenters, Oath Keepers, and Proud Boys. While in the minority, these groups were organized in small teams, borrowing gear, attire, and tactics from military and police SWAT teams. Conforming to Connell's concept of hegemonic masculinity, men in this group play a leading and dominant role based on hypermasculine performances of strength and aggression that men use to establish hierarchies, especially when there are no women present. Moreover, while they organized in small teams, these teams played an organizational and leadership role at the larger protest, exerting influence at the barricades, for example by speaking in megaphones, consulting with each other regarding tactics, and so on, in particular attempting to exert influence among unaffiliated or unorganized participants in the first category. Ethan Nordean (Seattle) and Joe Biggs (Florida), two of the highest-ranking Proud Boys, for example, both helped lead others to the barricades and encouraged them, over megaphones and through leadership by action, to breach the barricades, enter the Capitol and follow the crowd searching for lawmakers. Nordean was widely filmed during the riots acting as leader and organizer, providing tactical guidance to members and non-members alike; while Biggs is seen in videos using a megaphone to direct followers toward the barricades and engage in actions as needed (*Wall Street Journal*, 2021). The Oath Keepers were similarly organized, filmed moving in military stack formation, with Jessica Watkins playing an alleged leadership role, speaking over their radio channel about having a plan and sticking to it, discussed further in Chapter 10.

The violence that occurred at the barricades—small fences erected to establish a perimeter—was fairly minimal in comparison to what happened at the various direct entries into the Capitol buildings, where rioters smashed windows and fought hand to hand with police for hours, in an unpromulgated and relentless attack. This violence resulted in mass injuries and hospitalizations, predominantly of the police, with 140 injured and hospitalized (Jackman, 2021).

Male violence at the Capitol was not solely inflicted in a tactical formation to breach the building's security perimeter but also as a broader display of white supremacy and misogyny, amplified on the one hand by racist epithets hurled repeatedly by many different rioters at officers of color, and also in aggressions directed at women. In one video, a woman is seen lying in pain on the ground when a male protester looks at her, assesses the situation, and then tramples over her to get closer to the action. The sheer masculine anger and physical aggression exacted a high price from those who bore its brunt, leaving in their wake a stream of long-term injuries, post-traumatic stress, deaths, and suicides. It is these outcomes that the term toxic masculinity properly defines and decries. While the role of men and masculinity largely dominated the zeitgeist of the Capitol riot, mediatized as an outpouring of churning violence brewing within a hyper-masculinity hell-bent on combat, the role of women within this same outpouring also bears investigation, to be critically analyzed in the subsequent chapter.

Note

1 Rittenhouse is the 17-year-old white male who, on August 25, 2020 in Kenosha, WI, shot two people dead at a Black Lives Matter protest, and maimed another. He was acquitted of all charges.

References

Alberta, T (2019) *American carnage: On the front lines of the Republican civil war and the rise of President Trump.* New York, NY: HarperCollins.
Associated Press (2020) 'Trump tells Proud Boys: "Stand back and stand by",' 29 September [YouTube]. Available at: www.youtube.com/watch?v=qIHhB1ZMV_o (Accessed: 15 September 2021).
Bauman, Z (2013) *Liquid modernity.* Hoboken, NJ: John Wiley & Sons.
Bly, R (1990) *Iron John: A book about men.* Reading, MA: Addison-Wesley.
Connell, RW (2005) *Masculinities.* Cambridge, UK: Polity.
Easthope, A (1990) *What a man's gotta do: The masculine myth in popular culture.* New York, NY: Routledge.
Harrington, C (2021) 'What is "toxic masculinity" and why does it matter?,' *Men and Masculinities*, 24(2) [Online]. Available at: https://doi-org.ezproxy.lakeheadu.ca/10.1177/1097184X20943254 (Accessed: 28 September 2021).
Jackman, T (2021) 'Police Union Says 140 Officers Injured in Capitol Riot,' *Washington Post*, 27 January [Online]. Available at: www.washingtonpost.com/local/public-safety/police-union-says-140-officers-injured-in-capitol-riot/2021/01/27/60743642-60e2-11eb-9430-e7c77b5b0297_story.html (Accessed: 25 September 2021).
Jardine, A and Smith, P (eds.) (1987) *Men in feminism.* London, UK: Taylor & Francis Group.
Jhally, S and Katz, J (2000) *Tough guise: Violence, media, and the crisis in masculinity.* Amherst, MA: Media Education Foundation.
Kaufman, M (ed.) (1987) *Beyond patriarchy: Essays by men on pleasure, power, and change.* Toronto, ON: Oxford University Press.
Kellner, D (2008) *Guys and guns amok: Domestic terrorism and school shootings from the Oklahoma City bombing to the Virginia Tech massacre.* New York, NY: Routledge.
Kimmel, MS (ed.) (1987) *Changing men: New directions in research on men and masculinity.* Newbury Park, CA: Sage Publications.
Kutner, S (2020) 'Swiping right: The allure of hyper masculinity and cryptofascism for men who join the Proud Boys,' *ICCT Research Paper*, 33. doi:10.19165/2020.1.03.
McDonald, MM, Navarrete, CD and Van Vugt, M (2012) 'Evolution and the psychology of intergroup conflict: The male warrior hypothesis,' *Philosophical Transactions of the Royal Society B: Biological Sciences*, 367(1589) [Online]. Available at: https://doi.org/10.1098/rstb.2011.0301 (Accessed: 28 September 2021).
Pape, R (2021) 'Understanding American domestic terrorism mobilization potential and risk factors of a new threat trajectory,' The University of Chicago, 6 April. Available at: https://d3qi0qp55mx5f5.cloudfront.net/cpost/i/docs/americas_insurrectionists_online_2021_04_06.pdf?mtime=1617807009.
Pfeil, F (1995) *White guys: Studies in postmodern domination and difference.* London, UK: Verso.
RCW 9.41.045 (n.d.) 'Offenders under supervision of the department—Possession prohibited—Penalties' [Online]. Available at: https://app.leg.wa.gov/rcw/default.aspx?cite=9.41.045 (Accessed: 15 September 2021).

Romano, E (2021) 'How to Look Rugged: The Essential Men's Clothing Guide,' *DMARGE*, 30 January. Available at: www.dmarge.com/how-to-get-rugged-style (Accessed: 24 August 2021).

Rucker, P, Parker, A and Dawsey, J (2021) 'After Inciting Mob Attack, Trump Retreats in Rage. Then, Grudgingly, He Admits His Loss,' *Washington Post*, 7 January [Online]. Available at: www.washingtonpost.com/politics/trump-rage-riot/2021/01/07/26894c54 -5108-11eb-b96e-0e54447b23a1_story.html (Accessed: 26 August 2021).

Schallhorn, K (2018) 'Trump's Nicknames for Rivals, from "Rocket Man" to "Poca-hontas",' *Fox News*, 13 August [Online]. Available at: www.foxnews.com/politics/trump s-nicknames-for-rivals-from-rocket-man-to-pocahontas (Accessed: 16 September 2021).

Segal, L (2006) *Slow motion: Changing masculinities, changing men.* New York, NY: Springer.

The White House (2017) 'Remarks by President Trump on infrastructure' [Online]. Available at: https://web.archive.org/web/20201026023326/www.whitehouse.gov/ briefings-statements/remarks-president-trump-infrastructure/ (Accessed: 15 September 2021).

Wall Street Journal (2021) 'Video Investigation: Proud Boys Were Key Instigators in Capitol Riot,' *Wall Street Journal*, 26 January [Online]. Available at: www.wsj.com/video/series/ in-depth-features/video-investigation-proud-boys-were-key-instigators-in-capitol-riot/3 7B883B6-9B19-400F-8036-15DE4EA8A015 (Accessed: 1 September 2021).

Wedgwood, N (2009) 'Connell's theory of masculinity—its origins and influences on the study of gender,' *Journal of Gender Studies*, 18(4) [Online]. Available at: https://doi.org/ 10.1080/09589230903260001 (Accessed: 28 September 2021).

Zitser, J (2021) 'Far-right Group Proud Boys Claim They Will Attend January 6 DC Rally 'Incognito' and Wear All-Black to Blend in with Antifa Protesters,' *Business Insider*, 3 January [Online]. Available at: www.businessinsider.com/proud-boys-attend-janua ry-6-dc-rally-incognito-all-black-2021-1 (Accessed: 1 September 2021).

10

ALT-RIGHT QAMOMS, MOBILIZERS, MILITIAS, AND MARTYRS

Women at the Capitol Riots

iowyth hezel ulthiin and Sandra Jeppesen

Women have long played a fundamental role in right-wing groups. Kathleen Blee (2017, p. 74) has found that women's participation is hidden in plain sight, with masculine research bias in scholarship on right-wing organizations leading to the misperception that 'women are positioned as receptive to the mass appeal of fascism but lacking the agency to shape its direction.' Motivation to participate in these groups has been linked to a 'masculinist character: the far-right attracts men worried about their eroding power in the family, economy, and polity' (Blee, 2017, p. 75), where women are purportedly only there as wives, relegated to the organization of picnics. However, this assumption fails to explain the proliferation of women in far-right groups who increasingly play a particularly central, agentive, organizational, and ideological role (Blee, 2017, p. 77; see also Campion, 2020).

Of those who voted for Trump in the previous election, 53% of those were white women, surpassing other underrepresented groups (Anderson, 2018). Women who participated in the Capitol riots were also predominantly white, straddling two intersectional axes of identity expressed by membership in both an oppressed group (women) and a dominant group (whiteness). Thus they 'get the choice to be oppressed or not' (Anderson, 2018, p. 118), depending on whether they foreground race or gender in their activities. Some women involved in the Capitol riots embodied positions traditionally associated with masculine agency, such as CEOs, business owners, militia leaders, and political organizers, while others were social media influencers, march supporters, or participants; for the most part, they aligned themselves with whiteness, it seems, setting gender politics aside.

Alt-Right Feminism and Femininity

What would a gender politics of the alt-right look like? A fractured feminist landscape has emerged in the 21st century that includes versions of alt-right

DOI: 10.4324/9781003246862-13

feminisms. The 1990s saw the emergence of postfeminist ideologies, or the belief that earlier feminisms had created the material conditions of equality, meaning that feminism was no longer required. This thinking constituted part of the 'active process by which feminist gains of the 1970s and 80s [had] come to be under-mined' (McRobbie, 2004, p. 255). Diverging from postfeminism, neoliberal and intersectional feminisms also arose in the 90s, both becoming increasingly main-stream in today's social and political climate. While neoliberal feminism rightly argues that gender inequalities still exist, as gender biases are enacted by both men and women, on interpersonal and institutional levels, the solution it proposes is to increase corporate leadership positions for women (Sandberg, 2013). The systemic gendered oppression of marginalized groups is ignored in favor of advancing pri-vileged (often white) women who must take individual responsibility to fight gendered oppression in the boardroom. This form of neoliberal feminism is sometimes labelled 'white feminism' (Beck, 2021), in critiques that strive to account for racialized labor practices occurring under capitalism, as well as other barriers that constrain and limit women, including global location, race, social class, disability, immigration status, education, and LGBTQ2S+ identities. These critiques are assembled under the umbrella of intersectional feminism, focusing on intersectional axes of oppression, acknowledging multiple personal and structural oppressions that are mutually reinforcing (Collins and Bilge, 2016), and fighting these structures through a politics of liberation.

Women in alt-right groups tend to favor neoliberal rather than intersectional feminism, leaning towards an ideology called 'sex realism,' which advances 'the belief that women are not equal to men'; but that 'inequality does not necessarily make women lesser' (Campion, 2020, p. 161). This argument is based on notions of biological determinism and *a priori* 'makes [gender] equality neither possible nor desirable' (Campion, 2020, p. 161). Related to sex realism, women of the alt-right may embrace traditional feminine roles harkening back to an idealized past. This is reflected in the emergent subject position of the 'classic woman' or 'tradwife.' Adhering to 'classic' feminine ideals serves to 'coax and flatter women into con-forming to traditional gender roles' (Calogero and Jost, 2011, p. 212). More complicated than a backlash against feminism, the return to 'classic womanhood' may be seen as a reaction to an increasing insecurity that goads subjects into a myriad of reactionary stances in the search for solid ground (Rottenberg and Orgad, 2020). Seeking the promise of identity coherence, 'reasserting a narrowly defined version of femininity may be a way for some women to gain a sense of control over their lives' (Rottenberg and Orgad, 2020, para. 12). Despite obvious limitations on agential power in 'classic femininity,' such boundaries have an elusive draw.

The Intersection of Whiteness and Feminine Gender

This mélange of postfeminist, neoliberal, classic, and sex-realist perspectives com-bines with the fear generated by the great replacement conspiracy theory (discussed in previous chapters), encouraging white women to have increasingly large families based on the manufactured and racist need for 'white babies,' with women being 'heralded as the reproductive future of an [allegedly] imperiled people' (Campion, 2020, p. 161). As such, white women are granted power and agency through the nostalgic, reductionist, feminine roles of nurturer, mother, and caregiver which feature uncritical, unpaid domestic labor and, in their given forms, an undercurrent of sublimated racism. Included in this nostalgic femininity is 'the radical right's coded language on demographic panics which references a time when the country did not have so many immigrants or foreigners or people of color' (Christou, 2020, para. 12). In embracing such logics, women become powerful advocates for the white ethnostate, calling for a return to the dominance of hegemonic white masculinity, which has never fully been unseated.

Women's status, at the same time, becomes threatened by sublimated, unspoken racist–misogynist imaginaries which subjugate them in the limited roles of mother and wife, roles that are accessed through a reversion to racism. In this,

> Women learn the [racial purity] slogan as a defensive posture, one in which the rules of gender are suspended: women are called to racial actions that are otherwise unimaginable for them for reasons that are extraordinary. Racist activism for women is the upside-down carnival of possibility; for men it is the culmination of established notions of white manhood.
>
> *(Blee, 2017, p. 81)*

Through the collaboration of white women, aligned with (masculine) whiteness against their own gendered interests, white men can more fully entrench their power in both the domestic and public spheres. Yet despite these traditional gender dynamics, women in far-right spaces exert power and influence through their adoption of roles that serve as components powering the far-right machine. Campion (2020, p. 150) has found six distinct types of participation by women in the far-right, which she labels: 'violent actors, thinkers, facilitators, promoters, activists, and exemplars.' We explain this typology further in our analysis below.

Alt-Right Women in the Capitol Riots: Four Media Case Studies

Below we analyze four media case studies of alt-right women engaged in these six forms of participation in their involvement with the Capitol riots (see Table 10.1). The case studies are: 1) female Conspiracy Theorists, QAnon followers or QAMoms who promoted unrest online; 2) Republican Marjorie Taylor Greene who served to create the ideological framework for the riots and Women for America First who facilitated the 'March to Save America'; 3) Jessica Watkins who is an Oath Keeper and Ohio Militia leader, now held on conspiracy charges and labeled a ringleader in the mainstream media; and 4) Ashli Babbitt, a QAnon follower killed at the riots, now being held up as a

TABLE 10.1 Women's Forms of Participation at the Capitol Riots

Case study	Individuals	Affiliation	Forms of participation	Claim to fame
Conspiracy Theorists	Many	QAnon and others	Promoter, Exemplar	Access to hidden knowledge
Mobilizers	Marjorie Taylor Greene	Republican representative	Thinker, Facilitator	Dec 22, 2020 tweet calling for a 'grass-roots army'
Militia	Jessica Watkins	Oath Keepers	Facilitator, Promoter, Action	Alleged ring-leader up on conspiracy charges
Martyrs	Ashli Babbit	unaffiliated	Promoter, Martyr	Shot and killed by Capitol Police

Source: Copyright Sandra Jeppesen and iowyth hezel ulthiin.

martyr by the alt-right. While one might argue that the riots themselves were a product of conspiratorial thinking, a broader range of constituencies contributed to the spectrum of women active at the riots, from QAnon adherents to politicians and from militia groups to military, navy, and police veterans, with some overlaps among these groups. Out of the more than 700 arrested in the Capitol riots with a mere 12% being women (Hymes, McDonald, and Watson, 2021), one might argue the centrality of their roles actually outsized their contribution in numbers.

Women's gender performances tended toward traditional binaries, both in masculine tropes that involved anger, militarization, and aggressive discourses as well as in feminine tropes that included the classic woman or tradwife, the nurturer, and the supporter. We further argue that these performances were exemplary of what Anderson (2018) calls 'contained agency.' For Anderson (2018, p. 118), this 'occurs when oppression is localized to an individual's situation rather than identifying systemic, historic, and institutional frameworks for oppression.' Women in the Capitol riots exercised a contained agency that depended on alliances with—and sometimes performances of—hegemonic white masculinity, lacking a systemic or intersectional framework through which they might have been able to contest their own gendered oppression.

Women and QAMoms: Promoters and Exemplars

Many participants in attendance at the march and riots may be considered inspired believers,' not being part of military networks, gangs, or other organized clusters. These individuals were inspired to come alone to the 'March to Save America' for their own reasons (Program on Extremism, 2021). Many had succumbed to

QAnon and were then spurred on to alt-right radicalization, drawn to these spaces by largely innocuous-seeming causes such as #SaveTheChildren, which had, however, been co-opted by QAnon influencers (North, 2020). The hashtag would draw in concerned citizens, especially women who prided themselves on being mothers and caregivers, and in particular, survivors of sexual abuse who felt drawn to help children facing a similar fate (Dickson, 2020). Many in attendance at the Capitol march and riots would articulate slogans tied to QAnon narratives. However, we must remain cognizant of the fact that QAnon is a group without membership, functioning more as a way of seeing the world than an organization with any formal structure. It is also known as an umbrella conspiracy theory, able to draw together various streams of conspiracy thinking into one—albeit somewhat incoherent—stream.

Indicative of the conspiratorial narratives generated leading up to January 6th, @xashxnicoleofficial (2021), a TikTokker and mother, shared a video making this prediction:

> Christians will start getting executed just for being Christian. Life as we know it will be totally different and maybe this will be the final piece where God has this happen and then I think it would be the rapture happening and the end of the world.

This TikTokker is an example of a 'promoter,' which Campion (2020, p. 157) defines as 'individuals who engage in information sharing, dissemination, and provocation (commonly online), but who largely repackage and share ideas rather than create them.' Speculation regarding what the protest might become laid the groundwork of expectations among those in attendance who were ready, willing, and able to engage in armed scuffles with police, acting on the social imaginaries constructed by often-female 'promoters' on social media. After the riots, the same TikTokker seemed dazed, coming down off a high of frenzied expectation of supernatural imaginaries which never came to fruition. The confabulation around the alleged stolen election was as electric as it was hypnotizing, suspending the rioters in a spell with—they believed—liberatory potential.

QAnon conspiracy channels are rife with examples of female 'promoters' of the alt-right. A key example is Dr. Christine Northrup, who is well known for COVID denialism, anti-vaxxer messaging, and QAnon conspiracy narratives. In a video posted on Facebook on January 3rd, 2021, she played a song for her viewers, entitled 'Make them hear you' with lyrics intimating that the march on the Capitol was about getting the nation back as well as staying in 'fifth dimensional awareness,' thus avoiding 'infection' via the mainstream media (Northrup, 2021). All this is wedged between a section where she shows off her new kitten and another where she talks about doing a water fast. This and other conspiratorial narratives were powerful enough to bring women to Washington DC for the 'March to Save America' where they are captured in video and photographs wearing QAnon, Make America Great Again, and American Flag t-shirts and ball caps, made brave by their horror at the alleged 'deep state' corruption of the political elites, and expressing their support of Donald Trump who would, according to this particular social imaginary, fix everything. The power and rage of alt-right women at the march was incongruently targeted, focusing their anger not on the gendered oppression enacted by an outgoing President who himself stands accused of sexual assault and harassment, but instead on the alleged stolen election that they felt threatened their way of life. Thus, they aligned themselves with the power and dominance of whiteness and masculinity, represented not just by Trump but also by the alt-right in general and against their own interests.

In accordance with Campion's (2020) typography, women in QAnon serve as powerful 'exemplars' of traditional femininity. She argues that 'Exemplars are women in extreme and radical subcultures about whom cultural constructions have formed, in which they are celebrated as personifying the desired gendered identity' (Campion, 2020, p. 150). Idealized gendered performances exemplify the archetypes glorified by far-right groups such as goddesses, warrior women, and more, yet they consistently play a supporting role to leading aggressive performances, for example, of the predominantly male rioters. Women led rioters in other ways, in prayer and song, with one woman dressed as Lady Liberty herself, crying out for justice.

These emblematic female performances signal an allegiance with other more traditional forms of masculine power as expressed through the conservative ideals rallying under the leadership of Donald Trump. Women inspired to attend the riot may have been called to do so in a bid to establish an identity within a world on fire, who saw safety—even if there wasn't any to be found—amidst the ranks of a furious mob of middle-aged, white, male zealots. Yet, taking up roles of traditional femininity, as classic women or tradwives, may also skew a sense of their culpability as agential powers unto themselves. While women in far-right political circles may eschew certain liberal modes of female empowerment, their ability to construct narratives, inspire care, perform service, and show up in bodily force as supporters of a powerful, armed mob must not be overlooked. These women claim power in their wielding of traditional femininity, as promoters and exemplars communicating, and embodying a white-American-centric ideal for the collective future of 'their' nation.

Women for America First and Marjorie Taylor Greene: Thinkers and Facilitators

A key organizer of the protest march that became the Capitol riots, was a political group called Women for America First (WFAF), whose leader Amy Kremer was known for her role in the Tea Party. On their official website, WFAF posits, 'What makes our team so special? We are women. Women who know what it takes to get the job done. A group of women who know that it is critical to have our voices heard' (WFAF, 2021, para. 1). They boast decades of collective experience in politics, media, and grassroots activism, all of which was brought to bear in their role organizing the 'March to Save America' with calls to end the historic corruption of deep state power. Yet, their role would not be limited to planning the protest itself. Weeks before the riots, they organized a twenty-city tour across America. At one of their events, a member stated, 'We'd solve every problem in this country if on the 4th of July every conservative went and shot one liberal' (anonymous member as cited in Silverman, Lytvynenko, and Dixit, 2021). While this statement was greeted with an outcry on Twitter, it may have also served to mobilize their base.

WFAF later received a permit for the January 6th event that took place on the Ellipse in Washington D.C., helping to plan the event where Trump and Giuliani spoke before the march. Claims link the non-profit group to the Republican Party and the White House, as, for example, the WFAF staff on the day of the march included members hired and paid for by the Trump campaign (Lardner and Smith, 2021). However, Trump's re-election campaign officials are denying all involvement. One of the figures implicated was Caroline Wren, a GOP fundraiser, who is listed as the 'VIP Advisor' on the event permit and who was paid $20,000 per month by Donald J. Trump for President Inc. (Lardner and Smith, 2021). WFAF exemplifies the power of women to act as 'facilitators,' defined as 'individuals who act in an enabling, organizational, or logistics role, as part of, or on behalf of, a movement or group' (Campion, 2020, p. 156). WFAF carried out the logistics of the protest on January 6, not just organizing people to attend by funding buses, but also by providing a stage for incendiary rhetoric which would further inflame a public ready for a fight.

Another major figure in the lead-up to the riots was Marjorie Taylor Greene, who made one of the earliest tweets about the stolen election, later generating a trending topic and subsequent action (see Chapters 4 and 5). In a 90-minute video posted on YouTube on February 23, 2019, in a bid to solicit donations for a 'Fund the Wall' march, with support from the American Defence Force (a right-wing militia), Marjorie Taylor Greene stated:

> 'communist traitors and Islamist lovers,' would be 'cowering in fear,' saying, 'If we have a sea of people, if we shut down the streets, if we shut down everything. If we flood the Capitol Building. Go inside. These are public buildings. We own them.'
>
> *(Greene, 2019, cited in Sollenberger, 2021, para. 5)*

In this sense, Greene may be considered a 'thinker' a person who develops theories, or social imaginaries, that may be represented as ideological information within the alt-right. Campion (2020, p. 150) argues that female 'thinkers make original contributions to radical right theory or beliefs through the advancement of novel ideas.' Greene has been well established as a politician who consistently generates violent rhetoric, going so far as to call for the execution of political leaders (Steck and Kaczynski, 2021a). She famously supported extremist conspiracy theories (Steck and Kaczynski, 2021b), notably QAnon's most dangerous narratives. During the lead-up to the riots, Greene was seen by some as the initiator of the #StopTheSteal campaign, saying, 'The real cancer for the Republican Party is weak Republicans who only know how to lose gracefully' (Greene as cited in Funke, 2021). Leading up to the violence, Greene posted inciting statements on Parler (see Chapter 5), leading the way, as an alt-right 'thinker,' for other violent rhetoric on a platform that served to draw in fanatical outsiders. As discussed earlier, she wrote this inciting text:

> On January 6 on the House floor, I will OBJECT to fraudulent electoral votes from several states at the Capitol. But I cannot do this alone. I must have a grassroots army behind me. We have a rapidly growing group of House Members and Senators. But more pressure is needed!
>
> *(Greene, 2020)*

Using the violent imaginary of a grassroots army, Greene proposes ideological conspiracy theories, as well as acting as a formative facilitator of the violence that culminated at the Capitol building. Her role as a thinker and facilitator serve to underline the importance of women organizing large-scale events in positions of real or perceived legitimacy, as Greene is an elected representative, and WFAF is a well-resourced organization. Together they contributed to fomenting the rage that showed up in DC on January 6th and laying the groundwork for that—albeit largely masculine—rage to unravel.

Oath Keeper Jessica Watkins: Promoter, Facilitator, Activist

Jessica Watkins, a 38-year-old member of the Oath Keepers (see Figure 10.1), played an active role in organizing militia members to attend the riots—whether she is a violent ringleader, however, is another question. The Oath Keepers are understood to be:

> a loosely organized anti-government group with chapters around the country. … While the organization says that its mandate is defending the Constitution, several human-rights groups have identified it as one of the largest and most dangerous extremist groups in the country.
>
> *(Farrow, 2021, para. 3)*

The Oath Keepers are arguably the most visible element of the alt-right anti-government's 'patriot' trend in the US today and they were also highly visible at the Capitol riots. Watkins herself is a 'former Army ranger, Afghanistan war veteran, and volunteer firefighter' (Snodgrass, 2021). She 'served in an infantry unit in the US Army for three years and was deployed to Afghanistan in 2002, according to the Pentagon' (Cohen, 2021b), having left in 2004 after being forced out when 'her sexual orientation [sic; gender identity] was discovered' (Caniglia, 2021). Despite her removal from the military by a Trump law prohibiting transgender people from serving, Watkins became a staunch Trump supporter.

FIGURE 10.1 Jessica Watkins (left) and Shown in Militia Gear at the Capitol Riots (right)
Source: Copyright iowyth hezel ulthiin, ulthiin's impression of original image, Who is Oath Keeper Jessica Watkins via https://www.wikifyhollywood.com/2021/02/who-is-oath-keeper-jessica-watkins/.

Watkins attended the Capitol riots due to a mounting frustration over the fact that her bar, the Jolly Roger, was closed under lockdown orders. She shifted from working to spending time online, and quickly became a promoter, activist, and facilitator of the alt-right, expressing anti-lockdown rhetoric, vocalizing on social media, and organizing and attending events. She used Parler and Twitter to express her views, evidence that she was a social media promoter. She wrote on Parler, 'My small business is a bar. Empty on a Saturday. Thanks for nothing DeWine' saying, 'Guess I am going to go pack for DC now. See you there' (Watkins, 2021, cited in Caniglia, 2021). She was convinced that the Democrats had stolen the election, in a collision of QAnon and Stop the Steal conspiracies, expressing an at-times violent and somewhat incoherent discourse. She says, 'Biden may still be our president. If he is, our way of life as we know it is over. Our Republic would be over. Then it is our duty as Americans to fight, kill and die for our rights' (Watkins, 2021, cited in Caniglia, 2021, from court documents). She believed that Trump had called on 'patriots' to stand up and fight for democracy. She also used social media to organize the Oath Keepers as well as a militia she formed and led herself—the Ohio State Regular Militia—which aimed to support police and military in times of humanitarian crisis, however, they soon developed as a 'far-right group that has overlapping membership with other Oath Keepers' (Snodgrass, 2021), and shared white supremacist ideologies.

At the riots, Oath Keepers were seen in military gear, moving to the front of the rioters in a stack formation. A social media video of her with another Oath Keeper shows them expressing excitement about having breached the 'fucking Capitol'

(Watkins, 2021, cited in Garrison and Bensinger, 2021). Military gear worn by the Oath Keepers included insignia, combat helmets, reinforced gloves, bullet-proof tactical vests, ballistics goggles, and hand-held radios with headsets (Melendez, 2021), demonstrating that they were organized and ready for physical engagement. Just before the action, Watkins posted a selfie on Parler: 'Me before forcing entry into the Capitol Building. #stopthesteal #stormthecapitol #oathkeepers #ohio-militia' (Watkins, 2021, cited in Melendez, 2021). The use of the term 'forcing' suggests a dominating expression of power. She is subsequently heard on walkie-talkie radio, saying: 'We have a good group. We have about 30–40 of us. We are sticking together and sticking to the plan,' indicating she would be going silent after the breach of the Capitol building because she would be 'too busy' (Watkins, 2021, cited in Melendez, 2021), demonstrating her power in the Oath Keepers.

Prosecutors argue that she and other Oath Keepers prepared in the weeks leading up to January 6 as if they were going to war, recruiting and training members with the goal of blocking the certification of President Joe Biden's victory (Durkin Richer, 2021, para. 6). The Oath Keepers also allegedly had a 'quick reaction force' in place, a cohort of heavily armed 'patriots' available nearby—in case Trump called upon them. Continuing to post on social media after the riots, and secure in her belief that she would not be arrested, Watkins (2021, cited in Caniglia, 2021) boasted of her accomplishments publicly, saying: 'Yeah. We stormed the Capitol today. Teargassed, the whole 9. Pushed our way into the rotunda. Made it into the Senate even. The news is lying (even Fox) about the historic events we created today.' Watkins is portrayed in the media as the 'Alleged ringleader of the most serious paramilitary conspiracy stemming from the Capitol attack' (Cohen, 2021b).

It is no surprise that mainstream media coverage is scapegoating Watkins, a transgender woman, as an 'alleged ringleader,' reinforcing transphobia, particularly in light of the Chelsea Manning Wikileaks case[1]. According to Federal Judge Amit Mehta, Watkins 'was a recruiter and did recruit others to participate in the events of January 6' (Mehta, 2021, cited in Cohen, 2021b), and according to Justice Department lawyer Ahmed Baset, Watkins 'planned, participated and organized a major part of this insurrection' (Baset, 2021, cited in Cohen, 2021b). She has been charged with and pleaded not guilty 'to four federal crimes: conspiracy, destruction of government property, obstruction of an official proceeding and entering a restricted building—the Capitol' (Cohen, 2021b). Facing these accusations, Watkins later disavowed the Oath Keepers, having said that her participation was 'out of love for my country' (Watkins, 2021, cited in Cohen, 2021b). Watkins' friend, Adita Lynne Harless says in her defense, that 'Jessica's loyalty to her country and desire to serve may have allowed her to be taken advantage of by people with an agenda that Jess was, perhaps, not fully cognizant of' (Harless, 2021, cited in Caniglia, 2021), reiterating the idea that Watkins exercised a form of contained agency, failing to recognize the fundamental conditions of her own oppression. Watkins was refused a request to be released on bail awaiting trial, her issues 'complicated by the fact that she is a transgender woman struggling to adjust to being held in federal detention without bond' (Caniglia, 2021). Yet, despite her poor treatment in jail, the judge said Watkins 'is too dangerous to be released' (Durkin Richer, 2021, para. 4). She has gone on a hunger strike, being placed on a suicide watch 'not designed to treat one's mental-health issues,' according to her attorney, AJ Kramer, who also reported that Watkins 'was left naked in a cell with lights on 24 hours a day for four days in full view' (Kramer, 2021, as cited in Caniglia, 2021), a situation that could only be described as transphobic torture.

The fact that Watkins is transgender complicates our critical analysis of gender at the riots. Watkins' gender identity conforms to a feminine gender expression which relies on the gender binary. To claim that she is also performing stereotypical masculinity would risk reverting to her birth gender, a transphobic argument to be avoided. And yet the mainstream media is depicting her as a violent actor through her militia engagement, proximity to white male violence, and calls for violence on social media—this latter being surprisingly common among riot participants leading up to January 6th. At the riots, she herself never became violent. Rather, it seems she is being targeted by the state simply for her role as a facilitator and a promoter on social media.

Perhaps the actual violence in this case could be seen to be the State's violence against Watkins, through her interrogation and torture in jail. The failure of mainstream media to denounce the prison torture of a transgender woman, and her concomitant branding as a 'ringleader' is thus a double-edged sword. It points to the contained agency of alt-right women in leadership roles in male-dominated white supremacist groups, but at the same time, membership in extremist groups serves to justify her torture and maltreatment as a transgender woman in jail under dangerous circumstances where her very life may hang in the balance.

Ashli Babbit: Promoter, Activist, Exemplar

Under Campion's (2020, p. 150) framework, we can understand that activists 'publicly support radical right movements through direct action at rallies or meetings.' Women with military training could be considered activists within this lens. Ashli Babbitt, a 35-year-old woman and Air Force veteran, is one such activist. She was a QAnon follower and anti-masker, and traveled alone to Washington to participate in the March to Save America. Having served in the military for 14 years, with training in the handling of civil disturbances (much like the one she participated in), she went on to start a pool supply company with her family members, later becoming a staunch Trump supporter. She first got involved in alt-right politics online, which is where she was exposed to QAnon (Barry et al., 2021).

In the days leading up to the riots, she posted a video selfie addressing Democratic politicians on Twitter, saying, 'You can consider yourself put on notice. Me and the American people. I am so tired of it, I am woke, man, this is absolutely unbelievable' (Babbit as cited in Barry et al., 2021). The term 'woke' is typically used for intersectional anti-racist activists, those who have come to a consciousness of multiple intersecting oppressions as well as their own intersectional identities.

Babbitt, however, used the term to describe a burgeoning 'understanding' of the QAnon conspiracy and other disinformation. She reposted tweets calling for a 'violent uprising' (Babbitt as cited in Barry et al., 2021) at the Capitol on January 6th, similar to tweets of other participants now being used as evidence of conspiracy. Because of her social media activity, she can be considered a promoter of alt-right ideas. 'Promoters,' according to Campion (2020, p. 150), 'repackage and propagate radical right theories and beliefs on social platforms such as YouTube, Instagram, and Twitter,' as well as—during its brief inception that included the time of the riots—the alt-right platform Parler.

On the day of the Capitol riots, Babbitt was 'wearing snow boots, jeans, and a Trump flag wrapped around her neck like a cape' (Barry et al., 2021) when she attempted to breach the Speaker's Lobby of the Capitol through a smashed window. As the window was taken out by a male compatriot, she shouted a rallying cry, 'Go! Go!' using a military command to advance, and was hoisted up by two men to crawl through the window. Immediately upon her ingress through the window frame, she was fatally shot by a Capitol Police officer in her left shoulder (Fischer, Flack, and Wilson 2021), falling back into the small mob who had propelled her forward to her death (Barry et al., 2021).

Although Babbitt had struggled both financially and emotionally after her time in the Air Force, after her death, she has been hailed by the alt-right as a martyr, shifting from the role of activist and promoter to exemplar. After the Capitol riots, 'white supremacist and anti-government extremists began trying to use Ashli Babbitt's death as a clarion call for recruits' (Fischer et al., 2021, para. 1). However, despite her posts, 'there's no evidence she was a member of any organized extremist groups' (Fischer et al., 2021, para. 4). That fact notwithstanding, even as the riots were still in progress, Texas Oath Keeper and Three Percenter Larry Brock posted this on Facebook: 'Trying to find the name of a woman that was gunned down by Capitol Police today. She was unarmed and is the first Patriot Martyr in the Second American Revolution' (as cited in Fischer et al., 2021, para. 3). The manipulation of the meaning of her death can be seen as evidence of a troubling and insensitive gendered exploitation by male members of alt-right groups. Without even knowing who she is, Brock calls her a 'Patriot' and a 'Martyr,' referring to the Capitol riots as a 'Revolution.' The motives of those valorizing her actions do not serve Babbitt herself, her husband, or family and friends. Rather, they underline the use of women as cogs in a much larger machine, their lives and deaths serving as fodder for systematized gender exploitation among the alt-right (see Figure 10.2).

Emblematic of this distortion,

> Users on the social media sites Parler and Telegram began circulating an image of the so-called 'Babbitt Flag' which, according to the Anti-Defamation League, features a woman in front of the Capitol dome with a single drop of blood on her neck, where it was initially believed Babbitt was shot.
>
> *(Fischer et al., 2021, para. 7)*

FIGURE 10.2 Babbitt Flag
Source: Copyright iowyth hezel ulthiin, ulthiin's impression of original image, 'Babbitt Flag,'
which originated on the 4chan message board.

Babbitt becomes an 'exemplar' of white femininity. Exemplars, Campion (2020, p. 161) argues, serve to 'epitomize a desired, gendered, and idealized identity. They become symbols of the movement through sacrifice and martyrdom.' White supremacists and anti-government groups are using her death as evidence of white genocide and state-sanctioned brutality, suggesting that any opposition to the government will result in death (Fischer et al., 2021, para. 22–24). As Hughes argues, martyrs serve a particular purpose for extremists, saying they present 'a role model. Somebody who paid the ultimate price for the beliefs that the extremist group is promoting. And sometimes this has issues of gender and sex mixed into it' (Hughes, 2021, cited in Fischer et al., 2021, para. 32). Babbitt's death is being exploited by making her into a martyr in the service of male-dominated groups that she had literally nothing to do with. Her husband says that he is 'disgusted by what he [has] read about her online' (Fischer et al., 2021, para. 34), which suggests that the distortion of her image after her death serves the groups who have co-opted it with complete disregard for the wants and needs of those who loved her and who survive to witness her transformation into an online discourse of martyrdom that is beyond their control.

Conclusion

While there are certainly 'misogynist elements within and beyond the extreme and radical right, there are nonetheless women who are active, not passive, contributors to the ideological environment' (Campion, 2020, p. 164). Women in the Capitol riots served key roles as 'violent actors, thinkers, facilitators, promoters, activists, and exemplars' (Campion, 2020, p. 150). Their support and contributions to organizing a predominantly white-male violent force provided a framework creating broad mass appeal for extremist groups, providing social cohesion, planning, and serving as exemplars of female participation.

Yet, with 'contained agency' their understanding of their own conditions are limited by their inability to look to the source of their oppression, which might explain the contradictory narratives of the #savethechildren campaign, and sup porting a known sexual assault perpetrator in former President Trump. Instead of fighting gendered oppression, women mobilizing and participating in the Capitol riots seem to have bought into a narrative which further entrenches their gender position through binary modes of social engagement, either in the traditional role of procreators and facilitators on social media, for example, or the traditional masculine role as violent actors—one of the few concessions to feminist progress such as it is. Both binaries, in their extremity, provide toxic affordances for adherents within their social spheres. One may find that identity, security and self-realization 'can occur across the forms of participation, with identity to be found in violence as much as promotion, activism, or procreation' (Campion, 2020, p. 164). The main understanding to be drawn from the riots, in terms of female gender performances, is the extent to which these limited visions exclude more positive forms of engagement, confining participants to a very narrow band of destructive agency which only serves to undermine their own freedoms.

Note

1 Chelsea Manning, a transgender woman, is alleged to have provided state secrets to Wikileaks.

References

Anderson, WKZ (2018) 'Classifying whiteness: Unmasking white nationalist women's digital design through an intersectional analysis of contained agency,' *Communication, Culture and Critique*, 11(1), 116–132. https://doi.org/10.1093/ccc/tcy002.

Barry, E, Bogel-Burroughs, N and Philipps, D (2021) 'Woman Killed in Capitol Embraced Trump and QAnon,' *The New York Times*, 8 January [Online]. Available at: www.nytim es.com/2021/01/07/us/who-was-ashli-babbitt.html (Accessed: 12 August 2021).

Blee, KM (2017) *Understanding racist activism: Theory, methods, and research*. New York: Routledge.

Calogero, RM and Jost, JT (2011) 'Self-subjugation among women: Exposure to sexist ideology, self-objectification, and the protective function of the need to avoid closure,' *Journal of Personality and Social Psychology*, 100(2), 211–228. https://doi.org/10.1037/a 0021864.

Campion, K (2020) 'Women in the Extreme and Radical Right: Forms of Participation and Their Implications,' *Social Sciences*, 9(9), 149. https://doi.org/10.3390/socsci9090149.

Caniglia, J (2021) 'How an Ohio bartender's patriotism was warped by social media and a devotion to Trump, ending in conspiracy charges from the Capitol riots,' *Cleveland.Com*, 11 April [Online]. Available at: www.cleveland.com/politics/2021/04/how-an-ohio-barten ders-patriotism-was-warped-by-social-media-and-a-devotion-to-trump-ending-in-conspira cy-charges-from-the-capitol-riots.html (Accessed: 18 August 2021).

Christou, M (2020) '#TradWives: Sexism as Gateway to White Supremacy,' *Open Democracy*, 17 March [Online]. Available at: www.opendemocracy.net/en/countering-radical-right/ tradwives-sexism-gateway-white-supremacy/ (Accessed: 25 September 2021).

Cohen, M (2021a) 'Woman charged in Capitol riot asks judge to let her take vacation in Mexico,' *CTV News*, 3 February [Online]. Available at: www.ctvnews.ca/world/woman-charged-in-capitol-riot-asks-judge-to-let-her-take-vacation-in-mexico-1.5294192 (Accessed: 18 August 2021).

Cohen, M (2021b) 'Alleged Oath Keeper ringleader in Capitol siege ordered to stay in jail before trial,' *CNN*, 26 February [Online]. Available at: www.cnn.com/2021/02/26/p olitics/jessica-watkins-oath-keepers-capitol-attack/index.html (Accessed: 18 August 2021).

Collins, PH and Bilge, S (2016) *Intersectionality*. Cambridge UK: Polity Press.

Dickson, E (2020) 'Sexual-Abuse Survivors are Getting Sucked into QAnon,' *Rolling Stone*, 18 November [Online]. Available at: www.rollingstone.com/culture/culture-features/qa non-sexual-assault-save-children-conspiracy-theory-1090992/ (Accessed: 17 August 2021).

Durkin Richer, A (2021) 'Oath Keeper, an Army Veteran, Charged in Capitol Riot Renounces Militia Group,' *Military Times*, 28 February [Online]. Available at: www. militarytimes.com/news/your-military/2021/02/28/oath-keeper-an-army-veteran-charg ed-in-capitol-riot-renounces-militia-group/ (Accessed: 25 September 2021).

Farrow, R (2021) 'A Former Marine Stormed the Capitol as Part of a Far-Right Militia,' *The New Yorker*, 14 January [Online]. Available at: www.newyorker.com/news/news-desk/a-former-marine-stormed-the-capitol-as-part-of-a-far-right-militia (Accessed: 18 August 2021).

Fischer, J, Flack, E and Wilson, S (2021) '"Who shot Ashli Babbitt?" Inside the effort to make a January 6 martyr,' *WUSA9*, 3 July [Online]. Available at: www.wusa9.com/a rticle/news/national/capitol-riots/who-shot-ashli-babbitt-inside-the-effort-to-make-a-ja nuary-6-martyr-right-wing-paul-gosar-donald-trump-white-supremacist-anti-semitic-qa non/65-6641f710-99d0-42ba-b657-4c568e132ef1 (Accessed: 17 August 2021).

Funke, D (2021) 'What Rep. Marjorie Taylor Greene has Said About Election Fraud, QAnon and Other Conspiracy Theories,' *PolitiFact*, 2 February [Online]. Available at: www.politifact. com/article/2021/feb/02/what-rep-marjorie-taylor-greene-has-said-about-ele/ (Accessed: 17 August 2021).

Garrison, J and Bensinger, K (2021) 'Meet the Woman Facing the Some of the Most Serious Capitol Riots Charges,' *BuzzFeedNews*, 26 January [Online]. Available at: www.buzzfeed news.com/article/jessicagarrison/conspiracy-charge-ohio-militia-capitol (Accessed: 29 September 2021).

Greene, MT (2020) 'On January 6 on the House floor, I will OBJECT to fraudulent electoral votes from several states at the Capitol…' *Parler*, 22 December [Online]. Available at: https://parler.adatascienti.st/post/90e725e001cf45a6b9523ab2f1f0c148 (Accessed: 15 September 2021).

Hymes, C, McDonald, C and Watson, E (2021) 'What we Know about the "unprecedented" Capitol Riot Arrests,' *CBS News*, 11 August [Online]. Available at: www.cbsnews.com/news/us-capitol-riot-arrests-latest/ (Accessed: 17 August 2021).

Lardner, R and Smith, MR (2021) 'Records: Trump allies behind rally that ignited Capitol riot,' *WKBN*, 18 January [Online]. Available at: www.wkbn.com/news/national-world/records-trump-allies-behind-rally-that-ignited-capitol-riot/ (Accessed: 17 August 2021).

McRobbie, A (2004) 'Post-feminism and popular culture,' *Feminist Media Studies*, 4(3), 255–264. https://doi.org/10.1080/1468077042000309937.

McRobbie, A (2015) 'Notes on the perfect: Competitive femininity in neoliberal times,' *Australian Feminist Studies*, 30 (83), 3–20. https://doi.org/10.1080/08164649.2015.1011485.

Melendez, P (2021) '"Humiliated" Rioter Jessica Watkins Vows to Ditch the Oath Keepers: "Time to Let All of That Go",' *The Daily Beast*, 26 February [Online]. Available at: www.thedailybeast.com/jessica-watkins-claims-shes-no-longer-an-oath-keeper-in-detention-hearing (Accessed: 18 August 2021).

North, A (2020) '#SaveTheChildren is pulling American moms into QAnon,' *Vox*, 8 October [Online]. Available at: www.vox.com/21436671/save-our-children-hashtag-qanon-pizzagate (Accessed: 17 August 2021).

Northrup, C (2021) 'The Great Awakening Jan 3, 2021 Let Them Hear You from Ragtime… A good theme song. Limits of the PCR test,' *Facebook*, 3 January [Online Video]. Available at: www.facebook.com/watch/?extid=SEO——&v=1352378968441774 (Accessed: 25 August 2021).

Program on Extremism (2021) *This is our house: A preliminary assessment of the Capitol Hill siege participants*. The George Washington University. Available at: https://extremism.gwu.edu/sites/g/files/zaxdzs2191/f/This-Is-Our-House.pdf (Accessed: 28 September 2021).

Rottenberg, C and Orgad, S (2020) 'Tradwives: The women looking for a simpler past but grounded in the neoliberal present,' *The Conversation*, 7 February [Online]. Available at: http://theconversation.com/tradwives-the-women-looking-for-a-simpler-past-but-grounded-in-the-neoliberal-present-130968 (Accessed: 17 August 2021).

Sandberg, S (2013) *Lean in: Women, work, and the will to lead*. New York: Knopf Doubleday.

Silverman, C, Lytvynenko, J and Dixit, P (2021) 'The "Women For America First" Bus Tour Led to the Capitol Coup Attempt,' *BuzzFeed News*, 26 January [Online]. Available at: www.buzzfeednews.com/article/craigsilverman/maga-bus-tour-coup (Accessed: 17 August 2021).

Snodgrass, E (2021) '"Oath Keeper" Jessica Watkins Denounced the Extremist Group But Will Stay in Jail Before her Trial, Judge Says,' *Business Insider*, 26 February [Online]. Available at: www.businessinsider.com/oath-keeper-jessica-watkins-will-stay-in-jail-before-her-trial (Accessed: 2021).

Sollenberger, R (2021) 'In 2019, Marjorie Taylor Greene told protesters to "flood the Capitol," feel free to use violence,' *Salon*, 2 February [Online]. Available at: www.salon.com/2021/02/02/in-2019-marjorie-taylor-greene-told-protesters-to-flood-the-capitol-feel-free-to-use-violence/ (Accessed: 25 August 2021).

Steck, E and Kaczynski, A (2021a) 'Marjorie Taylor Greene indicated support for executing prominent Democrats in 2018 and 2019 before running for Congress,' *CNN*, 26 January

[Online]. Available at: www.cnn.com/2021/01/26/politics/marjorie-taylor-greene-dem ocrats-violence/index.html (Accessed: 25 August 2021).

Steck, E and Kaczynski, A (2021b) 'Georgia Rep. Greene's history of dangerous conspiracy theories and comments,' *CNN*, 4 February [Online]. Available at: www.cnn.com/2021/ 02/04/politics/kfile-marjorie-taylor-greene-history-of-conspiracies/index.html (Accessed: 17 August 2021).

Vanderbilt, A [@xashxnicoleofficial] (2021) 'Am I crazy? I've never felt more crazy ...,' *TikTok* [Online Video]. Available at: www.tiktok.com/@notsurewhattoputhere/video/ 6919496178870668550?is_copy_url=1&is_from_webapp=v1&referer_url=https%3A%2F %2Fwww.businessinsider.com%2F&referer_video_id=6919975959353429253 (Accessed: 17 August 2021).

WFAF (2021) 'Women For America First – Our Story,' Women For America First [Online]. Available at: https://wfaf.org/ourstory/ (Accessed: 17 August 2021).

11

RACE, RIOTS, AND THE POLITICAL IMAGINARY

Chenjerai Kumanyika

In the late afternoon of January 6th, 2021, toward the end of a Zoom meeting, I gave in to the temptation to check Twitter. Immediately, my timeline was filled with images of white people scaling the walls of the Capitol building and screenshots of broadcasts from major news outlets with the chyron, 'Capitol building breached.' As soon as the meeting ended, I pulled up the livestreams from CNN, MSNBC, and FOX news and searched for Facebook live feeds to begin watching the events as they unfolded. As I did this, I also called friends as we shared the bits of information, marveled at the spectacle, and began forming our sense of what these events meant. Since the occasion inspiring the protests was the certification of election results, I stayed up late into the wee hours of January 7th to see how this episode of rebellion would end. In the weeks that followed, I found myself continuing to try to make sense of the events that had transpired, to the detriment of other work that I needed to do.

In the months after the riots the usual onslaught of memes, essays, reporting, and previously unreleased footage flooded the Internet, offering a variety of analyses. These included assessments of what had motivated the rioters, various accounts of the police response or lack thereof, outrage at what these events meant for democracy, demands for a robust punitive response from the carceral state, and arguments about what race had to do with all of the above.

However, I felt that while many of these analyses—especially those concerning race—contained pieces of the truth, they were often incomplete and at times deeply misleading. Despite the seemingly conclusive spectacle of rioters breaking into the Capitol and the tragic finality of five people dying, the ideological character, symbolism and even some aspects of the facts on the ground were more complex than what appeared at first glance.

Some rioters displayed iconography that invoked symbolism of a deeply anti-authoritarian patriotism, even as they attempted to invalidate a vote, and called for

DOI: 10.4324/9781003246862-14

hangings in favor of the re-election of an authoritarian leader. While all of these rioters appeared to desire the re-election of Donald Trump, some also seemed motivated by conspiracy theories (QAnon and so on), while others were more directly focused on election conspiracies. Some rioters seemed to be there only for carnivalesque performances and symbolic rebellion, while others seemed prepared to kidnap and hurt politicians that they hoped to locate. Some police seemed to cooperate with rioters while far more participated in the violent suppression of the violent riots once they reached a fevered pitch. While the vast majority of the participants were white, many of them seemed to be financially secure and middle class, thus frustrating simple analyses of proletarian rebellion.

In a similar manner, the reactions of prominent conservatives to these events were also ambivalent. In the immediate aftermath, a few condemned the violent character of the protest, but few condemned the apparent fantastical theories of election conspiracy. There was an effort to mourn the police and rioters who were killed, but this didn't yield any unified rejection of the spirit of the protest or its most public champions, Donald Trump, Rudy Giuliani, Marjorie Taylor Greene and others.

While all of the above were alarming developments in the already alarming state of US politics, these events also seemed to be quite useful for Democratic party talking points. The openly anti-democratic fury of the conservative shock troops on the ground, and the elite Republicans who had invited them, the real threats against the lives of Democratic congress members and Mike Pence, the refusal of Republican elites to abandon the goals of the riots even after it was clear that rioters and police had both been killed—all made it easier for leaders of the Democratic party to depict the Trump-dominated Republican party as the clear and exclusive problem with US politics and to discourage critical thinking about their own record and agenda.

These conflicting currents within the overall spectacle allowed conflicting narratives from news media and social media trends to circulate and gain momentum. Many of these narratives contained true elements but ultimately were far too simplistic. All of this continues to make it difficult to understand some elements of what transpired and even more difficult to understand what is to be done. The current chapter is an opportunity to delve further into that inquiry and outline a few key takeaways.

The Context of the Capitol Riots: Two Faces of American Empire

The specifics of the event, who was or was not present, the specific actions that took place during the rebellion and the stop the steal campaign, and details of the days and months leading up to it are all important. However, the first mistake to avoid in understanding the Capitol riots is to limit our analyses to those directly related phenomena.

In order to form a coherent analysis of these events, it is necessary to take a step back from January 6th, 2021 and to acknowledge that what is now referred to as the Capitol riots occurred in the context of two contrasting faces of American Empire. One—whose most visible symbol is Joe Biden—has draped itself with some contours of social democracy and racial justice. The other—whose most visible symbol is Donald Trump—is led by a coalition of national and local corporate and Republican leaders and the currently dethroned but still influential former President. This latter face of American Empire has cast aside dog whistles and speaks explicitly in the language of Western Chauvinist patriarchal neo-settler colonialism. By using the term American Empire and speaking about what the two parties share, I'm speaking of a commitment first and foremost to a kind of external and internal neo-colonialism that ensures extraction and control of resources without the annoying interference of real democracy. This includes (but is not limited to) assuring, deepening and extending the influence of the military apparatus (even if specific military strategies change) and extending the capacities of the carceral apparatus, including policing, all in the name of security.

The imperial project also involves translating equality to mean 'equal access.' This means re-envisioning and reorganizing public goods and programs won in earlier political struggles, to be subsumed under various forms of private sector governance. Where the subjects of the imperial project resist domination of their resources or governments, these efforts will need to be reined in materially by the hard power of US military intervention, economically through sanctions and trade policy and monopoly, and rhetorically by the vague and deceptive concept of 'US national interests.'

Since the Capitol riots and Biden's election, developments like the 'retaliatory' drone strikes that killed ten Afghan civilians sent out as Biden's voice thundered 'We will hunt you down and kill you,' the abrupt ending of Covid-inspired housing and income protections, the refusal to engage the problem of police or prisons in any meaningful way, and the ugly expression of Biden-era immigration policy which saw Haitian asylum seekers being beaten by white border patrol officers on horseback—all represent a set of clearly neoliberal, colonial priorities that invite a more precise assessment.

What requires tremendous nuance to grasp is that the social democratic contours of the current US Democratic party—infrastructure proposals, superficial diversity efforts and racial symbolism, declarations in support of the working class—represent *both* the victories of leftist struggle in the US *and* the effort of the national Democratic party to maintain control of its domination over progressive politics. This is accomplished in some instances by real concessions coerced by organized movements, but also by paying lip service to these through the aesthetics and symbolism of multiculturalism and New Dealism.

This matters because both the movements from below and their incorporation by corporations and the Democratic party have given conservative politicians useful targets for physical and discursive attack. The explosive uprisings and urban rebellions drenched in (but not wholly determined by) the politics of Black Lives Matter and the expanding progressive caucus in the US Congress have all become important sources—and targets—of rage for conservatives.

With a basic proposition of these two faces of American Empire in place, an analysis of the Capitol riots can be shaped by the correct questions. A few key questions that I'm concerned with here are as follows. What political discursive projects are being constituted through the mediated representation of the Capitol riots? How might our initial impressions be challenged by a more patient analysis? How are we being invited to understand the role of white supremacy and race and what is missing from that? How can we understand the response of the police? How are both faces of American Empire using these events to further their political ends? Finally, what do these events teach us about the way forward?

Race and the Police Response

The first images that I saw of the Capitol riots were largely coming from short video clips and memes on social media and maybe some live streaming footage from major news networks. Based on that keyhole view of the first wave of media, it did seem like there was very little police presence and that the police that were present were either indifferent to or supportive of the protests. One particular image did show a police officer opening a barricade to let rioters in. Another showed a police officer dressed in riot gear gently escorting an elderly woman protester down the stairs out of the Capitol—with no visible intent to arrest or detain her.

When confronted with fragmented, anecdotal and incomplete images such as these, it is common to fill the gaps of information with pre-existing narratives that might explain them. In this case, these images of apparently indifferent or co-operative police officers synced up very well with the pre-existing sense that the many police are (ideologically influenced to be) implicitly or explicitly white supremacist Trump supporters who were sympathetic to the cause of the rioters.

Here were thousands of white folks—armed, angry, pissed-off white folks—confused in terms of disinformation, descending on the Capitol. Indeed, it is difficult to imagine anything close to this response if the rioters had been non-white or in any way associated with Black Lives Matter or other radical causes. The apparent contradiction is so clear because of the ubiquitous and wanton police violence that unfolded only six months earlier in the summer of 2020. In the context of the Capitol riots, memes contrasting these two different police responses appeared immediately (see Figure 11.1). The idea was that the police didn't stop the protest because they supported the cause—including its white supremacist layers.

It is important to note that this kind of analysis of the police response might appear to be identifying a kind of *structural racism,* because it focuses on the police and points to institutionalized ideological features of police culture. However, I think this more accurately describes a kind of *personal or individualized racism or bigotry* in which the attitudes of individual police determine their responses to the

FIGURE 11.1 Meme of violent riot police response to BLM (left) and meek USCP response to Capitol rioters (right)

Source: Copyright iowyth hezel ulthiin, ulthiin's impression of original meme images from www.scarymommy.com/police-response-compare-blm-protest-capitol-storm/, *photos copyright Jose Luis Magana/AFP/Saul Loeb/Getty.*

rioters when they encounter them. But this kind of 'racist police' analysis has very limited explanatory power.

This isn't to say that there wasn't a clear difference between how these rioters were treated versus how Black Lives Matter or leftist rioters have been treated. There is. Even given the challenges of coordinating multiple policing institutions and obstacles within the Trump administration, it feels certain that a protest with a more left leaning ideological character—especially one with a large Black participation base—would have been treated differently. Based on what we now know, I think it's more accurate to say that the prospect of thousands of white people mobilizing didn't motivate the necessary actors in advance to prepare to unleash the full expression of police power. Whether they were sympathetic or not, the Capitol police weren't prepared, they were outnumbered and overwhelmed.

One example of the limits of using a few anecdotal images to argue that police just let the rioters walk into the Capitol without putting up a fight is that overwhelming evidence now suggests that conclusion is incorrect. A few days after the riots, footage would emerge of scores of police (at least 56 DC Metropolitan Police Officers) involved in physical combat with rioters for over an hour and one police officer trapped inside an elevator in the Capitol groaning in fear and pain as he fought to escape. Officer Brian Sicknick was sprayed with bear spray while restraining rioters, and died from the effects of this attack the next day. Sicknick wasn't bear-sprayed because he was 'letting the rioters in'—quite the opposite. But the public perception of an unequal police response, based on racist attitudes of police, matters because it set the stage for the legitimizing response from the Biden administration.

A White Supremacist Riot?

Another analysis that circulated in both mainstream reporting and social media argued that the best way to understand the Capitol riots was that it wasn't really motivated by fears of election fraud, QAnon or other of the more visible concerns. At its core, many commentators argued, it was a white supremacist event. Indeed, the FBI confirmed that members of white supremacist groups (consistently described as 'extremists') and militias were present, participated in the violence and are facing federal charges (Naylor and Lucas, 2021). This analysis invites the public to imagine that these relatively marginal white supremacist militias organized the event, or that the masses of white people driven by white supremacy and drunk on Trump support took to the streets of Washington and stormed the Capitol. However, there is one element to note about this persuasive and partially correct narrative.

Naming white supremacy explicitly feels progressive or even radical and necessary especially in a context where 75 million Trump supporters and many in mainstream media seek to deny or distort the role of race in American politics. The problem is that the term 'white supremacy' is vague and without precision; it flattens the diverse ideological currents in the Capitol riots into a homogenous bigotry and beckons us to think that it was this bigotry that was the primary organizing principle.

One definition of white supremacy—the focus on white 'extremist' militias—leaves out several important factors. One thing it leaves out is the role of elite politicians in starting, funding, promoting and steering the 'stop the steal' campaign (see Chapter 5). It casts Republican elites that openly supported the protest such as Trump, Roger Stone, Rudy Giuliani, and Marjorie Taylor Greene, as simply egging on a pre-existing uprising. The term 'white supremacist' can be usefully applied to the 'stop the steal' campaign, but this is a very different kind of white supremacist leadership than the Proud Boys or Oath Keepers. It matters that in the immediate aftermath of the riots, some elite conservatives were able to conceal their own roles by blaming the 'March to Save America' on marginal bigoted militias.

The symbols present at the Capitol riots offer a different gateway into understanding what united the Capitol rioters. For example, Confederate flags (see Figure 6.4) can be seen throughout the riots. Its display is plentiful outside of conservative America, it is far from monolithic in its signifiers, and in many cases right-wing groups are in open opposition to one another on several issues. This flag, originally a specific battle flag, was not a symbol of the confederacy during the brief existence of this separate US government. But after reconstruction, and at several moments over the course of the twentieth century, the symbol was resuscitated and circulated as an ideological fetish to activate and constitute a nostalgic white solidarity.

When politicians raise the Confederate flag or threaten to take down a Robert E. Lee statue, the flag becomes a unifying force. The fetish draws together a block of conservative white voters who might have previously been in different political tendencies. Some potential constituents may consider themselves mainstream conservatives focused on 'bread and butter' issues, or they may be annoyed by debates about confederate statues, cancel culture, or what they've been told is critical race theory. Others may be concerned about alleged election fraud, while yet others may be involved in or sympathetic to the Oath Keepers, Proud Boys, Three Percenters, and so on. For all of these folks, the imagination of what could possibly be a more complete democracy is infuriating and galvanizing.

This is intensified when the crowd calling for or executing the toppling of statues includes Black women, queer folks, trans folks, anarchists, and others beating the drum against white supremacy. The combined spectacle of the statue toppling and the response against it draws together a reactionary block of people which becomes politically very useful. I say 'becomes useful' because conservative strategy is evolving as well, rather than fixed and unfolding in some kind of master plan—even conservatives are often extremely forward thinking about how to provoke and then rhetorically deploy protest. And the Confederate flag and other confederate symbols stand as a composite discursive rejection of a culturally transforming America.

This is relevant here because the various waves of anti-racist, anti-police brutality and anti-Trump protests on the left might have something to do with the rising anger and mobilization of folks on the right that contributed to the Capitol riots.

Another set of defining images of the riots were pictures of Jacob Chansley, aka Jake Angeli, an activist from Arizona. Chansley intentionally presented a stunning spectacle—his head was crowned with a horned fur hat, his face was painted red-white-and-blue, and his bare chest revealed a collage of tattoos. A statement from the DOJ added, 'This individual carried a spear, approximately 6 feet in length with an American flag tied just below the blade' (United States Attorney's Office, 2021).

There is, of course, much to be learned from these visual markers. His tattoos are symbols borrowed from Norse Mythology. They include the Yggdrasill tree, Thor's hammer, and Valknut—three linked triangles enclosed in a circle. It's not clear what these symbols mean to Chansley but there is an established tradition of far right and white supremacist organizations using these symbols to signal a (false) connection to Viking ancestry. The Shamanic markers such as the feather hanging from Angeli's right ear indicate a desire to inhabit and/or project a kind of indigeneity that is somehow connected to patriotism. For example, William Chaloupka (1997) has written about the county supremacy and militia movements as among 'the most visible forms of the populist right resurgence in American Politics.' These movements work through claims of sovereignty and resistance to federalism and thus the ability of white Americans to present themselves as indigenous to America—when politically convenient. Of course, this discursive and material imagination and material control of land and resources is directly linked to the discursive and material project of erasing actual native Americans. Most of the media stories and memes that mentioned Chansley focused on his outrageous look and his request for organic food during his initial period of incarceration. These mediatized details, along with his self-given title of QAnon Shaman, cast him as both entitled and delusional.

But another way to understand Jake Chansley's visual presentation is as a kind of misdirection from other components of his biography. Chansley served in the Navy—first as a supply clerk and then as an airman on the Kitty Hawk Super-carrier. After two years and 15 days in uniform, he was taken out of the Navy. According to Task and Purpose, Chansley was discharged after refusing to take the anthrax vaccine.

The Role of the Military in the Capitol Riots

The fact that Jacob Chansley—a former Navy airman (and anti-vaxxer)—was present at the riots was not an anomaly. In fact, this detail points to an extremely important aspect of the Capitol riots. According to NPR, of more than 140 individuals charged for participation in the riots, at least 27 of those (roughly 20%) have served or are currently serving in the military (Dreisbach and Anderson, 2021), including veterans such as Timothy Louis Hale-Cusanelli, for example, who was a Navy contractor with clearance with naval weapons and secret security clearances (Sisk, 2021). Georgetown University's Project on Extremism estimates that 43 alleged Capitol rioters had military experience (Milton and Mines, 2021). Reporting in February of 2021, Military.com found 32 veterans among the arrested rioters with 40% of those being affiliated with the Marines (Harkins and Seck, 2021). To put this into perspective, according to the 2018 census, only 7% of the broader population is affiliated with the military (Vespa, 2020). These military affiliations connect a variety of seemingly disparate individuals and disparate organizations. Additionally, digging into the large military participation in the riots offers clarity in several other areas.

Most importantly, it reflects decades of efforts by right wing and white supremacist organizations to recruit among the US military. In *Bring the War Home: The White Power Movement and Paramilitary America*, Kathleen Belew (2018) points out that the California Knights of the Ku Klux Klan was founded in the 1980s by a 20-year Army veteran—Frazier Glenn Miller. Miller employed 'the narrative, symbols and weapons of the Vietnam war' as he shaped the culture of the group. The Georgetown Project on Extremism reports that military individuals that participated in the riots were about four times more likely to be involved in domestic 'extremist' organizations such as the Proud Boys or Oath Keepers (Milton and Mines, 2021). NPR reports that roughly one third of active-duty troops said they had 'personally witnessed' racism in the ranks in recent months (Dreisbach and Anderson, 2021). These included swastikas, white supremacist tattoos, Nazi style salutes etc. Army reserve sergeant Hale-Cusanelli, mentioned above, is described in court documents as 'an avowed white supremacist and Nazi sympathizer.' But the signs of this have been around for several years. In February of 2020, a survey of over 1630 active-duty military by the Military Times reported that over one third of respondents had 'personally witnessed examples of white nationalism or ideological-driven race extremism' (Shane, 2020).

Ashli Babbitt—the Capitol rioter shot by police as she attempted to enter the speaker's lobby on the second floor of the Capitol building—was also a 14-year military veteran. According to friends, family and evidence from her social media accounts, she was taken in by QAnon and other far-right conspiratorial culture. However, she also noted in threads in 2018 that she had previously been an Obama supporter and was turned off voting Democrat by disdain for Hillary Clinton. If this is true, it suggests that not all far-right members of the military were life-long impenetrable white supremacists and that the perceived results of democratic governance were part of what alienated some Capitol riot participants.

The vast military experience within the ranks of the Capitol rioters also may explain why they were able to outmaneuver the small contingent of US Capitol Police. At least one fifth of the individuals arrested were far more experienced and prepared for the tactical conflict that ensued than the majority of the US population or even of conservatives.

Michael Brenes (2021) and historian Jennifer Mittelstadt (2015) insightfully point out that in addition to serving as a 'warfare state,' the US Military also has expanded to serve as kind of welfare state—providing a variety of social services such as healthcare, retirement benefits, housing assistance, education, childcare and other forms of support. This bond of dependency between the institutions of the military and the families of recruits reveals that their loyalty is not purely an ideological phenomenon. And as more Americans benefit from militarized (and increasingly privatized) support, these same Americans become ripe for recruitment by far-right groups and by mainstream authoritarian political figures.

It's worth reiterating and challenging here the vague claim of white supremacy or the simple idea that the Capitol rioters were motivated by the desire to make America great for white people. The more focused analysis of the role of the military allows us to home in on this particular recruitment ground for white supremacy and its expression and cultivation within a vast and widely-celebrated mainstream American institution.

There are many other aspects of the motivations and composition of the Capitol riots that could be focused on but I will now briefly turn to a few points about the response to the riots by both the Democratic and Republican branches of the American empire.

Election Fraud and Insurrection as the New/Old Conservative Playbook

On the afternoon of January 6th, as I watched enraged Trump supporters enter the Capitol, my mind began to wonder how Republican politicians would justify this. By this point in the afternoon, it was clear that one protester had already been shot and there was footage of rioters chanting 'hang Mike Pence' repeatedly. One group of rioters appeared to have carried a noose into the Capitol. It seemed undeniable that Trump and other leaders had provoked this response through repeated claims of election fraud and other forms of incitement. With media outlets determined to keep eyes on their channels by reporting each alarming and gruesome detail, this seemed like a low point in Republican politics.

The sense that it would be difficult for conservatives to recover from this deepened as footage of Trump supporters in open combat with police emerged. Indeed, several police officers had died in connection to the events of January 6th. Capitol Police officer Brian Sicknick died the day after he was 'overpowered and beaten by rioters' (Healy, 2021). In the months after the riots, Jeffrey Smith of the D.C. Metropolitan Police, Howard Leibengood of the US Capitol Police, and Gunther Hashida and Kyle DeFreytag of the DC Metropolitan Police all died by suicide.

In the first 24 hours after the riots, Republican politicians appeared to be finding ways to try to distance themselves from the violence of the riots—which had killed at least four people. While most affirmed the right to dissent but agreed with Democrats that this was the wrong way to do it, some went as far as to blame Black Lives Matter and Antifa. In fact, according to NPR, in the 24 hours following the riots the myth that the rioters were Antifa was shared 400,000 times on social media (Ryan-Mosley and Ohlheiser, 2021). This disinformation campaign was led by conservative pundits like Laura Ingraham, Sean Hannity and Tucker Carlson, and Rush Limbaugh, but also by politicians such as Matt Gaetz, Paul Gosar, and Mo Brooks. This idea mostly died down when FBI Director Christopher Wray flatly rejected the claim, stating that there was no evidence for it.

But it soon became clear that the events of the Capitol riots wouldn't douse the flames of the 'stop the steal' campaign. Writing on Townhall.com, conservative radio host Mark Davis initially distanced himself saying, 'No one should defend it or even attempt to excuse it under the guise of "hey, this is what you get when people get really mad …",' but then qualified this by saying that the behavior of the rioters 'does not erase the righteous grievance of millions of Americans who have lost faith in an election system cast to the winds of political opportunism' (Davis, 2021). Even as the FBI pursued and arrested hundreds of Capitol rioters, and several US Capitol Police officers testified in front of Congress, Republican leaders in several states continued to call the election results illegitimate, calling for new 'forensic audits' of election results and stoking anger among their base. Some onlookers referred to this as the new playbook of conservative politics.

Even in the heat of the riot's aftermath, most conservative leaders didn't distance themselves from the 'stop the steal' campaign. In fact, shackled to a myth- and rage-drunk base, Republicans have fervently embraced and attempted to institutionalize the 'stop the steal' campaign that gave rise to the riots. Some have called this pattern of planting seeds of fear about voter fraud, decrying election results, and attempting to overturn them as a new playbook of conservative governance. This assessment is partially correct.

'Stop the steal'—the war cry of the Capitol rioters—is at least as old as 2016. In that year Roger Stone used the phrase to pre-emptively invalidate a Hillary Clinton victory that never came about. Both Stone's operatives and Trump would introduce it again in 2018 in reference to Florida's gubernatorial races. When the phrase appeared in September of 2020, its popularity was once again driven by elites such as Stone, Trump and Greene. But although the expression and contemporary articulation of this strategy may be new, its core is old and deeply American.

These efforts to invalidate the will of the majority must be seen as the latest expression of voter disenfranchisement—a principle of American democracy. Fear of the governing power of the majority dates back at least as far as the constitutional convention where several delegates spoke out explicitly against mass voting rights, and even proportional representation, in Congress. Roger Sherman of Connecticut argued that people 'should have as little do as may be about government,' for the reason that they are 'constantly liable to be misled' (Bomboy, 2017). James Madison also distrusted the collective will of Americans and argued that only landed elites should be granted the power to steer the direction of the country (Mayville, 2015). One result of these debates that is not well-known by many is that the right to vote is not enshrined in the US Constitution.

Following this rather anti-democratic foundation, every stage of the potential enfranchisement of Black Americans and women has been met with resistance by those that supported a white supremacist, patriarchal, capitalist vision of America. This opposition did not follow neatly along party lines as it does now. For many years the Democratic party in America was the home of the most fervent anti-abolitionist and racist plantation elites. But poll taxes, literacy tests, and lynching defined the Black voting experience in America all the way up until at least the Voting Rights Act of 1965. Since that time the same goals have been pursued through an expanding matrix of redistricting, onerous and illogical Voter ID laws, poll watchers, pre-emptive voter-fraud fear campaigns, and baseless audits.

This strategy has at least three benefits for conservative leaders and Republican politicians. First, while audits have been a dismal failure in overturning the results of the 2020 election, similar audits in future close votes could be successful especially at the state and local levels. The long project of stacking the courts with conservatives is a strong incentive to push decisions regarding democratic elections into the less democratic jurisdiction of the courts.

What's more important than overturning elections is that facing over 74 million Republicans who voted for Trump, Republican voters could understandably feel that they must appear to be loyal to Trump and outraged about his loss in the election. Even if some conservative politicians believed that the election was legitimate, the success of the stop the steal campaign means that Trump support can only be expressed through public support of claims of election fraud. Supporting (baseless) audits is a way to perform loyalty to their constituents.

Third, the claims of election fraud have become a furnace of rage for the Republican base. For years Republicans have highlighted cultural issues such as abortion, gay marriage, various scandals such as Hillary Clinton's email usage and 'Benghazi,' gender and bathroom usage and currently, concerns about critical race theory and cancel culture (see Chapter 2) to keep their base enraged and thus engaged. Some have theorized that because Republican economic policies actually hurt large parts of their base, the rage-stoking cultural politics are increasingly essential. Indeed, Republican losses are sometimes understood by leaders as failure to generate enough rage. Who can forget South Carolina Senator Lindsey Graham's comments after Mitt Romney lost to incumbent president Barack Obama: 'The demographics race we're losing badly. We're not generating enough angry white guys to stay in business for the long term' (Helderman, 2012).

In short, claims of election fraud give Republican leaders an issue that impacts elections but also can be used to govern in between the elections. This is precisely how the stop the steal campaign is being used between 2020 and 2024.

When understood this way, the conservative playbook of 'stop the steal' politics shouldn't primarily focus our attention on spectacles like January 6th, or similar events in other states, protecting political procedures or election results. We should more accurately recognize this as a strategy of governance writ large. The rage about election fraud authorizes conservatives to further their agendas on a range of issues including voter registration, housing, education, healthcare and public health, the regulation of corporate entities, foreign policy and so on.

The Democratic Response: Strengthening the Carceral State as Racial Justice

One way to begin discussing the Democratic response to the riots is to revisit the image of Adam Johnson carrying off Nancy Pelosi's lectern (see Figure 6.3). Whether or not journalists understood this in the moment, one kind of discursive trajectory involved casting the moment where Johnson was caught walking out with the podium as a moment of horror and disorder. Mass evictions and homelessness, poverty and exploitation, private and military regimes that allow and facilitate sexual assault, wanton resource extraction, the separation of children from migrant families, rampant and flagrant police terror, pollution and disaster capitalism—those are things to be patient about. But *this*—walking out with Pelosi's lectern—is symbolic of disorder, the symbol that things have gone too far.

Similarly, there was a lot of ideological work being done in naming participants and critiquing the action of the riots. Should the participants be called protesters, insurrectionists, or, as Biden called them, 'domestic terrorists'? Also, how should the entering of the Capitol be described? To describe this as 'breaching' the Capitol building reproduces assumptions about who is allowed in the Capitol and who is not. So in that sense, to cast the entering of the Capitol by unauthorized members of the public as a key visual and primary problematic act sets up the discursive framing of order and the subsequent response. *Order was somehow restored* at the moment when the podium was returned to the Capitol, and when Nancy

Pelosi was widely shown in the news speaking at the podium confirming the electoral vote.

However, as mentioned earlier, in the days and months following January 6th, media outlets and individual commentators also pointed out the role of white supremacist groups and the discrepancy between the mild police response to the mostly white Capitol rioters and tremendous and violent police response to Black Lives Matter protests (see Figure 11.1). One CNN headline read 'How People of Color Can Cope with the Capitol Riot Hypocrisy.' It was clear that this kind of framing was at least partially intended to directly honestly confront white supremacy as an important factor in the riots.

But this trend of coverage, and calls for the punitive response to match what would have happened to Black rioters, set the stage for the response by the Biden administration and supportive leaders. Biden spoke explicitly on this in the following days: 'No one can tell me that if it had been a group of Black Lives Matter protesting yesterday, they wouldn't have been treated very, very differently from the mob of thugs that stormed the Capitol' (Biden, as cited in Bose and Brice, 2021). This debate is instrumentalized by the Biden Administration to set themselves on the side of righteousness with respect to racism. Biden's statement also engages in discursive struggle over the often-racialized word 'thug,' as we will recall Trump saying that his people were not 'thugs' like the BLM protesters of 2020 (see Chapter 9).

There are three further aspects of the response that I want to call attention to. First, in the week after the riots, the US Capitol Police—constructed as both a failure and as the primary victims of the riots—insisted that they lacked the resources necessary to confront this kind of threat, calling for further funding. This response, which strengthens the military and policing, was given a kind of racial cover by the aforementioned framing of racial hypocrisy. On January 7th, DC Mayor Muriel Bowser—an African American woman—held a press conference with Metropolitan Police Chief Robert J. Contee, an African American man. Bowser explained that violent attacks 'may not end on the 20th and that means a whole different level of policing' (NBC15 Madison, 2021). Bowser complained of a shrinking police force and asked for more funding and capacity to police first amendment free speech protests that she claimed were growing in number.

This trend of Black faces representing the DC police continued and intensified during the July 2021 House Select Committee Hearing about the attack. The news coverage of those hearings focused on the testimony of Black USCP officer, Harry Dunn. Dunn's emotional tendency focused heavily on race as he detailed the epithets that rioters shouted at him during the riot. Dunn's testimony was emotional; 'How the [expletive] can something like this happen?! Is this America? I began sobbing and officers came over to console me' (Dunn, 2021).

Dunn's moving testimony not only underscored the racial framing of the riots, but also cast the police in a heroic, progressive and victimized light, that was starkly different from the ubiquitous and disturbing coverage of the nationwide police brutality following the murder of George Floyd.

Hours after the first hearing of the House Select Committee investigating the Capitol attack, Congress introduced a $2.1 billion package. The framing of the bill revealed how politicians used the Capitol riots to discursively funnel a huge infusion of money into both policing and the military:

> This $2.1 billion package is designed to address the aftermath of the violent insurrection that took place on Jan. 6, heal the remaining scars of the COVID pandemic on the Capitol complex and provide the resources we need to ensure the safety of our Afghan partners as we conclude our mission in that country.
>
> *(Leahy, 2021)*

It is not clear how those funds were used in Afghanistan, given the tragic failure of the withdrawal effort. What is clear is that the Senate bill redirected $100 million for the Capitol Police, $300 million for new Capitol security measures, and more than $1 billion to the defense department, $500 million of which to the National Guard (Leahy, 2021).

The DOJ has also strengthened its surveillance capacity in response to the riots and its preparation for hearings. Unsealed court findings revealed that the DOJ subpoenaed cell phone data—including photographs and location data—from Google and used this to create maps to identify the location of accused rioters. US Sen Mark R. Warner, Chair of the Senate Intelligence Committee (and former telecommunications entrepreneur) urged mobile carriers, AT&T, T-Mobile, Verizon, Apple, Facebook, Gab, Google, Parler, Signal, Telegram, and Twitter to 'immediately preserve content and associated meta-data connected to Wednesday's insurrectionist attack on the United States Capitol' (Warner, 2021). These techniques—deployed with the approval of those seeking a punitive response to white supremacist rioters—are likely to be used going forward. Protesters who may come to the Capitol in the future, peacefully or otherwise, will not be excluded from these forms of discipline and surveillance.

Finally, Biden made it clear that he intends to prioritize a new law focused on domestic terrorism and put resources toward specialized anti-terrorism training for federal, state, tribal and yes, local law enforcement. The blueprint for such a law could be present in the failed Domestic Terrorism Prevention Act (S. 3190 and H.R. 5602) that would have created three new 'Domestic Terrorism Offices,' within DOJ. Senate Majority Leader Chuck Schumer (D-N.Y.) demanded that the Transportation Security Administration (TSA) 'put any #CapitolRiot participant on the TSA "No Fly" list' (Darnell, 2021).

Conclusions

The foregoing reflection points to a number of clear conclusions for individuals, organizations and movements pursuing social justice. First, the responses that are now being pushed by the Biden Administration currently appear focused on routing out domestic terrorism and upholding democratic procedures. However, if history is to be any guide, these procedures will be used with more lasting effects on radical and progressive movements and on Black, Brown, and poor people, Muslims and other perceived threats to American Empire. Already some documents emerging from Homeland Security discuss the importance of intervening in the radicalization of potential domestic terrorism. This goal resonates strongly with a long US history of ideological policing. While the frame of libertarianism and the individualizing frame of 'civil liberties' is inadequate to describe the role anti-terrorism projects play in the reconfiguring of US imperial aims, civil liberties advocates are correct in their attention to and refusal of the authoritarian core of the emerging framework under Biden's Democratic administration. Several such commentators have pointed out that the challenge of legal ways to apprehend, try and prosecute political dissidents—such as the Capitol rioters—is not a shortage of punitive resources but an anti-democratic surplus of invasive and criminalizing laws, policies, and statutes.

Second, this punitive response, which bolsters the US police and carceral apparatus, was at least initially given a kind of racial cover by the overly simplistic racial frameworks that circulated in the mainstream media about the event. If the rioters were shown preferential treatment by the state because they were white, then (by this logic) the only way to balance the scales is to bolster the police, military, carceral and legal capacities necessary to identify, arrest, and punish anyone reasonably associated with riot participation. This doesn't point to minimizing the role of white supremacy, becoming apologists for the Capitol rioters or denying that Black or radical protesters are treated differently. But it means recognizing that we are in a political-economic environment in which media and social media companies are incentivized to flood the internet and television with hot takes on the role of race, and liberal centrist actors are eager to perform racial solidarity by translating the racial mechanisms of empire as nothing more than bigotry that can be trained or incarcerated away. In this context, patient, historical, sophisticated accounts of the role of race in political events are greatly needed.

Turning to the rioters themselves, the large participation of active or retired military points to a more important antiracist and anti-empire goal. First, there is already a spectrum of movements that targets the ever-expanding budget of the Pentagon and the social costs of expensive never-ending wars. In light of wildly successful far-right recruitment efforts, these antiwar, antimilitary movements can also be seen as fighting a key nurturing ground for violent white supremacists. These movements should not only focus on dismantling the Pentagon budget, but also on pursuing strategies that hold open the possibility of recruiting members of the military and veterans into social movements. Several veterans' organizations against US wars have emerged showing that this strategy is possible and fruitful. But efforts to economically starve the bloated Pentagon budget and recruit military must face the reality of the military welfare state and continue to tackle the material factors that tether Americans to this institution.

Finally, the spectacle of the Capitol riots seemed conclusive because the images and sounds of violence and rage brought to us by a variety of media gave the public the sense that what was most important about these events was unfolding right before our eyes. However, consider the things that are threatening Black people's lives in Philadelphia. For example, where I live, attacks from white supremacists are not among the top concerns. A tour of the most oppressed areas of West Philadelphia, Southwest Philadelphia, and North Philadelphia won't feature Oath Keepers, Three Percenters or Capitol rioters. You will see police, poor people who can't afford adequate housing, lack of healthy food options, lack of healthcare, and school buildings filled with asbestos and falling apart.

In this time, where critical analysis and some left and progressive hot takes are shaped by the idea that the camera shows everything, and that the political task that is important is to just name what is happening on camera, the critique is that liberals and conservatives are reluctant to do that, especially around police violence. In this view, one that I disagree with, the main task of the left is simply to name what is on camera—to name the flagrant terror and murder that is right in front of us. That which is before our eyes.

What I hope that this chapter and this book make clear is that what is right in front of our eyes or what is on camera does *not* give us everything we need for critical analysis and radical transformative action. We often need a deeper historical analysis, theoretical frames, and a more grounded understanding of these events. In the case of an officer choking Eric Garner or George Floyd, the choking is on camera for us to see. But the problem is not the choking—or not only. The problem is the reality of the state and police, which is not on camera, and which is not going to be found in images and videos.

Similarly, with the Capitol riots, angry confused violent and some racist white folks are on camera. But much of what is taking place 'before our eyes,' before and beyond the immediacy of moments of looking, can shape what was put in front of our eyes by the media in those very moments. The clues are there but the evidence of what the state is, and what we must therefore fight, requires sustained, ongoing analysis, political education and revolutionary practice.

References

Belew, K (2018) *Bring the war home*. Cambridge: Harvard University Press.

Bomboy, S (2017) 'Senators Should Serve for Life, and Other Election Ideas from the Founders' [Online]. *National Constitution Center*. Available at: https://constitutioncenter.org/blog/sena tors-should-serve-for-life-and-other-election-ideas-from-the-founders-1 (Accessed: 12 October 2021).

Bose, N and Brice, M (2021) 'If Rioters Were Black, "Hundreds" Would Have Been Killed: Washington Reflects on Capitol Rampage' [Online]. Available at: https://www. reuters.com/article/us-usa-election-inequality-idUSKBN29D1HM (Accessed: 12 October 2021).

Brenes, M (2021) 'To Defeat the Radical Right, End American Empire,' *Jacobin*, February [Online]. Available at: https://jacobinmag.com/2021/02/far-right-us-imperialism-milita ry-capitol-riot (Accessed: 12 October 2021).

Chaloupka, W (1996) 'The county supremacy and militia movements: Federalism as an issue on the radical right,' *Publius: The Journal of Federalis*, 26(3), 161–175.

Darnell, T (2021) 'Schumer: Put everyone involved in Capitol riots on federal No-Fly list,' *The Atlanta Journal-Constitution* [Online]. Available at: www.ajc.com/news/nation-world/schum er-put-everyone-involved-in-capitol-riots-on-federal-no-fly-list/PIJ2CNZUDNEPNGXAD MUWHTI37A/ (Accessed: 12 October 2021).

Davis, M (2021) 'A Day of Rage, a Day of Shame,' *Townhall.com*, 7 January [Online]. Available at: https://townhall.com/columnists/markdavis/2021/01/07/a-day-of-rage-a -day-of-shame-n2582723 (Accessed: 12 October 2021).

Dreisbach, T and Anderson, M (2021) 'Nearly 1 in 5 Defendants in Capitol Riot Cases Served in The Military,' *NPR*, 21 January [Online]. Available at: www.npr.org/2021/ 01/21/958915267/nearly-one-in-five-defendants-in-capitol-riot-cases-served-in-the-mil itary (Accessed: 12 October 2021).

Dunn, HA (2021) 'Written Statement of Harry A Dunn, Private First Class, Hearing Before the Select Committee to Investigate January 6th Attack on the United States Capitol,' *NPR*, 7 July [Online]. Available at: https://legacy.npr.org/2021/07/27/dunn_testimony. pdf (Accessed: 12 October 2021).

Harkins, G and Seck, H (2021) 'Marines, Infantry Most Highly Represented Among Veterans Arrested After Capitol Riot,' *Military.com*, 26 February [Online]. Available at: www.military.com/daily-news/2021/02/26/marines-infantry-most-highly-represented-a mong-veterans-arrested-after-capitol-riot.html (Accessed: 12 October 2021).

Healy, J (2021) 'These Are the 5 People Who Died in the Capitol Riot,' *The New York Times*, 11 January [Online]. Available at: www.nytimes.com/2021/01/11/us/who-die d-in-capitol-building-attack.html (Accessed: 12 October 2021).

Helderman, R (2012) 'As Republican Convention Emphasizes Diversity, Racial Incidents Intrude,' *The Washington Post*, 29 August [Online]. Available at: www.washingtonpost. com/politics/2012/08/29/b9023a52-f1ec-11e1-892d-bc92fee603a7_story.html (Accessed: 12 October 2021).

Leahy, P (2021) 'Address on the Bipartisan Emergency Capitol Security Supplemental Appropriations Bill,' US Senator Patrick Leahy of Vermont, 29 July [Online]. Available at: www.leahy.senate.gov/press/address-on-the-bipartisan-emergency-capitol-security-su pplemental-appropriations-bill (Accessed: 12 October 2021).

Mayville, L (2015) 'Fear of the few: John Adams and the power elite,' *Polity*, 47(1), 5–32.

Milton, D and Mines, A (2021) '"This is War:" Examining Military Experience Among the Capitol Hill Siege Participants,' George Washington University. Available at: https://doi. org/10.4079/poe.04.2021.00 (Accessed: 12 October 2021).

Mittelstadt, J (2015) *The rise of the military welfare state.* Cambridge: Harvard University Press.

Naylor, B and Lucas, R (2021) 'Wray Stresses Role of Right-Wing Extremism In Hearing About Jan. 6 Riot,' *NPR*, 3 March [Online]. Available at: www.npr.org/2021/03/02/ 972539274/fbi-director-wray-testifies-before-congress-for-1st-time-since-capitol-attack (Accessed: 12 October 2021).

NBC15 Madison (2021) 'Washington, DC Mayor Muriel Bowser Briefing Regarding the Riot at the US Capitol Yesterday' *Facebook*, 7 January [Online]. Available at: www.fa cebook.com/watch/live/?ref=watch_permalink&v=459012095261092 (Accessed: 12 October 2021).

Ryan-Mosley, T and Ohlheiser, A (2021) 'How an Internet Lie About the Capitol Invasion Turned into an Instant Conspiracy Theory,' *MIT Technology Review*, 7 January [Online]. Available at: www.technologyreview.com/2021/01/07/1015858/capitol-invasion-antifa -conspiracy-lie/ (Accessed: 12 October 2021).

ShaneII, L (2020) 'Signs of White Supremacy, Extremism Up Again in Poll of Active-Duty Troops,' *militarytimes.com*, 6 February [Online]. Available at: www.militarytimes.com/news/pentagon-congress/2020/02/06/signs-of-white-supremacy-extremism-up-aga in-in-poll-of-active-duty-troops/ (Accessed: 12 October 2021).

Sisk, R (2021) 'Army Reserve Sergeant Charged in Capitol Riots Alleged to Be White Supremacist,' *Military.com*, 19 January [Online]. Available at: www.military.com/daily-news/2021/01/19/army-reserve-sergeant-charged-capitol-riots-alleged-be-white-suprema cist.html (Accessed: 12 October 2021).

United States Attorney's Office (2021) 'Three Men Charged in Connection with Events at US Capitol' [Online]. Available at: www.justice.gov/usao-dc/pr/three-men-charged-connection-events-us-capitol (Accessed: 12 October 2021).

Vespa, J (2020) 'Census Bureau Releases New Report on Veterans' United States Census Bureau,' 2 June [Online]. Available at: www.census.gov/newsroom/press-releases/2020/veterans-report.html (Accessed: 12 October 2021).

Warner, M (2021) 'Warner Urges Wireless Carriers and Technology Companies to Preserve Evidence Related to the Attack on the US Capitol,' Mark R Warner, US Senator from the Commonwealth of Virginia, 9 January [Online]. Available at: www.warner.senate.gov/p ublic/index.cfm/2021/1/warner-urges-wireless-carriers-and-social-media-companies-to-p reserve-evidence-related-to-the-attack-on-the-u-s-capitol (Accessed: 12 October 2021).

INDEX